WHAT THEY SAY

EXECUTIVES IN CHINA-ICELAND TRADE AND ECONOMIC COOPERATION

中冰企业家风采录

张守凤◎主编　　赵　芳　张　环◎副主编

中英双语版
BILINGUAL EDITION

中国经济出版社
CHINA ECONOMIC PUBLISHING HOUSE
北　京

图书在版编目（CIP）数据

中冰企业家风采录 / 张守凤主编. -- 北京：中国经济出版社，2022.8

ISBN 978-7-5136-7057-9

Ⅰ. ①中… Ⅱ. ①张… Ⅲ. ①企业家 - 事迹 - 中国 - 现代 ②企业家 - 事迹 - 冰岛 - 现代 Ⅳ. ① K825.38 ② K835.355.38

中国版本图书馆 CIP 数据核字（2022）第 150660 号

策划编辑　崔姜薇
责任编辑　郭书芳
责任印制　马小宾
封面设计　久品轩

出版发行　中国经济出版社
印 刷 者　北京力信诚印刷有限公司
经 销 者　各地新华书店
开　　本　710mm × 1000mm　1/16
印　　张　18.25
字　　数　250 千字
版　　次　2022 年 8 月第 1 版
印　　次　2022 年 8 月第 1 次
定　　价　88.00 元
广告经营许可证　京西工商广字第 8179 号

中国经济出版社　网址 www. economyph. com　社址 北京市东城区安定门外大街 58 号　邮编 100011
本版图书如存在印装质量问题，请与本社销售中心联系调换（联系电话：010-57512564）

《中冰企业家风采录》编委会

序言 | FOREWORD

手捧《中冰企业家风采录》书稿，心中委实有些激动。让我激动的原因之一是，济南大学冰岛研究中心的这本书是为了庆祝中冰建交50周年而编辑出版的。我与张守凤教授编译的《诗的国度：冰岛诗歌选》也是为了同样的目的。我不得不说，冰岛研究中心的工作人员都是促进中冰关系的有心人，他们早在2019年就开始筹划有关庆祝活动。我感觉得到他们心之热，他们的热心也一直催促着我，让我更勤奋地工作。

原因之二，这本书所记录的是为中冰关系精耕细作的人们。书中所采访的15位成功人士，都是善于开拓、非常勤奋的企业家。书中所展现的冰岛人士都曾长期在中国工作和生活，长期与身边的中国人打交道，他们喜欢中国，有的可以说是热爱中国。他们为了工作，不可避免地要向冰岛人介绍中国，介绍自己在中国的所作所为。毛一玮和谢莹莹在对冰岛中国贸易协会主席Jonina Bjartmarz的采访中，写下了这样的文字："在合作之前，首先要打破偏见。'我（Jonina）曾经在中国住过一段时间，并从事一些进口贸易的生意。我很了解中国，有很多中国朋友，我也学到了很多。但当我终于回到冰岛的时候，我发现人们看待中国的方式还是老样子。'由于中冰民众长期存在的认识偏差，两国之间的交流与合作存在一些阻碍。"据我所知，当中冰关系出现困难时，在被采访的冰岛人士中，有人仗义执言，与冰岛有关领导人直接交涉，讲明情况。

原因之三，这本书对冰岛在全世界最有影响的公司进行了介绍。譬如碳循环国际公司，是一家致力于可再生能源的研发和生产的公司，据有关资料显示，目前该公司已拥有可再生能源和循环二氧化碳排入物转化成甲醇的技术，可为汽车、船舶等提供绿色清洁能源。据报道，浙江吉利控股集团在冰岛首都雷克雅未克已与该公司签署了一项总额为4500万美元的投资协议。将来冰岛的这项技术，若用于吉利所生产的甲醇燃料汽车上，将大大改善我国的空气质量。再譬如，我参观过马瑞奥（Marel）公司，该公司是冰岛最大的食品加工公司，2021年在上海开设了中国开放创新中心，是件很值得庆贺的事。冰岛的地热技术世界领先，联合国在冰岛开办的地热学院为我国培养了很多地热人才。2018 年，中国光大控股有限公司宣布通过旗下基金对冰岛企业极地绿色能源集团进行 7000 万美元的投资，极地绿色能源集团与中国石化集团子公司共同运营着中国的地热行业龙头企业——中石化绿源地热能开发有限公司。

济南大学冰岛研究中心成立于 2014 年，对冰岛的环境、生物资源、地热等的研究已取得突出成绩。该中心目前加强了对北极航道的研究，开展了许多与之相关的专业活动。值得一提的是，济南大学已经与冰岛比弗雷斯特（Bifrost）大学达成了合作协议，该合作将会进一步促进中国对冰岛的研究，也会加强冰岛对中国的研究。眼前的这本书是该中心精心打造的一部面向普通读者的作品。希望愿意了解中国与冰岛关系以及中国与北欧各国关系的读者能在阅读本书中有所收获。

这本书的采访者是在校学生中的志愿者。这个做法值得提倡，因为它给学生参与实践、与国内外企业界人士直接接触的机会。这种机会对学生的成长是极其有益的。

我借上述文字，祝愿济南大学冰岛研究中心在今后的研究中取得更大的成绩。虽然冰岛是个小国，但它却是一个文学和诗歌的大国，是保护本国语言的大国，是环境保护的大国，是读书和出书方面的大国，是科技发明的大国，是群众体育运动的大国。研究和利用好冰岛在社会发展方面的经验，加强同冰岛在各方面的交流，对构建人类命运共同体、实现我们第二个百年奋斗目标和伟大的中国梦有很高的参考价值。

王荣华

中国前驻冰岛大使、国际儒学联合会顾问、

济南大学客座教授、外交笔会理事、

国际中西哲学比较研究会会员

2022 年 7 月 20 日

I was somewhat excited when reading the manuscript of "*What They Say — Executives in China-Iceland and Economic Cooperation*". The first reason for my excitement is that the manuscript had been compiled for publication by Icelandic Research Center of University of Jinan to mark the 50th anniversary of the establishment of diplomatic relations between China and Iceland. The *Kingdom of Poetry: Selected Icelandic Poems* translated by Professor Zhang Shoufeng and me was also for the purpose. I have to say that everyone in Icelandic Research Center had totally set their mind on bettering the relations between China and Iceland. They began to plan relevant celebration events as early as 2019. I had been warmed up by their devotion, and their enthusiasm had been urging me to work harder.

The second reason is that the manuscript had recorded those who have worked hard for and cultivate the good relations between China and Iceland. The fifteen successful persons interviewed in the book are all entrepreneurs who had ploughed deep and farmed with great care in the relations. The Icelanders described in the book had all worked and lived in China for a long time, and they have been in frequent contacts with Chinese around them. They like China, and some can be said to have deep love for China. They inevitably have to familiarize Icelanders with China and what they have done in China for their work. In their interview with Jonina Bjartmarz, Managing Director of Iceland-China Trade Promotion Association, Mao Yiwei and Xie Yingying wrote: "Before taking actions for cooperation, we must first get rid of any prejudice. 'I (Jonina) have lived in China for a long time and engaged in import trade business. I know a lot about China. I have many Chinese friends, and I have learned a lot. But when I finally got back to Iceland, I found that the way people looked at China was still the same.' Due to the long-standing misunderstanding between people in China and Iceland, there are great obstacles to the exchanges and cooperation between the two countries." As far as I know, when there was some difficulties in the relations, someone who had been interviewed spoke out boldly to relevant Icelandic leaders in a direct manner to clarify related matters.

The third reason is that Iceland's most influential companies in the world are introduced in the book. For example, Carbon Recycling International (CRI) is a company committed to the research and development as well as production of renewable energy. According to relevant data, the company, at present, has owned the technology to convert renewable energy and recycled carbon dioxide emissions into methanol, which can provide green and clean energy for cars, ships and others. It is reported that Zhejiang Geely Holding Group has signed an investment agreement of total amount of US$ 45 million with CRI in Reykjavik. In the future, if the technology of Iceland is applied in methanol-fueled cars produced by Geely, it will greatly improve the air quality of our country. For another example, I have visited Marel, the largest food processing company in Iceland. It established the Marel's Shanghai Progress Point in 2021, which is something worth celebrating. Iceland leads the world in geothermal technology. The geothermal Institute established by the United Nations in Iceland has trained many geothermal talents for our country. In 2018, China Everbright Ltd. announced that it would invest US$ 70 million in Iceland Arctic Green Energy Corporation, an Icelandic enterprise, through its funds. Arctic Green Energy Corporation and a subsidiary of China Petrochemical Corporation jointly operate Sinopec Green Energy Geothermal Development Co., Ltd. (SGE), a leader in China's geothermal industry.

Founded in 2014, Icelandic Research Center of University of Jinan has made outstanding achievements in the research of Iceland's environment, biological resources, geothermal energy and others. At present, the Center has strengthened the research on the Arctic waterway and carried out many professional activities related to it. It is worth mentioning that University of Jinan has reached a cooperation agreement with Bifrost University in Iceland. The cooperation with the Icelandic university will further promote our research on Iceland and strengthen the research on China by the Icelandic side. The book in front of me is a work carefully designed by the Center for ordinary readers. I hope that readers who are willing to know about the relations between China and Iceland as well as those between China and Northern Europe can benefit from the book.

The interviewers of the book are volunteers among students in universities. The practice is worth advocating because it gives students the opportunity to participate in social practice and have direct contact with business people at home and abroad. This kind of opportunity is extremely beneficial to the growth of college students.

I would like to use the above words to wish Icelandic Research Center of University of Jinan greater achievements in its future research. Although Iceland is small as a state, it is big in literature and poetry, big in protecting its own language, big in environmental protection, big in reading and publishing, big in scientific and technological inventions, and big in mobilizing her masses in sports. The research and possible application of Icelandic experience in its social development, the strengthening of exchanges in all aspects with Iceland would be very valuable for the cause of building a community with a shared future for mankind and realizing our second Centennial goal and the great Chinese dream.

Wang Ronghua
Former Ambassador to Iceland,
Advisor to the International Confucian Association (ICA),
Guest Professor of University of Jinan,
Member of Council of the Diplomatic Pen,
Member of International Society for Comparative Studies of Chinese and Western Philosophy (ISCWP)
July 20, 2022

前言 | PREFACE

自1971年中国与冰岛正式建立外交关系以来，双方在经贸、旅游、文化、教育、科技等诸多领域务实合作，取得了积极成果。

——经贸往来逐年加强。2005年，冰岛在西欧国家中率先承认中国市场经济地位。2006—2021年，中国已连续16年成为冰岛在亚洲最大的贸易伙伴。2013年《中华人民共和国政府和冰岛政府自由贸易协定》签署，这是中国和欧洲国家签署的第一个自由贸易协定，对中欧经贸关系的发展具有重要的示范作用，这标志着正式建立了中冰自由贸易区。2015年7月，浙江吉利控股集团宣布以4500万美元入股冰岛碳循环国际公司，实现了中国对冰岛直接投资零的突破。2020年，中国和冰岛双边贸易额为5.6亿美元，是1971年的2360倍。

——旅游业态逐年向好。1978年，中冰友好交流协会组织第一批冰岛游客到中国旅游。近年来，中国赴冰岛游客大幅增加。2014—2018年，中国（包括港澳台地区）赴冰岛游客由每年2.6万人次增至13.35万人次，年均增长72.52%。2019年，来自中国的游客数量已近9.9万人次，中国成为冰岛第七大游客来源国，连续8年成为冰岛在亚洲的最大客源地。

——文化传播逐年活跃。2014年双方文化部门签署了《中冰文化合作谅解备忘录》。两国在对方国家举办画展、邮票展等多项展览，互派文艺团体进行访问演出。2018年，冰岛国家男子足球队闯进世界杯及在世界杯上的出色表现为中国人民所钦佩，两国足球交流更加活跃。2019年中国“欢乐春节”活动首次走进冰岛，引发热烈反响。冰岛的《萨迦》《埃达》等著作译成中文在华出版。《道德经》《论语》《西游记》等中国经典名著也被翻译成冰岛语在冰岛出版发行。

——教育事业逐年兴盛。早在20世纪七八十年代，中国即开始派出留学生赴冰岛学习冰岛语。2006—2007年，冰岛阿克雷里大学和冰岛大学相继设立了汉语课程和汉学专业。2008年，冰岛大学“北极光”孔子学院正式成立，冰岛民众学习汉语的兴趣越来越高。2019年，中国和冰岛两国政府签署关于相互承认高等教育学历学位的协议，这对促进两国在教育领域的合作，特别是留学生的交流具有重要意义。

——科技合作逐年密切。中冰两国在地热、环保、地震、海洋学、北极科研等方面的合作成果丰硕。20世纪80年代，冰岛开始为中国培训地热技术人员。2005年，中冰签署《中华人民共和国国家环境保护总局与冰岛共和国环境部环境合作谅解备忘录》和《中国地震局和冰岛环境部地震研究合作谅解备忘录》。2012年，双方签署的《中华人民共和国政府与冰岛政府关于北极合作的框架协议》是北极国家与中国签署的第一个涉及北极事务的法律文件。2018年，中—冰北极科学考察站正式启用，成为继“中国北极黄河站”后，中国在北极地区设立的第二个科考站，必将在北极科研合作方面发挥重要作用。

为更好服从服务于国家外交大局，进一步助力中冰两国双边各领域务实合作，2014年济南大学成立了冰岛研究中心。该中心是中国教育部备案的国别与区域研究中心。目前，冰岛研究中心已吸引了国内外数十名学者担任中心研究人员，针对冰岛及中冰关系开展了多项研究，竭力为中冰双边合作建言献策。冰岛研究中心积极主动与中外使馆以及高校建立联系，聘请多位中国前驻外大使和海内外专家作为顾问和客座教授，为开展有深度、有高度的智库研究奠定了良好基础。

2021年是中冰建交50周年。为增进中冰两国相互了解，弘扬当代中冰企业家自强不息、敬业奉献、顽强拼搏的精神，展示中冰企业家在推动中冰两国经贸往来等方面所作出的积极贡献，济南大学冰岛研究中心组织本校23名学生志愿者，采访整理了15位致力于中冰两国经贸往来的中国和冰岛企业家的商业故事和创业故事，编写了《中冰企业家风采录》一书。

本书的编撰于2021年6月正式启动，2022年5月完成。书中采访的15位企业家非常具有代表性，他们是两国各行业中的翘楚，他们在不同领域积极履行社会责任、体现企业担当，发挥了桥梁纽带作用。书中每一篇文章都是一个精彩的奋斗故事，讲述了每一位企业家艰辛的拼搏人生，或激励斗志，或启迪人生，为我们丰富精神世界、增强精神力量提供了文化滋养。希望此书的出版能够深化中冰友谊、拉近两国人民距离、加深对中冰经贸关系的了解与认识，激励中冰两国企业家在双边贸易、投资、旅游、科技、教育等诸多领域合作过程中作出新的更大贡献。同时，希望两国年轻人从企业家们精彩的人生中受到激励和启发，从而创造出属于自己的丰富人生。

由于时间匆忙，本书难免有不足之处，敬请广大读者批评指正！

编者

2022年5月

Since the formal establishment of diplomatic relations between China and Iceland in 1971, the two countries, through practical cooperation, have made positive achievements in many fields, such as trade, tourism, culture, education as well as science and technology, etc.

—Economic and trade exchanges between two countries are being strengthened year by year. In 2005, Iceland became the first Western European country to recognize China's market economy status. From 2006 to 2021, China has become Iceland's largest trade partner in Asia for 16 consecutive years. *Free Trade Agreement between the Government of the People's Republic of China and the Government of Iceland* was signed in 2013, which is the first free trade agreement between China and European countries. It plays an important exemplary role in the development of China-EU economic and trade relations. China-Iceland free trade zone was also officially established. In July 2015, Zhejiang Geely Holding Group announced that it had become the shareholder of Carbon Recycling International (CRI) by their investment of US$ 45 million in CRI, which achieved a breakthrough of zero outward direct investment from China in Iceland. In 2020, the bilateral trade volume between China and Iceland reached US$ 560 million, 2,360 times that of the year of 1971.

—The tourism industry is growing year by year. In 1978, China-Iceland Friendship Exchange Association arranged for the first batch of Icelandic tourists to travel in China. In recent years, Chinese tourists to Iceland have increased sharply. From 2014 to 2018, Chinese tourists (including tourists from Hong Kong, Macao and Taiwan) to Iceland increased from 26,000 to 133,500 per year, with an average annual increase of 72.52%. In 2019, the number of tourists from China has reached nearly 99,000. China has become Iceland's the seventh largest source of foreign tourists in the whole world and the largest source of tourists in Asia for eight consecutive years.

—Cultural communication is becoming active year by year. In 2014, the cultural departments of two countries signed *Memorandum of Understanding on Cultural Cooperation between China and Iceland*. The two countries held many exhibitions in each other's countries, such as art exhibitions and stamp exhibitions, and sent theater troupes to each other for performances. In 2018, the Icelandic men's national football team qualified for the World Cup and performed well in the World Cup, which was admired by Chinese people, so football exchanges between both countries became more active. In 2019, "Happy Chinese New Year" entered Iceland for the first time, causing an enthusiastic response. Icelandic works such as *Sakya* and *Edda* have been translated into Chinese and published in China. Chinese classics such as *Tao Te Ching*, *the Analects of Confucius* and *Pilgrimage to the West* have also been translated into Icelandic and published in Iceland.

—Education is booming year by year. As early as the 1970s and 1980s, China began sending students to Iceland to learn Icelandic. From 2006 to 2007, University of Akureyri and University of Iceland successively offered Chinese courses and established Sinology major. In 2008, the Northern Light Confucius Institute at University of Iceland was officially established, and Icelandic people are increasingly interested in learning Chinese. In 2019, the governments of both China and Iceland signed an agreement on mutual recognition of qualifications concerning higher education, which is of great significance to promote the cooperation in the field of education between two countries, especially the exchange of foreign students.

—Scientific and technological cooperation is becoming close year by year. China and Iceland have made rich achievements in cooperations in geothermal energy, environmental protection, earthquake, oceanography, Arctic scientific research, etc. In the 1980s, Iceland began to train geothermal technicians for China.

In 2005, memorandums of understanding on the cooperation of environment and seismic research between China and Iceland were signed. In 2012, China and Iceland signed *the Framework Agreement on Arctic Cooperation*, which is the first legal document involving Arctic affairs between China and an Arctic State. In 2018, China-Iceland Arctic Science Observatory was officially opened. It becomes China's second research station in the Arctic region after the "Chinese Arctic Yellow River Station" and is bound to play an important role in the cooperation on Arctic research.

In 2014, Icelandic Research Center was established at University of Jinan to better serve the overall situation of national diplomacy and further assist the practical cooperation in various fields between China and Iceland. The Center is a national and regional research center registered by Ministry of Education of the People's Republic of China. At present, Icelandic Research Center, having attracted dozens of scholars at home and abroad as researchers of the center, not only carries out a number of studies on Iceland and the bilateral relations, but also makes every effort to offer advice and suggestions for the bilateral cooperation between China and Iceland. The Icelandic Research Center actively establishes contacts with Chinese and foreign embassies and universities. Meanwhile, it hires many former Chinese ambassadors to foreign countries as well as experts at home and abroad as consultants and visiting professors, which lays a good foundation for in-depth and high-level think tank research.

The year of 2021 marks the 50th anniversary of the establishment of diplomatic relations between China and Iceland. Icelandic Research Center of University of Jinan under Ministry of Education of the People's Republic of China organized 23 student volunteers to interview and sort out the business experiences and entrepreneurial stories of 15 entrepreneurs who are committed to economic and trade exchanges between China and Iceland. Icelandic Research Center compiled the book *What They Say — Executives in China-Iceland Trade and Economic Cooperation* to commemorate the 50th anniversary of the establishment of diplomatic relations between China and Iceland. The target of the book is to further enhance mutual understanding between the two sides, vigorously carry forward the spirit of constant self-improvement, professional dedication and tremendous tenacity in the life of contemporary China-Iceland entrepreneurs, as well as show the positive contributions made by Chinese and Icelandic entrepreneurs in promoting bilateral economic and trade exchanges.

The compilation of the book was officially launched in June 2021 and completed in May 2022. The 15 interviewed entrepreneurs in the book are very representative. Based on their own duties, they perform their social responsibilities, build bridges to boost China-Iceland relations and contribute to practical cooperation in various fields. Every chapter of the book is a wonderful struggle story, and every entrepreneur has a hard time. Whether the inspiration of fighting spirit or enlightenment of life, they provide cultural nourishment for us to enrich our mental world and enhance our spiritual power.

We hope that the publication of the book will deepen the awareness and understanding of the two peoples on China-Iceland economic and trade relations, shorten the distance between the two peoples, further deepen China-Iceland friendship, strengthen cultural exchanges as well as help Chinese and Icelandic entrepreneurs to make new and greater contribution to the cooperation process of bilateral trade, investment, tourism, science and technology, education, etc. Meanwhile, we hope that the young people of both countries will be encouraged and inspired by the wonderful lives of entrepreneurs and enrich their own colorful lives.

Due to the tight schedule, there are inevitably some deficiencies in the book. Your criticism and correction will be highly appreciated!

Editors

May, 2022

目录 | CONTENTS

01

不务空名，足履实地

——访冰岛碳循环国际公司在华合资公司总经理夏红星

石油大王洛克菲勒曾经说过："我们的命运由我们的行动决定，而绝非完全由我们的出身决定。"自改革开放以来，我国诞生了一大批白手起家的杰出职业经理人，他们凭借自己的聪明才智，开创了一片天地，而资深职业经理人夏红星就是其中之一。20 世纪 90 年代，夏红星踏着改革开放的浪潮，单枪匹马闯进能源行业，并且在这个行业奋斗了 20 多年。在采访中，他热情地与我们分享他在工作中的趣事和自己的见解，每当说到能源和环保行业时，他总是侃侃而谈。勇于创新、坚持不懈、求真务实、承担社会责任和可持续发展是企业赖以生存的基础，也是夏红星始终坚持的发展理念。

长风破浪会有时——积累

"不积跬步，无以至千里；不积小流，无以成江海。"资深职业经理人夏红星的职业履历充分印证了这句话。夏红星曾供职于江苏省江阴市一家民营企业 10 年，之后，他又先后在德国鲁奇公司、英国石油公司和法国道达尔公司三家国际大型能源公司任职，深耕能源行业 20 多年，对能源利用和环境保护有着专业而独到的见解。"我在能源公司工作了 20 多年，对二氧化碳一点儿也不陌生，更能体会到节能减排的重要性。"基于这种忧患意识，2017 年，夏红星入职冰岛碳循环国际公司（Carbon Recycling International，CRI）在华合资公司，致力于减排和环保事业。

2007 年，夏红星团队曾在国际煤炭与能源新产业博览会上接受记者采访时说道："煤炭与能源新产业博览会搭建了一个很好的平台，使企业与国际上先进的技术转让商、技术提供商有了面对面交流的机会。我们之前也和山西的一些煤矿企业进行了接触，发现这些企业经营得都很好。我特别希望这次能找到注重环保的合作伙伴。"可见，夏红星很早就意识到了环境保护的重要性，并一直致力于节能减排事业。在英国石油公司工作时，夏红星团队曾与中科院大连物化所合作，最主要的目标就是实现煤炭的清洁利用和高效利用，如何让1千克煤炭创造出更多的经济价值、排放最少的二氧化碳。这次合作真正将产学研融合在一起，从根源上提高煤炭的利用效率。

作为能源行业从业者，夏红星对节能减排有着更为深刻的理解。“正如《资本论》中所说，资本家的第一桶金都是血淋淋的，西方能源公司早期的发展可能不是那么光彩，但他们成长起来后还是有一定社会责任感的。这些能源公司承受着非常大的社会压力，其中最大的压力就来自二氧化碳的减排。”在采访中，夏红星讲述了一件让他印象最深刻的事。在他任职于法国的道达尔公司期间，道达尔公司曾在中国内蒙古投资建设全球首个煤制烯烃一体化工业化项目，合资投资额约40亿美元，但项目进行了六七年便终止了，最主要的原因之一与二氧化碳排放有关。“这个项目每年的二氧化碳排放量接近600万吨，这个数字是非常吓人的。道达尔公司是世界第四大石油公司，这一个项目排放的二氧化碳总量占公司全球所有项目的10%。”这无疑会给中国的环境带来巨大的压力，对中国的环境治理来讲，可谓雪上加霜。

人类无时无刻不呼出二氧化碳，二氧化碳的排放是不可避免的。因此，减少二氧化碳排放是不是治标不治本，关键在于如何将排放的二氧化碳吸收、转化。2017年，夏红星主动从道达尔公司转入冰岛碳循环国际公司，组建其在中国的第一家合资公司，主要研究领域也从当初的研究排放二氧化碳转移到现在的减少二氧化碳排放。冰岛碳循环国际公司总部位于冰岛首都雷克雅未克，掌握二氧化碳加氢制甲醇的先进技术——从工业排放物和可再生能源中提取二氧化碳，并提炼成超低碳液体汽车燃料和可再生甲醇。企业的核心目标是创造效益，效益的产生来源于企业的核心竞争力，而核心技术往往在核心竞争力中起着决定性作用。冰岛碳循环国际公司开发的ETL技术（二氧化碳制甲醇技术）是目前全球唯一工业在产的二氧化碳加氢制甲醇项目，这为冰岛碳循环国际公司在能源行业立足奠定了基础，同时也为其带来超过普通企业的客户关注度以及市场广泛度。

冰岛碳循环国际公司为应对气候变化、治理大气污染提供了可操作的解决方案，公司雄心勃勃，想让二氧化碳加氢制甲醇装置在全世界开花结果。但利用可再生资源这一概念在当时的中国还未发展起来，冰岛国际碳循环公司无从下手。夏红星说：“作为一家外资民营企业，政府支持力度相对较弱，我们必须自力更生。”为此，夏红星带领团队成立了上海麦芬隆公司，对中国市场进行了深入的调研和考察。“我们花了将近一年的时间，才基本上确定了公司未来的发展战略，瞄准了市场开拓方向。”2019年，夏红星拿下了冰岛碳循环国际公司在华合资公司的第一个示范项目，二氧化碳加氢制绿色甲醇工业化生产装置在河南安阳正式施工建造。2021 年 5 月 26 日，时任冰岛驻华大使古士贤先生（Gunnar Snorri Gunnarsson）一行人参观了项目现场，对甲醇项目工地进行了实地考察。夏红星对项目做了详细介绍，该项目是全球第一套规模化利用温室气体减排的绿色环保、低碳循环经济示范项目，对提升安阳市在河南省乃至全国的绿色环保形象具有十分重要的示范意义。

夏红星（前排左二）为古士贤大使（前排右二）讲解在建项目

没有经历，任何新的东西都无法深知。20 多年的能源行业从业经历造就了今天的夏红星，也成就了冰岛碳循环国际公司在华合资公司。正是这宝贵的经历，让夏红星深刻认识到节能减排的重要性、洞察到能源行业未来的发展趋势。凭借丰富的经验和知识以及敏锐的市场洞察力，夏红星顺应节能减排这一呼吁，开启了职业生涯的新阶段。

君子藏器于身，待时而动——机遇

夏红星加入冰岛碳循环国际公司后，赶上了中国绿色低碳发展政策的热潮。2020 年 9 月，国家主席习近平在第七十五届联合国大会一般性辩论上发表重要讲话，宣布中国二氧化碳排放力争于 2030 年前达到峰值，努力争取 2060 年前实现碳中和。2021 年 7 月，全国碳排放权交易市场开市。低碳在中国掀起了一股新热潮。从这一方面看，夏红星加入冰岛碳循环国际公司、进入中国市场的决定显得极具前瞻性。“我当时也不知道它会来得这么快，但我坚信，我加入冰岛碳循环国际公司的决定是正确的，我很看好这个产业方向。”

“中国是一个人口大国，也是能源消费大国，能源利用效率不高。同时，我们的能源紧缺，能源安全问题令人担忧。纵观这几个方面，中国政府肯定会朝着减少碳排放的方向前进。”对于中国大力推动碳减排，夏红星有自己的见解。“中国政府做这件事是经过深思熟虑的，碳减排对我们国家的产业来讲，既是压力，也是动力，问题的关键在于企业如何看待碳减排。短期来看，资源型企业会承受较大压力，但长期来看，减少碳排放将促进产业结构调整，实现可持续发展。”

作为一个富煤、缺气、贫油的国家，我国能源结构以煤炭为主，用煤就免不了排放二氧化碳。20 世纪 90 年代的中国正值改革开放的热潮，当时中国工业化如快马奔驰，发展迅速，但这给环境带来了巨大的压力，中国的碳排放总量仅占全球的 11%，而 2019 年中国的碳排放量达到了全球的 28%。“我国煤炭的利用效率可能还达不到发达国家的 60%，也就是说 1 千克煤的热量在日本可以创造 1 万元人民币的价值，但在中国可能只有三四千元人民币。我们的碳排放量是这些发达国家的几倍。因此，我们也在国际上承受了非常大的压力。”

2021 年，全国碳排放权交易市场上线交易。当被问到如何看待碳排放权交易市场的开放时，夏红星说：“无论对个人、企业、国家，还是对世界来说，这都是一件令人振奋的事。碳排放权交易市场其实是起杠杆的作用，来调节经济和社会行为。”碳排放权交易市场通过碳的价格水平影响企业的生产活动，高价将会驱使企业朝着减排的方向发展。积薄而为厚，聚少而为多。当越来越多的企业受到碳排放权交易市场的影响时，势必会影响产业结构，促进全球经济持续均衡发展，减少二氧化碳排放。在夏红星看来，碳排放权交易市场的开放，不仅会为宏观发展带来机遇，也会对个人产生深刻影响。“期望碳排放权交易市场使节能减排的理念深入人心，影响每个人的行为习惯，形成环保主义情怀。”

培根曾经说过："善于识别与把握时机是极为重要的。在一切大事情上，人在开始做事前要像千眼神那样察看时机，而在进行时要像千手神那样抓住时机。"夏红星和冰岛碳循环国际公司能享受到政策红利绝非偶然，是他们超前的眼光和科学的决策，使他们能够抓住这一机遇，在环保行业里大显身手、大展宏图。

君子强学而力行——务实

"格物致知，求真务实"是一种态度，这种态度在一定程度上依赖于工作者自身的素质。没有哪个人生下来就适合做某事，都是在自我修炼中逐渐养成的。一名优秀的职业经理人正需要在这样的修炼中慢慢养成一种求真务实的态度，去分析自己身边的各种信息。20 世纪 90 年代，社会上出现创业热潮，在当时的背景下，可能由于资源禀赋的不同，或者偶然的机遇导致一些人的成功。然而，在如今全球化的大背景下，首先要明白自己处于什么位置，距离目标还有多远，如何到达彼岸。必须能够生存，才可以在生存的基础上发展自己。这也与夏红星多次提到的务实精神不谋而合。

在被问及对当代年轻职业经理人的建议时，夏红星是这样说的："首先，年轻职业经理人应该判断他们到底喜欢什么。其实，他们需要更多地了解各方面的知识，然后结合知识再去做一件自己喜欢的事，一开始做错没有关系，可以多尝试几次，然后才能发现他们更喜欢做哪一个。"古语讲："君子强学而力行。"说的就是缜密思考，把所学和所用有机结合起来。学习不是最终目的，学以致用才是更重要的。对于当代年轻人，夏红星给予了这样的寄语："要把科学的梦想变成现实，要树立正确的价值观，充满好奇，坚持不懈，戒骄戒躁，永远向上。"做人如此，做企业也是一样。不能靠高谈阔论，要脚踏实地，一步步地探索，扎实做事。做企业最根本的是做出好产品，提供好的服务，有良好的经济效益。"这样一路走来总有收获，走着，走着花就开了。"

2021 年 9 月 27 日，夏红星带领冰岛碳循环国际公司与江苏斯尔邦石化有限公司签署了 10 万吨级的绿色甲醇项目，深刻践行务实精神。

夏红星（前排右一）参与二氧化碳制光伏膜材料项目启动仪式

先天下之忧而忧——责任

职业经理人作为企业的领导者，是社会的精英群体，他们必须处理好个人与社会的关系。只有具备强烈的责任感与使命感，以助力社会发展为己任，超越传统的经济利益最大化的思维，将个人利益和企业经营融入社会的整体利益，才能得到社会各方的信任与尊敬，从而实现更大的发展。做一个成功的职业经理人，应该且必须具备责任心这一基本的企业家精神，要对社会起到一定的引领作用。“如果只是有能力，而不承担社会责任，那么这个职业经理人还不足以拥有成为成功职业经理人的条件。当前，中国存在一大批值得我尊敬并以其为标杆的职业经理人，这些职业经理人的共同点是，他们会把自己更多的时间和精力投入创造社会价值上。”夏红星认为，责任永远是第一要义，社会责任更是重要。明确自身的社会角色和社会定位，对社会的期望和要求积极回应，培育有强大的正能量的企业文化，坚持依法合规经营、互利合作，带领企业取得良好的经营业绩，为中国乃至全球经济社会的可持续发展作出更大的贡献，是新时代赋予中国职业经理人的历史重任，也是职业经理人社会责任的核心内涵。

夏红星也一直在自己的领域践行责任担当。为促进我国节能减排事业的发展，夏红星走访全国各地，多次参加煤化工相关会议，如第七届中国新型煤化工国际研讨会暨煤化工产业低碳与高质量发展论坛、焦炉煤气综合利用技术研讨会暨关键配套装备专题推介会等会议，并致力于推广二氧化碳制甲醇的规模化普及与应用，为中国二氧化碳减排事业添砖加瓦。在能源方面，夏红星也有自己独到的见解，并且为国家新能源发展提出了建议。他认为，当下中国对于新能源汽车的补贴比例过高，并且不可持续，而且这项政策也受到很多质疑。“客观地讲，目前的许多新能源可能并不能够维持下去。但是，如果把补贴新能源的资金分散开来，可以撬动许多个甲醇装置的建设，这对国家能源与环境是大有益处的。”同时，夏红星从自己的观点出发，认为新能源是否会成为未来的主流仍是未知。

对当代年轻人，夏红星是这样说的：“如果一个人不关心政治，不关心社会，这其实是一个不负责任的人，当代年轻人可能会不太理解。他们觉得做好本职工作就可以了，其实并不是这样的，每一个年轻人都应该关心政治。”少年强则中国强，少年智则中国智！如果青少年都不关心国家政治，那么一个国家就很难健康地成长，其未来将令人担忧。

“务实”与“社会责任”一直是夏红星强调的两个基本的人生价值观，无论是对个人，还是对企业或者国家而言都如此。夏红星坚信，“可持续发展”是企业最大的社会责任，企业包括职业经理人在承担社会责任的过程中，就是应该通过多种方式与政府合作打造良性循环。“国有所需，企有所呼”是一个企业必备的信念。夏红星已经成功带领着 CRI 踏上了中国的减排道路，并且致力于成为行业的引领者。

（刘旻璞　孟伟）

Not Seeking Empty Fame but Doing Solid Work

— Interview with Xia Hongxing, General Manager of Carbon Recycling International's Joint Venture in China

Oil magnate Rockefeller once said, "Our destiny is determined by our actions, not by our origins." Since the reform and opening up, a large number of outstanding self-made professional managers, who have carved out their own careers with their own intelligence, have been born in China. Xia Hongxing, a senior professional manager, is one of them. In the 1990s, Xia Hongxing, following the wave of reform and opening up, broke into the energy industry alone and struggled in this industry for more than 20 years. In the interview, he enthusiastically shared with us his interesting stories and opinions in his work. Whenever he talked about the industry of energy and environmental protection, he always poured out words. Innovation, perseverance, pragmatism, social responsibility and sustainable development are not only the basis for the survival of the enterprise but also the development concept that Xia Hongxing always adheres to.

A Time Will Come to Ride the Wind and Cleave the Waves —Accumulation

"A journey of a thousand miles may not be achieved without accumulation of each single step, just as the enormous ocean may not be formed without gathering every brook or stream." The history of senior professional manager Xia Hongxing fully confirms the remark. Xia Hongxing once worked in a private enterprise in Jiangyin City, Jiangsu Province for 10 years, and then successively worked in three large international energy companies: Germany Lurgi Gmbh, British Petroleum PLC and French TotalEnergies. He has been deeply involved in the energy industry for more than 20 years and has professional and unique opinions on energy utilization and environmental protection. "I have worked in the energy industry for more than 20 years. Carbon dioxide isn't strange to me, I can better understand the importance of energy conservation and emission reduction." Based on the awareness of potential dangers, Xia Hongxing joined the joint venture of Carbon Recycling International (CRI), Icelandic firm, in China in 2017, and was committed to the cause of emission reduction and environmental protection.

In 2007, Xia Hongxing's team said in an interview with reporters at the International Coal & Energy New Industry Expo: "The International Coal & Energy New Industry Expo has built a good platform for enterprises to have face-to-face communication with international advanced technology transferors and providers. We have also contacted some coal mining enterprises in Shanxi before and found that those enterprises are doing well. I especially hope to find some partners who pay attention to environmental protection this time." It can be seen that Xia Hongxing has long realized the importance of environmental protection and has been committed to the cause of emission reduction. When working for BP PLC, Xia Hongxing's team cooperated with Dalian Institute of Chemical Physics (DICP) of the Chinese Academy of Sciences for realization of the clean and efficient utilization of coal and the method of making a kilogram of coal create more economic value but emitting the least carbon dioxide. That cooperation truly integrates enterprises, universities and research institutes, and improves the utilization efficiency of coal from the root.

As a practitioner in the energy industry, Xia Hongxing has a deeper understanding of energy conservation and emission reduction. "As *Das Kapital* said, capital comes dripping from head to foot, from every pore, with blood and dirt. The early development of Western energy companies may not be so glorious, but they still have a certain sense of social responsibility after they grew up. These energy companies are under great social pressure, and the biggest pressure comes from the reduction of carbon dioxide emission." In the interview, Xia Hongxing told the most impressive thing to him. During Xia Hongxing's tenure at French TotalEnergies, TotalEnergies invested in the world's first industrial integration project of coal to olefin in Inner Mongolia, China, with the joint investment of about USD 4 billion, but the project was terminated after 6 or 7 years. One of the main reasons for the termination is related to carbon dioxide emissions. "The annual carbon dioxide emission of the project is close to 6 million tons, which is very frightening. The project emits 10% of the total carbon dioxide emissions of all the global projects of TotalEnergies, the world's fourth largest oil company." This will undoubtedly bring great pressure on China's environment and even worse for China's environmental governance.

Human beings exhale carbon dioxide all the time, which makes carbon dioxide emissions inevitable. Therefore, whether the reduction of carbon dioxide emissions is a palliative rather than an ultimate solution depends on how to absorb and transform the emitted carbon dioxide. In 2017, Xia Hongxing resigned from TotalEnergies and joined Icelandic Carbon Recycling International (CRI) to form its first joint venture in China. His main research field has also shifted from the original emission of carbon dioxide to the current absorption and consumption of carbon dioxide. Headquartered in Reykjavik, the capital of Iceland, CRI has mastered the advanced technology of carbon dioxide hydrogenation to methanol — extracting carbon dioxide from industrial emissions and renewable energy, and refining it into ultra-low-carbon liquid as vehicle fuel and renewable methanol. The core goal of enterprises is to make a benefit, which comes from the core competitiveness of enterprises, and the core technology often plays a decisive role in the core competitiveness. ETL Technology developed by CRI is currently the only industrial carbon dioxide hydrogenation to methanol project in the world, which provides a foundation for CRI to gain a foothold in the renewable and sustainable energy industry. Meanwhile, it also brings more customer attention and wider market than ordinary enterprises.

CRI has provided operable solutions to deal with climate change and control air pollution. It is full of ambition and wants to make carbon dioxide hydrogenation to methanol plants blossom and bear fruit all over the world. However, the concept of using renewable resources had not been developed in China at that time, and CRI could not find a way to start its business. Xia Hongxing said: "As a foreign-funded private enterprise, the government support is relatively weak, and we must rely on our own efforts." For this purpose, Xia Hongxing led the team to set up Maifenlong (Shanghai) Environmental Engineering Technology Co., Ltd. to conduct in-depth research and investigation on the Chinese market. "It took us nearly a year to basically determine the Company's future development strategy and aim at the direction of market development." In 2019, the industrial production equipment of carbon dioxide hydrogenation to methanol, the first carbon dioxide recycling demonstration project of the joint venture of CRI, was officially constructed by Xia Hongxing's company in Anyang, Henan. On May 26, 2021, Mr. Gunnar Snorri Gunnarsson, the ambassador of Iceland to China, and his party visited the site of the demonstration project and made a field visit to the construction site of methanol project. Xia Hongxing introduced the project in detail. The project is the world's first set of green and environmental protection and the demonstration project of low-carbon circular economy for large-scale use of greenhouse gas. It has very important demonstration significance for improving the green environmental protection image of Anyang in Henan Province and even the whole country.

Without experience, you can't know well anything new. More than 20 years of working experience in the energy industry has created today's Xia Hongxing and the joint venture of CRI in China. It is the Xia Hongxing's valuable experience that makes Xia Hongxing deeply realize the importance of energy conservation and emission reduction and gain insight into the future development trend of the energy industry. With rich experience and knowledge as well as keen market insight, Xia Hongxing complied with the appeal of energy conservation and emission reduction and opened a new stage of his career.

A Gentleman Hides His Tools in His Body and Waits for the Time to Move — Opportunity

Xia Hongxing caught up with the upsurge of China's green and low-carbon development policy after joining CRI. In September 2020, Mr. Xi Jinping, President of the People's Republic of China said at the General Debate of the 75th Session of the United Nations General Assembly that "China aim to have CO_2 emissions peak before 2030 and achieve carbon neutrality before 2060." In July 2021, China's national carbon trading market started online trading. Low carbon has set off a new upsurge in China. From this aspect, Xia Hongxing's decision to join CRI and enter the Chinese market seems very forward-looking. "I didn't know it would come so soon at that time, but I firmly believe that my decision to join CRI is correct, and I am optimistic about this industrial direction."

"China is a country with a large population and a huge energy consumer. Its energy efficiency is not high. Meanwhile, our energy shortage and security are worrisome. Looking at these aspects, the Chinese government will certainly move in the direction of carbon emission reduction." Xia Hongxing has his own views on China's efforts to promote carbon emission reduction. "The Chinese government has done this after careful consideration. Carbon emission reduction is both a pressure and a driving force for our country's industry. The key to the question lies in how enterprises view carbon emission reduction. In the short term, resource-based enterprises will bear great pressure, but in the long run, carbon emission reduction will promote the adjustment of industrial structure and achieve sustainable development."

As a country rich in carbon, short of gas and poor in oil, China's energy structure is dominated by coal, so coal use will inevitably emit carbon dioxide. In the 1990s, China was in the great upsurge of reform and opening up. At that time, China's industrialization was developing rapidly like a galloping horse, but it brought great pressure to the environment. China's total carbon emissions in the 1990s accounted for only 11% of the world, while China's carbon emissions reached 28% of the world in 2019. "The utilization efficiency of China's coal may not reach

60% of that of developed countries, that is, the heat of a kilogram of coal can create a value of RMB 10,000 in Japan, but that may only be RMB 3,000 or 4,000 in China. Our carbon emissions are several times that of these developed countries, so we are under great pressure internationally."

In 2021, the national carbon emissions trading market launched online trading. When asked how to view the opening of the carbon trading market, Xia Hongxing said: "it is an exciting thing for individuals, enterprises, our country and the whole world. The carbon trading market actually acts as a lever to adjust economic and social behaviors." The carbon trading market affects the production activities of enterprises through the price level of carbon, and the high price will drive enterprises to develop in the direction of emission reduction. Many a little makes a mickle. When more and more enterprises are affected by the carbon trading market, the effect on the industrial structure is bound to occur, which can promote sustained and balanced economic development and reduce carbon dioxide emissions in the world. In Xia Hongxing's view, the opening of the national carbon emissions trading market will not only bring opportunities for macro development but also have a profound impact on individuals. "The carbon trading market is expected to make the concept of energy conservation and emission reduction deeply rooted in the hearts of the people, affect everyone's behavior and habits, and form a feeling of environmentalism."

Bacon once said: "It is extremely important to be good at identifying and grasping opportunities. In all big businesses, people should look at their opportunities like thousands of eyes before starting to do things, and seize the opportunity when they go on." It is no accident that Xia Hongxing and CRI can enjoy the dividend policy. It is their advanced vision and scientific decision-making that enable them to seize the opportunity, distinguish themselves and achieve their ambitions in the environmental protection industry.

The Gentleman Shall Study and Practice Hard — Pragmatism

"Studying the nature of things, seeking truth and advocating practice" is an attitude, which depends on the quality of workers to a certain extent. No one is born to do something, but slowly learns in the process of self-cultivation. An excellent professional manager needs to develop a realistic and pragmatic attitude in such practice to analyze all kinds of information around him. The upsurge of entrepreneurship in the 1990s may lead to some person's success because of personal different resource endowments or accidental opportunities. However, in today's context of globalization, we must first understand where we are, how far we are from our goals and how can we reach the other shore. We must be able to find a gap and space that are suitable for our survival before we can develop ourselves on the basis of survival, which also coincides with the pragmatic spirit mentioned by Xia Hongxing many times.

When asked about the suggestions for contemporary young professional managers, Xia Hongxing said, "First of all, young professional managers shall judge what they like. Actually, they need to know more about all aspects of knowledge, and then do something they like in combination with the knowledge of their own. It doesn't matter if they make a mistake at first. They can try it several times before they can find out which one they prefer to do." As the old saying goes, "The gentleman shall study and practice hard", which means that the gentleman always think carefully and organically combine what he has learned with the profession that he is engaged in. Learning is not the ultimate goal, learning for practical use is more important. For contemporary young people, Xia Hongxing gave such a message: "People shall turn life into a scientific dream and realize the dream by establishing correct values, being full of curiosity, persevering, guarding against arrogance and impetuosity, and going up forever." One shall get along with people quite well, so does an enterprise with others. We shall not talk incessantly but explore step by step and do solid work in a down-to-earth way. The most fundamental thing for an enterprise is to make good products, provide good services and have good economic benefits. "In this way, you will harvest, and the flowers will keep themselves blooming all your way."

On September 27, 2021, Xia Hongxing led Carbon Recycling International

(CRI) to sign a 100,000-ton green methanol project with Jiangsu Sierbang Petrochemical Co., Ltd. profoundly practicing the spirit of pragmatism.

Be the First to Worry the Woes of the people — Responsibility

As the leaders of enterprises, professional managers are an elite group of the society, and they must deal with the relationship between the individual and society well. Only with a strong sense of responsibility and mission, to help social development as their own responsibility, surpass the traditional thinking of maximizing economic interests, and integrate individual interests and enterprise operations into the overall interests of the society, can they get the trust and respect of all social parties, so as to achieve greater development. To be a successful professional manager, they should and must possess the basic entrepreneurial spirit of responsibility and play a leading role in the society. "If a professional manager only has the ability, but does not undertake the social responsibility, then he is not enough to become a successful one. At present, there are a lot of professional managers in China that I respect and look up to. One point they have in common is that they devote their time and energy more to creating the social value." Xia Hongxing believes that responsibility is always the most important, and the social responsibility is even more. Clarifying the personal social role and positioning, responding positively to expectations and demands of the society, fostering a strong positive enterprise culture, adhering to law-based and compliance operations and mutual beneficial cooperation, leading the enterprise to achieve good business performance, and making greater contribution to the sustainable economic and social development of China and even the world at large, are the historical responsibilities of new era for Chinese professional managers and also the core connotation of their social responsibility.

Xia Hongxing has been practicing responsibility in his own field as well. To promote the development of China's emission reduction cause, he visited throughout the country and participated in coal chemical industry related meetings for many times, such as The 7th China New Coal Chemical Industry International Symposium and Coal Chemical Industry Low carbon and High Quality Development Forum, Seminar on Comprehensive Utilization of Coke Oven Gas and Special Promotion Conference on Key Supporting Equipment. He has also been committed to promoting the large-scale popularization and application of methanol from carbon dioxide, contributing to the cause of carbon dioxide emission reduction in China. Xia Hongxing also has his own views on energy, and he has put forward suggestions for the new energy development for the country. He believes that China's current subsidies for new energy vehicles are too high and unsustainable, and that the policy is also being questioned. "Objectively speaking, many new energy resources today may not be sustainable. However, if the subsidy funds for new energy are dispersed, so as to leverage the construction of many methanol units, it is of great benefit to the national energy and environment." At the same time, Xia Hongxing, starting from his own point of view, thinks that it remains to be seen whether new energy will become the mainstream of the future.

This is what Xia Hongxing said for contemporary young people: "If one does not care about politics, or society, this is actually an irresponsible behavior. Young people today in particular may not understand. They think they can just do their job well. That's not really the case, every young person should be concerned about politics." Juvenile strong and China strong, Juvenile wise and China wise! If even the juveniles don't care about national politics, then it will be difficult for a country to maintain healthy growth, and its future will be worrying.

Xia Hongxing participated in seminar on comprehensive utilization of coke oven gas

Whether for the individual, enterprise or the country, "pragmatism" and "social responsibility" have always been two essential life values that Xia Hongxing emphasizes. He believes "sustainable development" is a topic that must be concerned to operate an enterprise. In the process of undertaking social responsibility, enterprises, including professional managers, should work together with the government in various ways to create a virtuous cycle. "When the country needs, the enterprise can respond" is an essential belief for enterprises. Xia Hongxing has successfully led CRI on the road to emission reduction in China, and he is committed to becoming a leader in this industry.

(Liu Minpu　Meng Wei)

02

明德任责，致知力行

——访冰岛中国贸易协会主席 Jonina Bjartmarz

“我生来就是高山而非溪流，我欲于群峰之巅俯视平庸的沟壑。我生来就是人杰而非草芥，我站在伟人之肩藐视卑微的懦夫！”这是“七一勋章”获得者张桂梅校长创立的华坪女子高中的校训。21世纪以来，女性的声音被越来越多的人听见，她们奋斗在各行各业，用自己的力量推动着人类前进的每一步。Jonina Bjartmarz，从创办律师事务所到从政再到下海经商，她的每一步对自己来说都是一次挑战。在采访中，Jonina热情地和我们分享了她的所见所闻所感，她对于中国和冰岛的贸易、能源和环保问题总有特别的见解。敢于挑战、勇于创新、不甘平庸、不惧使命，这是她人生经历的代名词，也带给我们铿锵坚定的女性力量。

人生如逆旅，我亦是行人

“世界是一面镜子，你是什么样的人，就能够折射出什么样的世界。”冰岛中国贸易协会主席Jonina Bjartmarz的人生经历充分诠释了这句话。大学毕业后，Jonina Bjartmarz和她的丈夫共同经营律师事务所超过15年。1999年，她创办了冰岛女企业家协会并担任协会的会长，并先后担任过冰岛国会议员、冰岛环境部长和北欧合作部长。“冰岛中国贸易协会将中国和冰岛之间的贸易联系起来，我创立的女企业家协会也将女性联合了起来，并鼓励她们做得更多更好。我愿意和别人一起工作，帮助他们成长。”在国际合作共赢的意识下，目前Jonina担任冰岛中国贸易协会的主席，致力于中冰两国经贸往来和交流合作。

“我觉得过去的选择对我来说是一个挑战。”正如她所言，Jonina的人生充满了各种未知与挑战。在学习期间，Jonina就经常在医院、社会服务机构、儿童服务机构等地实习，帮助有需要的人。正是因为这段经历，她迫切地想学习法律知识，为有需要的人提供援助。在通过大学预科考试后，她选择去法学院进修。“这对我来说是一个不小的挑战，因为最初只有

10% ~ 15% 的学生能够通过第一年的学业考核，而律师行业是一个男性主导的行业。”但是，越努力就会越幸运，Jonina 顺利地从法学院毕业，并获得律师资格证书，并于 3 年后成为冰岛律师协会的会员。

Jonina 积极面对人生的每一个选择。在担任律师的过程中，Jonina 始终担负着应尽的社会责任。“我以前经常和媒体打交道，在我从政的前几年，由于我担任冰岛家长协会的主席，不得不处理学校及其他方面的事情。我的社交能力很强，所以我经常出现在媒体面前，面对各种各样的争论。”正是因为她良好的表达和社交能力，Jonina 才被政党发现。“这对我来说也是一个挑战。这是我从未想象过的事情。我的丈夫也劝说我为什么不去试一试呢？如果我试都不试，以后一定会后悔的。”因此，Jonina 尝试了，也成功当选了议员。

2008 年金融危机期间，即使远在中国经商，Jonina 仍然挂念着她的祖国。“当时我住在中国，我非常担心冰岛，因为冰岛的金融状况很糟糕。我一直在想办法把更多的外汇带到冰岛。在我看来，发展旅游业是一个办法。通过旅游业，将为冰岛带来更多的游客、更多的外汇。所以，我在 2008 年创立了旅游公司。直到 2015 年，公司才有了起色。”与其他企业家不同，Jonina 的从商动机很单纯。她自始至终也坚持着本心，为那些需要帮助的人服务。

在合作之前，首先要打破偏见。“我曾经在中国住过一段时间，并从事一些进口贸易的生意。我很了解中国，有很多中国朋友，我也学到了很多。但当我终于回到冰岛的时候，我发现人们看待中国的方式还是老样子。”由于中冰之间长期存在的认识偏差，两国之间的交流与合作存在一些阻碍。在女企业家协会，Jonina 和协会成员经常举办展览会，代表们会介绍各自的公司，推销各自的商品和业务。

此外，Jonina 尤其注重女性意识的崛起。“我们也鼓励越来越多的女性创业，鼓励她们为成为企业主而不是雇员。”在这些女企业家身上，她好像看到了曾经的自己，一个曾经努力想打破男性对律师行业主导地位的自己，一个曾经想从政，为弱势群体打开话语权的自己。也正是因为自己先前的经历，她尤其想给还在拼搏创业的女企业家们一些帮助。“我穿越的风景和穿越我的风景构成了我”，正是过去的种种挑战锻造出现在的 Jonina，使她能够以更开阔的视野看待人和事。这些宝贵的经历也让她明白了互相尊重、互利共赢的重要性，开启了她人生的新纪元。

读万卷书，行万里路

经营旅行社的经历是Jonina人生中浓墨重彩的一笔，对Jonina来说，旅行中遇到的每个人、每件事都很有趣，同时也补充了她对这个世界的感知。

冰岛位于北大西洋一角，人口只有30多万，但自然风光优美，物产丰富。在冰岛，如墨的夜空中时常会出现璀璨壮丽的极光，色彩缤纷，变幻无穷。这里夏季清风徐来、满目绿茵，冬日银装素裹、冰封千里。美丽的风景无疑是游客的天堂，因此旅游业已成为冰岛的支柱产业。Jonina所做的就是将世界各地的游客带到这美丽的风景面前，向世界各地的游客展示来自大自然的魅力。Jonina说道，"我们在开展业务的过程中会遇到许多不同的人，与人互动的过程很有趣，这也是我喜欢这个行业的原因。我认为，我是一名教育家。在旅行的过程中，人们不仅仅是在旅行，同时也在体验当地文化，扩宽自身的见识，补充自己对这个国家和世界的看法，完善自身。"

旅游的过程也是一个不断打破偏见的过程。Jonina说，有一些首次来到中国的冰岛人，他们的反应非常有趣。由于冰岛是个人口较少的国家，所以长期以来，人们对中国的印象大多来自其他西方国家。当中美关系紧张的时候，冰岛人看到了更多来自西方，尤其是美国的宣传，因此会对中国和中国人产生偏见。所以，当一些冰岛人第一次到中国旅行，他们会发现实际的中国和预想中的很不一样。Jonina谈到了自己的一次经历："我有一个同事，她第一次来北京，我问她有什么期待？她说她希望有蓝天及没有污染的环境。我说，你想象中的是所有人都穿着旧衣服，还有拥挤的街道。但事实是，你会看到很多年轻人穿着漂亮的衣服，街道也不拥挤，一切都比你想象中的要好得多。但是，我告诉她们这些还不够，人们需要体验。这就是我的工作。"

在旅游业方面，Jonina是忠实的"可持续旅游"的支持者。在采访过程中，Jonina不断强调，我们应该怀着"可持续旅游"的理念去旅行，尤其是去冰岛这样环境脆弱的国度旅行。就像我们在冰岛可以看到一些宣传越野驾驶的广告，实际上这在冰岛属于犯罪行为。冰岛人深刻地意识到未受破坏的自然的非凡价值，因此他们身体力行地节约资源、保护环境，可持续发展的思想已根植于冰岛人的心里。

Jonina认为："我们的自然是一种资源，'可持续旅行'意味着游客不要留下足迹，自己带来的东西在离开的时候也应该全部带走。这不仅是从保护自然和文化的角度考虑，也是从社会效益和经济效益的角度出发。人们必须有可持续的意识。”这也让我们看到 Jonina 身上的社会责任感。只有保护环境，节约资源，走绿色可持续发展道路，才能保持旅游业的长久发展，保持一个地区的长治久安。

机会乘今日，雌雄决此行

松下幸之助有言：“假如机遇来临，你要好好把握，开创你的前程。”《中华人民共和国政府和冰岛政府自由贸易协定》（以下简称《协定》）的生效无疑对双方来说都是机遇。《协定》自 2014 年 7 月 1 日正式生效以来，极大地促进了中国和冰岛的贸易往来。中国近年来与冰岛的经贸关系不断改善，在很多相关领域特别是优势互补的领域已经开展合作。作为冰岛中国贸易协会主席，Jonina 抓住机遇，积极地促进双边贸易额的增加，发挥着关键的推动作用。

2018 年 10 月 29 日，Jonina 带领冰岛女企业家协会代表来华访问并在冰岛驻中国大使馆举办推介会，就食品、药品、水产品方面进行了热切商谈。中冰海鲜贸易进一步扩大。谈到此次经历，Jonina 赞不绝口。“这很有趣，而且在很多方面都非常成功。这些女性都是我们协会中的成员，还有一些女性携丈夫一起前来，我们是一个大概 20 人的团体。其中，有些女性是首次来到中国。我们关注到中国举办了中国国际进口博览会（China International Import Expo）等等，所以我们决定与大使馆合作。冰岛驻中国大使馆为这些企业家们组织了这次会议，以拓展在中国合作与发展的渠道。这次会议取得良好效果。”

不只是冰岛代表团来访中国，Jonina 也接待了许多访问冰岛的中国经贸代表团。例如，2019 年 10 月，Jonina 在冰岛接待了来自中国湖北省荆州市的经贸代表团，举办了冰岛—中国贸易促进会、冰岛投资环境推介会等系列经贸洽谈交流活动，结合双方优势和需求，在文化旅游、水产品深加工、运动用品和婴童服装等方面进行深度交流。

Jonina 对于如何与其他国家的企业家打交道颇有经验，当被问及对年轻企业家的建议时，Jonina 认为：“首先您需要增加对其他国家的了解，了解那里的文化和历史。这样你就知道对方来自哪里，并且明白对方做生意的方式。无论是在冰岛还是在中国都有一些不诚信的人，你需要了解你的生意伙伴的背景。最好的办法就是在进行任何业务往来之前先走访看看。我经常鼓励人们去中国，见识更多的人，看看当地城市如今的样貌，读一些中国历史。这同样适用于想在冰岛做生意的中国人。”做生意需要拿出诚意，尤其是在跨国贸易存在不少困难的情况下，唯有双方诚信合作，众人拾柴火焰高，中冰两国贸易在未来才会发展得更好。

在推动中国与冰岛经贸往来、促进冰岛贸易发展的过程中，Jonina 始终把握机遇、恪尽职守、不惧挑战，用自身行动演绎了何为“践行初心，不负使命”。

未来已来，将至已至

冰岛已成为世界上使用清洁能源最多的国家之一，并有信心成功完成能源转型。目前，冰岛一般只将可燃燃料用于车辆和船舶。“在过去的50年里，冰岛几乎没有使用过煤炭。冰岛采取了多项措施来减少受到全球气候变暖的影响，但从全球的角度来看，由于冰岛是一个小国，我们的贡献微乎其微。”Jonina 认为，在全球变暖的大环境下，冰岛能做的是为各国树立榜样，通过国际合作共同应对环境问题。中国在能源转型过程中遇到了不少困难和挑战，某些城市甚至采用拉闸限电来达成碳排放目标。对此，Jonina 表示：“在过去，因为烧煤，甚至房屋都是黑色的。但自从我们使用地热来供暖后，情况就大不相同了。空气质量开始变好，城市环境也得到改善。地热能也是一种相对便宜的供暖方式。在未来，我们希望履行我们的承诺和责任。我们能够做到的，为世界各国树立榜样，分享我们在地热方面的经验。我觉得这才是我们真正有贡献的地方。”可喜的是，目前中冰两国已经在能源领域广泛开展了交流合作。中石化已经开始利用冰岛的地热技术和经验，在中国打造“无烟城”，并开发其他项目。在碳循环方面，冰岛碳循环国际公司已经在中国投资。2021 年 9 月，冰岛和中国签署技术合同，江苏斯尔邦石化有限公司与冰岛碳循环公司合作，从工业尾气中回收二氧化碳来生产新能源材料。

未来，能源领域意味着无限的挑战和可能。对于处在转型阵痛期的中国，Jonina 表示，“我由衷地希望中国在能源转型的战役中可以成功。因为中国是世界上最大的工业化国家，中国比其他国家都更有义务去做，也比其他国家在这方面面临更多的困难。”目前，中国和冰岛正在不断加深能源领域的交流与合作。

冰岛作为欧盟碳交易市场的重要组成部分，在碳定价和碳交易方面有着许多先进经验。Jonina 认为，“当我们的对外贸易快速增长的时候，我们需要承担相应的国际责任。在某种程度上，碳交易市场很有效。这个交易体系主要包含的是欧洲国家，就像已经编号的座位。我不知道在中国国内，该如何建立这种碳交易体系。因为中国是一个多省市的国家，运作的方式会有所不同”。中国的全国碳交易市场刚刚起步，目前只有少数行业被纳入碳交易体系。2021 年 7 月，国务院启动了发电行业全国碳排放权交易市场上线交易。在未来，通过研究和学习欧洲碳市场经验，中国碳交易市场必将稳步扩大行业覆盖范围，借助市场机制，有效降低碳排放。

现阶段，冰岛的地热能开发已经十分成熟，对能源转型起到了重要作用。当前中国也在积极开发地热能，加速去碳化能源转型。2018 年，Jonina 在冰岛组织了一场与地热相关的研讨会，参会成员主要是来自中国山东的专家。研讨会为期 5 天，议程包括与冰岛能源局的座谈会和地质调查。与会期间，她带领专家们实地考察了冰岛各处地热的不同用途。中国和冰岛两国地理位置差异显著，地热能利用条件也有很大差别。冰岛位于美洲板块和欧亚板块的边界地带，两大板块的交界线从西南向东北斜穿全岛，因此，冰岛地热资源丰富。冰岛的地热温度很高，最高温度可达到 250℃。较高温度的地热能可以用来发电。然而在中国，地热温度在 50 ~ 100℃，不能用来发电，但可以用于供暖、温泉等。

Jonina（左四）与山东相关专家就地热问题展开讨论

冰岛成功地利用地热能开发旅游业，从而实现了经济与环保的协调发展。在冰岛，来自发电厂的多余地热水，经过地下高热火山熔岩层，与许多化学和矿物结晶混合，最终形成潟湖。冰岛蓝湖就是其中最大、最吸引游客的一个。除此之外，冰岛人还利用地热能建造泳池。对冰岛人来说，游泳和一日三餐同样重要。首都雷克雅未克虽然只有 17 万人居住，但却拥有 10 多个大型公共游泳池。剩余的地热能还用来给房屋供暖和融雪。冰岛还利用地热能建设了绿色温室和农业学校，发展生态农业，种植蔬菜、水果。“有了地热能和温室，一切皆有可能。”Jonina 骄傲地表示。对于中国而言，参考冰岛的成功经验，在地热采暖、温泉疗养、旅游等领域发展相当迅速，北京小汤山等地已成为地热能使用示范基地。

“当然，我们必须考虑到二氧化碳的排放问题。在研讨会的最后一天，来自中国的成员与冰岛当地的企业家和能源专家等进行了交流。其间，有中国专家问我，和烧煤比，地热能的成本是多少？很显然，他没有把碳排放考虑在内。就像我们所说，地热能的启动成本很高，但是从长远的角度来看，由于地热几乎没有碳排放，经济效益会更好。”对于目前推广地热能遇到的困难，Jonina 希望企业家们团结起来，担负起社会责任，为共同的地球、共同的家园而努力。

“责任”是 Jonina Bjartmarz 反复强调的词，也是她贯穿一生的信条。易卜生曾言：“社会犹如一条船，每个人都要有掌舵的准备。”时代的船桨已经传递到每个人手中，未来已来，将至已至。

（毛一玮　谢莹莹）

Shouldering Important Responsibilities via Broadening Knowledge to the Utmost and Enacting with Strength

— Interview with Jonina Bjartmarz, President of the Icelandic Chinese Trade Council

"I was built to be a mountain not a creek, rising to the high peaks with the small valleys at my feet. I was born to be great, not worthless, standing on the shoulders of the giants, the petty cowards beneath me." This is the motto of Huaping Girls' High School founded by the Principal Zhang Guimei, the winner of the "July 1 Medal". The voice of women has been heard by more and more people since the 21st century. They are struggling in all walks of life and pushing forward every step of human progress with their own strength. Jonina Bjartmarz has challenged herself from starting a law firm to going into politics to going into business. In the interview, Jonina enthusiastically shared with us what she saw, heard and felt. She always had special opinions on Iceland-China trade, energy and environmental protection. Daring to challenge and innovate, unwilling to mediocrity and not afraid of mission are synonymous with her experience and also bring us sonorous and firm female strength.

Life Is an Uphill Battle, and I'm a Foot-solider like Everyone Else

"The world is a looking-glass, and gives back to every man the reflection of his own face." Jonina Bjartmarz, the President of the Icelandic-Chinese Trade Council. Her life experience fully confirms the remark. After graduating from university, Jonina Bjartmarz ran a law firm with her husband for more than 15 years. In 1999, she founded and served as president of the Icelandic Women Entrepreneurs Association. Then, she successively served as a Member of the Iceland Parliament, Minister of Environment and Minister of Nordic Cooperation. "The Icelandic Chinese Trade Council has linked the trade between China and Iceland, just like the Association of Women Entrepreneurs I founded, which unites women and encourages them to do more and better. I am willing to work with others and help them grow." With the awareness of international cooperation, Jonina currently serves as the president of Icelandic Chinese Trade Council. She is committed to economic and trade exchanges between China and Iceland.

"I think the past choice is a challenge for me." As she said, Ms. Jonina's life is full of unknowns and challenges. While studying, Ms. Jonina often worked as an intern in hospitals, social service organizations, children's service organizations and other places to help who are in need of assistance. She was eager to learn legal knowledge and provide assistance to those in need due to this experience. After passing the matriculation exam, she chose to study in law school. "This was quite a challenge for me, as initially only 10%–15% of students made it through the first year of their studies, and the lawyer industry was a male-dominated profession." The harder she worked, the luckier she became. Jonina finished law school and got a lawyer qualification certificate and 3 year later became member of the Icelandic Attorneys Association.

Jonina actively faces every choice in her life. In the process of being a lawyer, Jonina has always shouldered due social responsibilities. "I used to deal with the media. In my first few years in politics, I had to deal with school and other things because I was the chairman of the Icelandic Parents Association. I have strong social skills, so I often appear in front of the media and face all kinds of arguments." It was because of her good expression and social skills that Jonina was discovered by the party. "This was also a challenge for me. This was something I never imagined. My husband also persuaded me to try it. If I don't try, I will regret it later." So Jonina tried and was successfully elected as a member of the parliament.

During the financial crisis in 2008, even though Ms. Jonina was doing business in China, she still missed her motherland. "I was living in China at the time and I was very worried about Iceland because the financial situation there was terrible. I kept thinking of ways to bring more foreign exchange to Iceland. In my opinion, developing tourism was one way. Through tourism, it would bring more tourists and more foreign exchange to Iceland. So I started a travel company in 2008. It was not until 2015 that the company began to pick up." Unlike other entrepreneurs, Ms. Jonina has simple business motivation. From beginning to end, she insisted on serving those in need.

Before cooperating, we must first break the prejudice. "I have lived in China for a few years and been engaged in import trade business. I have learned a lot about China. I have many Chinese friends, and I have learned a lot. But when I finally got back to Iceland, I found that the situation was still the same." Due to the long-standing prejudice towards China, there are some obstacles to the exchanges and cooperation between both countries. In the Association of Women Entrepreneurs, Ms. Jonina and members of the Association often hold exhibitions, where delegates introduce their companies and products.

In addition, Ms. Jonina paid particular attention to the rise of female consciousness. "We are also encouraging more and more women to start businesses and to become business owners rather than employees." In these female entrepreneurs, she seems to see herself, who once tried to break the male dominance of the lawyer industry, and who once wanted to go into politics to open the voice of the vulnerable groups. Because of her experience, she especially wanted to give some help to women entrepreneurs who are starting their business. "The landscapes that I travel through and that travel through me constitute me". It is the challenges of the past that forged Jonina, enabling her to view people and things with a broader vision. These valuable experiences also made her understand the importance of mutual respect, mutual benefit and win-win results, and opened a new era in her life.

Jonina (first from the right) took a photo at an altitude of 5,200 m on Mount Everest

Learn as Much as You Can and Do All You Can

The experience of operating a travel agency is one of the challenges in Jonina's life. Everyone and everything she met during the trip is very interesting and informative, which also complements her perception of the world.

Iceland is located in the corner of the North Atlantic, with a population of only more than 300,000, but it has excellent natural scenery and abundant products. In Iceland, splendid auroras often appear in the inky night sky, which are colorful and changeable. A gentle breeze whistles through the green grove in summer, and all over here are thousand miles of freeze and snow-bound land in winter. It is undoubtedly that the beautiful scenery is a paradise for tourists, so tourism has become the pillar industry of Iceland. What Jonina has done is bringing tourists from all over the world to this beautiful scenery and show the charm from nature to tourists. Jonina said, "We will meet many different people in the course of business, and the process of interacting with people is very interesting, which is why I like this industry. I think I am an educator. During the journey, people are not only traveling, but also experience the local culture and achieving aspirations for more knowledge, varied experience and improvement."

The process of traveling is also a process of constantly breaking prejudice. Jonina said that there were some Icelanders who came to China for the first time, and their reactions were very interesting. Since Iceland is a country with a small population, most of the impressions about China have long been from other western countries. When Sino-U.S. relations are tense, Icelanders see more propaganda from the West, especially the United States, so they will be biased against China and Chinese people. So when some Icelanders travel to China for the first time, they will find that the actual China is very different from the expected. Jonina talked about a personal experience, "I had a colleague who was visiting Beijing for the first time, and I asked her what she was expected? She said she wanted a blue sky and a pollution-free environment. I said, what you imagine is that everyone is wearing old clothes and there are crowded streets. But the truth is, you will see lots of young people in beautiful clothes, and the streets will not be crowded, and everything will be much better than you expected. However, it is not enough for me to tell them

Jonina experienced Chinese traditional clothing

above. I think people need more experience. This is my job."

In terms of tourism, Ms. Jonina is a loyal supporter of "sustainable tourism". During the interview, Ms. Jonina constantly stressed that we all should travel with the idea of "sustainable tourism", especially when traveling to a country with fragile environment like Iceland. Just like we can see some advertisements that promote off-road driving in Iceland, in fact, it is a crime in Iceland. Icelanders are deeply aware of the extraordinary value of unspoiled nature, so they've been very good at conserving resources.

Jonina said, "Our nature is a kind of resource, and 'sustainable travel' means that tourists should not leave footprints, and all the things they bring should be taken away when they leave. This is not only from the perspective of protecting nature and culture, but also from the perspective of social and economic benefits. People must have a sense of sustainability." This also shows us the sense of social responsibility in Ms. Jonina. Only by protecting the environment, saving resources and taking the road of green and sustainable development can we maintain the long-term development of tourism and the long-term stability of a region.

Taking the Opportunity, Today to Fight It Out

Konosuke Matsushita has a saying, "If opportunities come, you should take good care of yourself and start your career." The signing of *Free Trade Agreement between the Government of the People's Republic of China and the Government of Iceland* is a significant opportunity for both sides. Since the Agreement came into force on July 1, 2014, it has greatly promoted the trade between the Government of the People's Republic of China and the Government of Iceland. In recent years, economic and trade relations between China and Iceland have been continuously improved, and cooperation has been carried out in many related fields, especially those with complementary advantages. As the president of the Icelandic Chinese Trade Council, Jonina seizes the opportunity to actively promote the increase of bilateral trade and plays a key role in promoting it.

On October 29, 2018, Jonina led representatives of the Association of Women Entrepreneurs to visit China and held a promotion meeting at the embassy, where they had an enthusiastic discussion on food, medicine and aquatic products, thus promoting the further expansion of Iceland-China seafood trade. When it comes to this experience, Ms. Jonina is full of praise. "It's interesting and very successful in many ways. These women are members of the association, and some women come with their husbands. We are a group of about 20 people, some of whom came to China for the first time. We noticed that China had launched the China International Import Expo and so on, so we decided to cooperate with the embassy. The Embassy of Iceland in China organized this meeting for these entrepreneurs to expand channels of cooperation and development in China. The meeting was very effective."

Not only did the Icelandic delegation visit China, but Jonna also received many Chinese economic and trade delegations visiting Iceland. For example, in October 2019, Jonina received an economic and trade delegation from Jingzhou City, Hubei Province, China in Iceland, and held a series of economic and trade negotiation and exchange activities such as the Icelandic-Chinese Trade promotion Conference and Iceland Investment Environment Promotion Conference. Combined with the advantages and needs of both sides, Jonina conducted in-depth exchanges in cultural tourism, deep processing of aquatic products, sporting goods and baby clothes.

Jonina has a lot of experience in dealing with entrepreneurs from other countries. When asked about her advice to young entrepreneurs, Jonina said, "First of all, you should increase your knowledge about other countries, their culture and history. In this way, you will know where the other party comes from and how the other party does business. There are some dishonest people no matter what in Iceland or China, and you should know the background of your business partners. The best way is to visit before doing any business. I often encourage people to go to China, see more people, see what local cities look like today and read some

Chinese history. The same applies to Chinese who want to do business in Iceland." We need sincerity in doing business, especially when there are many difficulties in cross-border trade. Only many hands make light work can the China-Iceland trade develop better in the future.

In the process of promoting economic and trade activities between China and Iceland and promoting the development of Iceland's trade, Jonina has always grasped the opportunities, fulfilled her duties and interpreted what it means to "remain true to our original aspiration and keep our mission firmly in mind" with her own actions.

The Coming Future

Iceland has big ambition. It is on track to successfully complete its energy transition and has already become one of the countries that uses the most amounts of clean energy in the world. Nowadays, Iceland in general only uses combustible fuel for vehicles and shipping. "In the past 50 years, Iceland has hardly used coal. Iceland has taken an array of measures to reduce the impact of global warming, but from a global perspective due to being a small nation, our contribution is minimal." Ms. Jonina believes that in the context of global warming, what Iceland can do is to set an example for all countries and deal with environmental problems through international cooperation. China has encountered many difficulties and challenges in the process of energy transition. Some cities have even adopted power rationing in order to achieve carbon emission targets. In response, she said, "In the past, houses were even black because of coal burning. But since we used geothermal heating, the situation has been very different. The air quality began to get better and the urban environment has also been improved. Geothermal energy is also a relatively inexpensive way of heating. In the future, we hope to fulfill our commitments and responsibilities. What we can do is to set an example to countries around the world and share our experience in geothermal energy through innovation. I think this is where we really can contribute." Fortunately, China and Iceland have carried out extensive exchanges and cooperation in the field of energy. Sinopec has begun to apply geothermal technologies and experience from Iceland to build "pollution-free cities" and develop other projects in China. In terms of carbon cycle, Carbon Recycling International (CRI) in this industry have turned to make investments in China. In September 2021, Iceland and China signed a Technical Contract, under which Sierbang Petrochemical based in Jiangsu Province, cooperates with Carbon Recycling International (CRI), would recover carbon dioxide from industrial tail gas to produce new energy materials.

In the future, the energy field presents unlimited challenges and possibilities. For China in the throes of transition, Ms. Jonina said, "I sincerely hope that China can succeed in the battle of energy transition. Given China is the largest industrialized country in the world, China has more obligations than other countries and faces more difficulties than them in this regard." At present, China and Iceland are deepening exchanges and cooperation in the field of energy.

As an important player on the EU carbon trading market, Iceland has abundant advanced experience in carbon pricing and carbon trading. Jonina said, "When our foreign trade increases rapidly, we need to bear corresponding international responsibilities. To some extent, the carbon trading market is very effective. This trading system mainly includes European countries, just like numbered seats. I wonder how to establish such a carbon trading system in China. Considering China is a country with many provinces and cities, the mode to make this system operate will be apparently different." China's national carbon trading market has just kicked off. Currently, only a few industries have been incorporated into the carbon trading system. In July 2021, the State Council launched the online trading of the National Carbon Emission Permits Trade Market in the power generation industry. In the future to come, by studying and learning from the experience of European carbon market, China's carbon trading market will steadily expand the industry coverage and effectively reduce carbon emissions with the help of market mechanism.

At current stage, Iceland's geothermal energy development has been very mature and has played an important role in energy transition. Currently, China is also proactively developing geothermal energy and accelerating its energy transition through decarbonization. In 2018, Ms. Jonina organized a geothermal related seminar in Iceland. The participants were mainly experts from Shandong Province, China. The seminar lasted for 5 days, with agenda including a symposium with the National Energy Authority of Iceland and geological surveys. During the seminar, she led experts to investigate the different uses of geothermal energy in Iceland. There are significant geographical differences between China and Iceland, so are the utilization conditions of geothermal energy. Iceland is located in the border zone between the American Plate and the Eurasian Plate. The junction line of the two plates obliquely crosses the whole island from southwest to northeast. Therefore, Iceland is abundant in geothermal resources. Iceland's geothermal temperature is very high. The maximum temperature can reach to 250℃. Geothermal energy with higher temperature can be used to generate electricity. However, the temperature of geothermal energy in China ranges from 50 to 100℃, which cannot be used for power generation, but can be used for heating, hot springs and so on.

Iceland has successfully utilized geothermal energy to develop its tourism, thus realizing the coordinated development of economy and environmental protection. In Iceland, the excessive geothermal water from the power plants passes through the underground high-temperature volcanic lava layer and mixes with various chemical and mineral crystals, forming lagoons in the end. Among these lagoons in Iceland, Blue Lagoon is the largest and the most attractive. In addition, Icelanders also utilize geothermal energy to build swimming pools. For Icelanders, swimming is as important as three meals. Although Reykjavik, the capital city, has a population of 170,000, yet it has more than 10 large public swimming pools. The remaining geothermal energy is properly utilized to heat houses and melt snow. Iceland has also used geothermal energy to build pollution-free greenhouses and agricultural schools so as to develop ecological agriculture and to grow vegetables and fruit. "With geothermal energy and greenhouses, nothing is impossible." said Ms. Jonina proudly. For China, referring to the successful experience of Iceland, it has developed rapidly in the fields of geothermal heating, hot spring recuperation and tourism. Beijing Xiaotangshan and other places have become demonstration base for the utilization of geothermal energy.

"Absolutely, we must take into consideration of the issue of carbon dioxide emissions. On the last day of the seminar, members from China exchanged views with local entrepreneurs and energy specialists of Iceland. In this process, one Chinese expert asked me, what is the cost of geothermal energy compared with that of coal burning? Obviously, he didn't take carbon emissions into account. As we said, the start-up cost of geothermal energy is high, but the economic benefits in the long run will become better because almost no carbon dioxide is produced." Considering the difficulties encountered in promoting geothermal energy, Jonina hopes that all entrepreneurs will unite to shoulder social responsibilities and work together for our common earth, the only home for humanity.

"Responsibility" is a word repeatedly emphasized by Jonina Bjartmarz, and it is also her creed throughout her life. Ibsen has a saying that "Society is like a ship. Everyone should be prepared to take the helm." Now, the oars of the times have been passed to all of us, so let's prepare ourselves for the coming future.

(Mao Yiwei　Xie Yingying)

03

从两周到十二年，由冰岛至中国

——访绿钻（中山）科技有限公司总裁

Sigurdur Bragi Gudmundsson

“2009 年我去中山市帮助绿钻（中山）科技有限公司。当时他们说，只需要我两至三周的时间，如果我不去帮助他们，他们的公司将会面临融资，抑或是倒闭。所以我来到了中山市。意料之外，我发现这是座美丽的城市，我喜欢上了在这里工作的人们，自然也喜欢上了待在中国。两周后我返回了冰岛，但我再次决定，再花三个月的时间继续挽救这家叫绿钻（中山）科技有限公司的企业。后来，如你所见，两周不仅延长到三个月，而且到现在，我已经来到这家企业十二年了。”

这是 Siggi 在采访中的一段自我介绍，简短描述了这位来自冰岛的国际友人与绿钻（中山）科技有限公司之间的，由冰岛至中国、从两周到如今的十二年的传奇故事。

Siggi，全名 Sigurdur Bragi Gudmundsson，是一位深耕中国市场多年的冰岛友好企业家，时任绿钻（中山）科技有限公司（以下简称绿钻）总裁。截至 2021 年，Siggi 已在俄罗斯、立陶宛、拉脱维亚、冰岛等多个国家的多个公司担任过总裁、首席执行官，也曾任职于数个董事会；在教育事业方面，更是任职于冰岛雷克雅未克大学的董事会十余年之久。

数年来，Siggi 在掌管绿钻相关事务之余，也密切关注国际形势，热心推动中国和冰岛两国民间友好交流，为中冰民间外交发展贡献一份独特的力量。在公司管理方面，Siggi 有着独特的顾问心得，他善于分析企业管理中出现的问题并及时找出对策，他戏称自己的工作为“企业医生”。他奔波于遭遇困境的企业之间，确认问题并试图拯救他们。

作为国际友人，Siggi 无疑也热爱着中国。在采访内外，Siggi 数次强调他对中国文化、环境、工作氛围等方面的喜爱。他愿意分享自己的工作经验，也乐于帮助每一位来自冰岛和中国的年轻企业家。看了 Siggi 的故事，相信你我不论阶层、处境，都能有所收获。

广泛学习，跟上时代的步伐

俗语说，“万丈高楼平地起”，大学几乎是每一位精英有所成就的起点，是年轻人踏入社会前最好的训练场。冰岛的大学政策与中国不尽相同。为了获取更好的教育资源，冰岛政府鼓励人们前往其他国家学习先进的理论知识。当时年轻进取的 Siggi 便前往了雅典市的一所优秀工程院校——俄亥俄大学。

俄亥俄大学创立于 1804 年，是美国卡内基基金会评出的“一类研究型大学”之一，也是美国高校学科评估刊物 *PRINCETON REVIEW* 评出的美国最好大学之一。Siggi 成功走进了这所大学，获得了很多人梦寐以求的高学历，也增加了深厚的知识储备。

当时的 Siggi 还没有如现在一样丰富的工作经验，和很多现在懵懵懂懂、刚刚进入大学校园的大学生一样，他认为毕业以后，自己在工作中会有 80% 的概率用上工程学的知识，15% 的概率用上经济学知识，而仅有 5% 的概率应用哲学知识。所以，他主修了工程学专业，同时辅修了经济学与哲学专业。然而，Siggi 参加工作后发现，哲学远比他当初想象的要重要也实用得多，他现在所能知道的同学中，只有大约 30% 的人还在从事与工程有关的工作。

“众里寻它千百度，蓦然回首，那‘路’却在灯火阑珊处”，这正是对 Siggi 大学之路最贴切的描述。一门被认为是“额外”学科的哲学，却在他工作后，成为他的引路明灯，为其在黑暗的未来中指明了方向。Siggi 的路，也是许多已经为自己寻觅到一条好似正确的道路、正兴致盎然地向新生活整装待发的年轻人在未来所可能要走的路。

Siggi 认为，尽可能多地学习各方面的知识也许会是个好方法，有备而无患。而从社交能力来说，人缘好的人总是会有更多的机会，而且永远不会过时。所以，对于那些正处在迷茫中的学生们，Siggi 建议他们尽可能多地学习各种不同的知识，并磨炼他们的社交能力。如其所说，“我们很难知道在未来会是什么将我们拉出社会的泥潭，帮助我们脱颖而出。”

当然，“欲穷千里目，更上一层楼。”Siggi 在大学后，并没有止步不前，而是始终不忘持续精进，跟上时代变化的步伐。Siggi 绝不忽视学习的重要性，他做了一个形象的比喻，“我们可以看到，在几十年前，公司可能花了十年的时间去研究一台世界上最好的打字机，但他们不会想到，打字机将在不久后被电脑所取代。现在，我们几乎见不到打字机了。以前人们会说，要专注在一个确定的目标上，但现在的生活变化太快了，我们需要跟上时代变化的步伐，需要保持灵活、时刻做好改变的准备，并不断地增进自己。”自 1984 年 Siggi 从大学毕业以后，他一直工作到 2007 年，持续了相当长的时间，并且秉持着“活到老，学到老”的理念，他认为他需要更新自己的理论知识。于是，在 2007 年，Siggi 辞去了当时他所在的 Plastprent 公司的总裁职务，卖掉了自己的股份，进修了冰岛最大的大学——雷克雅未克大学的 AMP 课程（高级管理课程）。他还兼任了雷克雅未克大学的董事会成员，同时担任两个角色，帮助他从不同角度不断提升自己。

当然，Siggi 绝不否认工作的重要性。他认为，在就业初期，人们的学习曲线由大学中的陡峭变得趋于平缓，因而如何持续自身的学习状态十分重要。也许在初入社会时，像 Siggi 一样，先找到一份适合的工作，找到一个自己可以学习的榜样，也是十分必要的。工作中认识的人往往比初出校门的学生更成熟，具有阅历，向他们学习往往比缓慢摸索更具效率，更容易达到持续精进的目的。

“欲穷大地三千界，须上高峰八百盘”。学得广，学得对，学得与时俱进，就是 Siggi 对学习所下的定义。

不惧风险，成为“企业医生”

1984 年，Siggi 从俄亥俄大学毕业之后，得益于高学历的加持与深厚的知识储备，直接被一家名为 Plastprent 的公司聘用，并于 1984 年至 1989 年持续在 Plastprent 担任工程师。随后因不满公司的运行模式，Siggi 跳槽至新公司 Sigurplast，成为一名 CEO，开始了另一段不同的职业生涯。

“你们可以称呼我在 Sigurplast 的工作为‘企业医生’，我只在公司出现重大危机时去帮助解决问题并维持运行。我将我那时的工作总结为确认问题的存在、分析问题的源头与寻找解决方案三部分。”

可以用一个诙谐的句子来描述 Siggi 的职业生涯，“我是一块砖，哪里需要就往哪里搬”。Siggi 凭借超强的本领成功运营了 Plastprent 和 Sigurplast 公司，早期“企业医生”的职业生涯也为 Siggi 积累了富足的实践经验，为后续收到绿钻的求助并成功拯救、维持绿钻长期运营构筑了坚实的知识根基。Siggi 在 Sigurplast 的解决方案运行得十分顺利，这也帮助 Siggi 积累了足够的资金。于是，Siggi 在 Sigurplast 入职十年后，回归并收购了 Plastprent，同时成为两家公司的总裁。

“千锤万凿出深山，烈火焚烧若等闲。”在问题面前，不惧风险与困难，勇敢面对，理智解决，这成就了 Siggi，也成就了他所挽救下来的公司。

扎根中国，因热爱而前进

设想有一天，我们有了稳定的事业，不再需要为钱发愁时，我们是否还有想追求的东西？事业成功、财富自由之际，我们是否还会继续前进？又会是什么支持我们前进呢？一直以来，对钱财、对资产的渴望，对权利地位的渴求，似乎成了大多数人前进的动力。有人对顶层人士“对钱不感兴趣”的言论嗤之以鼻，认为其是在卖弄、吹嘘与炒作。资产与权利似乎成了一些人人生的唯一目的地。若真是如此，那么 Siggi 在 2007 年之后的故事，将成为其中的特例。

2007 年，Siggi 赚得了足够的钱，于是他选择从公司辞职，卖掉他的股份，转而回归家庭，去致力于后代的教育。他将自己两年的时间全心奉献给了两个孩子，带他们去了西班牙、美国以及其他一些国家学习，直至与绿钻合作。

对于签约绿钻的往事，Siggi 回忆道：“2005 年，我曾到过中国北京，那是我第一次去中国，那时我跟随一个 20 人的小团队。我来自冰岛东海岸一个非常非常小的城市，在我成长的年代，那里只有 800 人（2005 年北京常住人口约为 1536 万人），而北京，对于那时的我来说，城市太大了，我无法适应在那里的生活。所以，2009 年，当他们（绿钻的董事会）让我来中国时，我说我不感兴趣，我认为中山市会是个太大而喧闹的城市，而我那时只想和我的孩子一起享受生活。事实上，他们多次邀请我来中国。于是之后，在他们向我询问期望报酬时，我写下了我认为他们一定不会接受的数字，令我惊讶的是他们竟然接受了！因此，我签下了一个两周的协议，只到中山市两周时

在 Siggi（前排左四）的领导下绿钻公司的英德之旅

间。然而，在那之后，我很快爱上了中山这座城市。中山是一座平静而祥和的城市，我很喜欢在那里工作的人们，我看到了这家公司的未来。所以就如之前说的，我先将两周延长至三个月，到现在（在这家企业）几乎有十二年了。”

中山市宁静祥和的环境、绿钻公司同事的热心帮助以及公司良好的合作氛围给当时的 Siggi 留下了十分深刻的印象，以至于他改变了自己的想法，致力于拯救这家他喜爱的公司。

2010 年，Siggi 在中山市买了自己的房子，而他的其中一个儿子也来到位于中山市的中港英文学校，学习包括汉语在内的知识。

他不再在乎利益，而只想在中山这个城市工作，只想和他的同事们一起工作、一起前进。幸运的是，他成功了。绿钻不仅持续运营了 12 年，而且一跃成为当下顶尖的鞋材制造厂商，也拥有了自己的防滑科技专利，他们做到了真正的东山再起。

时至今日，Siggi 在采访中回忆起中山依然会十分激动，他太怀念那里的一切，但因为新冠肺炎疫情，他已经太久没有回来了。

直面困难，妥善解决问题

中文是世界上最难学的语言之一，对于不懂中文的 Siggi 来说，拯救绿钻并非一件易事。对外，文化的差异、市场类型与规模的变化等等都需要时间去适应。而对内，一个从国外空降而来的顶头上司也着实难以令所有人信服。

刚来中国，Siggi 不认识任何人，不会说中文，对有关鞋类市场的时尚潮流的信息也是一概不知，很多工作对他来说都更加艰巨。所以那时，他和董事会的意见经常是不一致的，于是导致了一些矛盾，总是需要试着去协调。以往在他国企业的顾问经验不再完全适用，这次 Siggi 要做出一些额外的、特殊的改变，一些他人难以做到的、独特的改变。“我还记得，当我不得不换掉绿钻的总经理时他那不屑的眼神。”幸运的是，Siggi 现在依旧在中国工作得非常好，也与中国同事相处得很融洽。

Siggi（后排左二）和他的管理团队

除去公司内部董事会的矛盾外，绿钻公司当时的运行效率并不高，在与各类友商企业沟通合作时，绿钻花费了大量的资金，而相对的合作进度却始终难以推进。对于公司的内部运行事务，Siggi 回忆道：当时每天都会有 20 封甚至 30 封的邮件等着他批阅，工作效率十分低下。“后来，我告诉我亲爱的同事们，我们不应该将时间浪费在写邮件来向我申请投资低于 1000 元的项目，我也告诉我的管理人员，他们需要自己做出决定。事实证明，我没有看走眼，他们确实是一群刻苦而有潜力的人。他们认真听取并实践了我的建议。所以现在我再也不会收到同事们发来的申请投资低于 1000 元的邮件了。我现在每天只需处理大约 5 封邮件，我愿意放权给他们，因为我百分之百相信他们。在我看来，他们现在总能做出正确的决定。他们发挥了潜能，变得更高效，更独立，也更能担负责任了。没有他们，我也不能将公司运营得这么好。”

初期的种种困难十分棘手，Siggi 甚至称其为“不可能完成的任务”。面对这种境况，仅靠自身知识与“企业医生”的经验红利显然是不够的。扶大厦之将倾，需要先稳固根基，好在 Siggi 并不需要只依靠他自己，他还有一些热忱、聪明、诚实和勤奋的同事们，这使公司扭亏为盈成为可能。

“中国和冰岛存在一些文化差异，在这方面，我想说的是我的同事们教会了我太多。我常举的一个例子是，我的司机弄丢了车钥匙。那时我的经理们建议我从他的工资中扣除（赔偿钥匙的）500 元。由于在冰岛时，我们并没有扣除员工工资的习惯，尽管我的经理们反对，但我仍说我不会扣除那位司机的工资。我并不能根据冰岛的文化来判断中国的事情的对错。直至今日，我仍想知道当时我的决策是否正确。我是否表现得太过仁慈？我的员工是否会因此而认为我不够强硬？或许我的经理们的做法才是正确的。多年以后，我仍然无法确定评价这件事。现在我可能会更多地听取经理们的意见。这件事情让我意识到，在这些规矩上会存在一些差异，这就像哲学课本第一页中说的，永远不要从自己的角度去寻找集体问题的答案，也永远不要以自己文化的观点来评判另一种文化。不过现在一切也都进行得很好，我很喜欢这里的文化习俗。”

曾经的障碍难以跨越，好在那已是曾经的障碍。相较之下，如今的新冠肺炎疫情，似乎是更为棘手的难题。

“如果你问我当下最大的挑战是什么，我会说那就是新冠肺炎疫情。首先，因为疫情，自 2019 年 12 月以来，我就已无法见到我亲爱的同事们了，甚至无法回到中国，我们必须在 Skype 和微信上开会，很多事情可能会被推到截止日期才能做完。即使是在冰岛，几乎 90% 的人都会打两次疫苗，但这也没能完全解决问题。时至今日，我仍然需要经历一个长达三周的检疫隔离才能回到中国，这无疑是场煎熬。”

“幸运的是，疫情只给我们的管理带来很小的影响，之前可能销售额下降了 40%，但到 2021 年，我们又重新盈利了，很高兴我们的工作能力没有受到更多的影响。”

新冠肺炎疫情破坏了一众年轻人的创业梦想。工厂倒闭、企业停工、资金链断裂，给各行各业的企业家们带来了重重难题。谁能想到，在科技迭代如此迅速的 21 世纪，人们会怀念以前不戴口罩的自由生活？

接受失误，做领头的牧羊犬

在谈及管理时，Siggi 用到这样一个有趣的类比：“牧羊人的牧羊犬通常有两种类型，其中一些喜欢走在羊群后面，并且赶着最后的羊（甚至以咬着落后羊的后腿的方式）让它们跑得快一点；另一种总是走在羊群的最前面，用它出色的判断力为羊群指引方向，带领着羊群前进。我更喜欢第二种牧羊犬，因为我喜欢成为那个被追随的人，而非去‘咬人’的那个。”

成为决策者与开拓者是需要勇气的，而 Siggi 似乎天生具备这种勇气。对处在悬崖边缘的绿钻来说，未来的道路仿佛都像被迷雾笼罩一般无从得知。这时，第一种牧羊犬催促它加速前进，以致在迷雾中越陷越深，只有消逝的终点在等待着它。它需要一个当机立断的引路人、开拓者，为它指明方向，而 Siggi 显然是后者。

驾驶飞机的 Siggi

绿钻为 Siggi 提供了前进的意义，重新点燃了他内心的火花。Siggi 作为领导者，与迷失的绿钻人一同找到了涅槃重生之路。开拓者的勇气使他敢于承担这个责任，不断精进生活的知识根基。他把不可能变为可能。

除去在工作中的管理者角色外，Siggi 在业余时间还是一名赛车手和飞行员。在赛车中，人们需要在高压下迅速做出决定，很难在每个弯道都处理得非常好，失误在所难免。而 Siggi 失误时，他总会立刻忘记刚才的意外，把注意力放在下一个弯道。“拘泥于上个错误的人终将会错失他的下一个翻盘机会。”人们很难在后悔的情况下将一件事做到完美，公司运营也是一样。接受你的错误，然后去思考下一步的路。做小决定的时候快一些，做大决定的时候慢一些。当事情进展顺利时要悲观一些，而遇到重大困难时则要乐观一些。这些 Siggi 在赛车中总结的经验，在生活中也给了他很多启发。

siggi 和他的越野车伙伴

直至今日，绿钻已成为世界防滑鞋垫与外底制造业的领军企业之一。曾经的它面临融资倒闭，企业分崩离析，Siggi 的到来给它带来了新的希望。如今，它已向着世界防滑技术顶点的新高峰前进，翻过曾经那绝望的山峰，等待着它的是崭新的光辉未来。

采访中途，出于礼节，我们向 Siggi 提及赠送纪念品的意向。Siggi 出人意料地想让我们寄些中国的食物给他，尤其是湖南菜。在近一个半小时的采访中，Siggi 十余次强调他对中国、对中山以及绿钻的喜爱。Siggi 这样说道：“我想强调的是，你知道的，我是多么喜欢中国。我急切地希望回到中国。我想念那里的湖泊与蓝天。我现在尤其想念我的同事们，他们是我见过的、共事过的、最高效的、最棒的了，能与这些中国人共事是我最幸运的事了。”

难得遇见如此热爱中国的国际友人，他拥有从两周延长至十二年的勇气，正是他的勇气、坚毅之心带给了他这十二年在中国的光辉岁月，这不禁令人心生敬意。愿疫情早日退去，以使 Siggi 以及更多冰岛人得以偿愿。

（黄梓杰　何静萱）

From Two Weeks to Twelve Years, from Iceland to China

— Interview with Sigurdur Bragi Gudmundsson, President of Green Diamond (Zhongshan) Technology Co., Ltd.

"I went to Zhongshan City in 2009 to help Green Diamond (Zhongshan) Technology Co., Ltd. The owners said it would only take me two to three weeks to check things out there. If I didn't help them, their company would face the financing or go out of business. So I came to Zhongshan. Unexpectedly, I found it a beautiful city, I like the people who work there and of course like staying in China gradually. I returned to Iceland two weeks later, but I again decided to spend another three months on saving this enterprise called Green Diamond (Zhongshan) continuously Technology Co.,Ltd. And then, as you can see, those two weeks have not only extended to three months, they have now come to twelve years."

This is a self-introduction of Mr. Siggi in the interview, which briefly describes the story between this international friend from Iceland and Green Diamond (Zhongshan) Technology Co., Ltd. This is a legendary story from Iceland to China, from two weeks to the present twelve years.

Mr. Siggi, named Sigurdur Bragi Gudmundsson in full, is a friendly Icelandic entrepreneur who has been deeply engaged in the Chinese market for many years, and also the president of Green Diamond (Zhongshan) Technology Co., Ltd (hereinafter referred to as Green Diamord). Until 2021, Siggi has served as president, CEO of various companies in Russia, Lithuania, Latvia, Iceland and other countries. Also he has served on several Boards of Directors, including the Board of Directors of University of Reykjavik in Iceland for over ten years.

These years, in addition to taking charge of the related affairs of Green Diamond, Siggi also pays close attention to the international situation, enthusiastically helps promote the friendly exchanges between people of China and Iceland, and makes a unique contribution to the development of people-to-people diplomacy between two countries. Siggi is good at analyzing corporate management problems and finding timely solutions. He jokingly calls his job "enterprise doctor". He had his own unique experience in identifying problems and trying to rescue companies that are in trouble.

As an international friend, Siggi undoubtedly loves China. Both in and out of interviews, Siggi has repeatedly emphasized his love for Chinese culture, environment, working atmosphere and other aspects. He is willing to share his experience and help every young entrepreneur from Iceland and China. After reading his story, I believe that you and I, regardless of plight and stratum, can gain something.

Learning Widely and Keeping Pace with the Times

As the saying goes, "Great oaks from little acorns grow". College is the starting point for almost every elite to make achievement and the best training ground for young people before they enter the society. The college policy of Iceland is different from that of China. In order to obtain better educational resources, the Icelandic government encourages people to study advanced theoretical knowledge in other countries. At that time, young and ambitious Siggi went to Ohio University, an excellent engineering college in Athens, USA.

Founded in 1804, Ohio University is one of the America's Carnegie Foundation's "First-class Research Universities", and also one of the best universities in America appraised by *PRINCETON REVIEW*, a journal of academic assessment in American colleges and universities. Siggi made it to the university, obtained the high degree that many people dream of, and added a profound knowledge reserve.

Siggi didn't have as much experience as he does now at that time. Like many college students who are now ignorant and have just entered the university campus, he reckoned that after graduation he would have an 80% chance of using engineering, a 15% chance of using economics and only a 5% chance of practical philosophy. So he majored in engineering and minored in economics and philosophy. But in fact, after going to work, Siggi began to find that philosophy was far more important and useful than he had thought. Among his classmates he knows now, only about 30% are still engaged in the job solely related to engineering.

"Find it thousands of times, suddenly look back, the 'path' just lies where the lights are dim". That's how Siggi's path to college is best described. Philosophy, which is regarded as an "extra" discipline, turned out to be his guiding light in the dark future after he started to work. Siggi's path is also the one that many young people may follow to find the right path for themselves when they are eagerly preparing for a new life.

He thinks that it might be a good idea to learn as much as you can about everything, because a good watch can prevent misfortune. And in terms of social skills, popular people will always have more opportunities, and it never goes out. Therefore, for students who are struggling, Siggi advises them to learn as many different knowledge as possible and hone their social skills. As he said, "It's hard to know what will pull us out of the mire and help us stand out in the future."

Of course, "To see a thousand miles; one should ascend another story." Siggi did not come to a halt at college, but kept improving to keep up with the changing times. He never ignores the importance of learning. As a figurative metaphor he made, "As we can see, a company might have spent a decade working on improving typewriter a few decades ago, but they did not expect that typewriters would soon be replaced by computers. Now, we hardly ever see typewriters anymore. People used to talk about focusing on a certain goal, but life changes so quickly these days, and we need to keep up with changing times, stay flexible, always be ready for change, and constantly improve ourselves." After graduating from college in 1984, Siggi worked until 2007. It lasted quite a long time. With the concept of "never too old to learn", he thought he needed to update his theoretical knowledge. So in 2007, Siggi resigned as president of Plastprent, sold his shares and studied AMP (Advanced Management Program) course, at University of Reykjavik, the largest university in Iceland. He also served on the Board of Directors of the University, taking on two roles that helped him improve himself from different perspectives.

Siggi, of course, never denies the importance of work. He believes that at the beginning of employment, people's learning curve flattens, not as steep as it was in college, so it's important to keep up the learning state. Perhaps when one first comes into society, it is necessary to find a suitable job first and find a role model to learn from, just like Siggi. The people we know at work are often more mature and experienced than the students who just left school. Learning from them is often more efficient than exploring slowly, and it will be easier to achieve the purpose of continuous improvement.

To know the wide world, we have to reach the peak. Learning broadly, correctly and with the changing times is Siggi's definition of learning.

Taking Risks and Becoming an "Enterprise Doctor"

After graduating from Ohio University in 1984, Siggi was hired directly by a company called Plastprent thanks to his advanced education and deep knowledge. He continued to work as an engineer at Plastprent from 1984 to 1989. Dissatisfied with the way the company operated, Siggi then moved to a new company,

Sigurplast, he began a different career.

"You can call me an 'enterprise doctor' because of the way I worked in Sigurplast, I was hired there to fix the problems and keep the company going when there was a major crisis. I summarized my work at that time into three parts: confirming the existence of the problem, analyzing the source of the problem and looking for solutions."

A witty sentence can be used to describe his career, "I'm a brick, and being moved to where I'm needed." With great ability, Siggi successfully operated Plastprent and Sigurplast. The early career of "enterprise doctor" has also accumulated rich practical experience for him, which has built a solid knowledge foundation for the subsequent successful rescue of Green Diamond and the maintenance of Green Diamond's long-term operation. Fortunately, Siggi's solution in Sigurplast ran smoothly, which helped him accumulate sufficient funds. So Siggi returned to buy Plastprent a decade after leaving Plastprent and joining Sigurplast, and became the president of both companies.

Siggi (first from the right) and his colleagues happily took pictures

You come out of deep mountains after hammer blows; under fire and water tortures you are not in woes. Siggi and the companies he has saved, have been able to face problems bravely and rationally without fear of risks and difficulties. It is this spirit that makes them themselves.

Taking Root in China and Moving Forward with Love

Imagine one day, when we have a stable career and don't have to worry about money anymore, is there something else we want to pursue? Will we move forward when our careers are successful and our wealth is free? What could it be to keep us going? For a long time, the desire for money, assets, rights and status seems to be the motivation for most people to move forward. Some dismiss the notion that those at the top are "not interested in money" as ostentation, boasting and hype. Assets and rights seem to be the only destination for some people. If so, Siggi's story after 2007 will be an exception.

In 2007, Siggi made enough money, so he quitted the company, sold his shares and returned to his family to concentrate on educating the future generations. He devoted two years of his life to his two children, taking them on trips to Spain, America and many other countries to study, until his collaboration with Green Diamond.

For signing Green Diamond, Siggi recalled: "I went to Beijing in 2005, which was my first trip to China, with a small team of about 20 people. I come from a very, very small city on the east coast of Iceland. When I grew up, there were only about 800 people was living there (the permanent population of Beijing in 2005 was about 15.36 million). Beijing was just too large for me to live in I felt at that time. So when they (Board of Directors of Green Diamond) asked me to go to China in 2009, I said I wasn't interested, I thought that Zhongshan was too big city for me, and I just wanted to enjoy life with my kids. Actually, they invited me many times to go to China. Then when they asked me about my expected salary, I wrote down a number I thought they would not accept, but to my surprise they did! So I signed a two-week agreement to go to Zhongshan for only two weeks. However, I fell in love with this city soon after that. Zhongshan is a quiet and peaceful city. I like the people who work there and I see a future for this company. So as I said before, I first extended two weeks to three months, and now it's been almost 12 years."

At that time, Siggi was deeply impressed by the quiet and peaceful environment of Zhongshan, the warm-hearted help of colleagues in Green Diamond Company and the good cooperation atmosphere of the company, so that he changed his mind and devoted himself to saving this company he loved.

In 2010, Siggi bought his own house in Zhongshan, and one of his sons went to China (Hong Kong) English School in Zhongshan studying among other things, Chinese.

Siggi no longer cared about benefits, but just wanted to work in the city of Zhongshan, and to work with his colleagues and move forward together. Fortunately, he succeeded. Green Diamond not only continued to operate for 12 years, but also became the current top insole manufacturer, and it also has its own non-slip technology patent. They made a real comeback.

Even now, Siggi still got emotional when he recalled Zhongshan in the interview. He misses it so much. However, because of COVID-19, he hasn't been back for too long.

Face Difficulties Bravely and Solve Everything Properly

Chinese is one of the most difficult languages in the world to learn. So for Siggi, who doesn't speak Chinese, saving Green Diamond wasn't easy. Externally, it takes time to adapt to cultural differences and market type and size changes. And internally, since boss arriving from abroad, it is really hard to convince everyone that it will work.

When Siggi arrived in China, he didn't know anyone, didn't speak Chinese and didn't have any information about fashion trends in the footwear market, making many jobs even harder for him. So at that time, he and the board were often at odds with each other, which led to some kind of conflict, and he always needed to learn to reconcile. His previous experience as a consultant in other countries was no longer fully applicable, and this time Siggi had to make some extra, special changes, and some unique changes that were difficult for others to make. "I still remember his disdain when I had to replace the general manager of Green Diamond, and I also remember his angry and contemptuous eyes." Fortunately, Siggi is now still working well in China and getting along well with his Chinese colleagues.

In addition to the conflicts within the company's board, the operation efficiency of Green Diamond was not high at that time. It spent a lot of money in communication and cooperation with various friendly enterprises, but the relative progress of cooperation was always difficult to advance. Also for internal operation of the company, Siggi recalled it being rather unproductive with him receiving 20 or even 30 emails a day from his coworkers waiting to be read. "Later, I told my dear coworkers not to spend our time by writing emails asking me for approval of investment that was less than RMB 1,000. I told my managements that they need to make their own decision. It turned out I was right. They were hard-working, powerful people who listen to my advice and put it into practice. So now for instance I won't get emails from my coworkers that is less than RMB 1,000. I now only have about 5 emails a day to deal with because I trust my coworkers 100% and they have always taken the right decisions at a given time in my opinion. They fulfilled their potential and became more efficient, independent and more responsible as well. Without them, I couldn't have run the company as well as I had."

The initial difficulties in Green Diamond were so intractable that Siggi called them the "mission impossible". Faced with such situation, relying on his own knowledge and the experience of "enterprise doctor" was obviously not enough. To right a falling mansion, a solid foundation is first needed. Fortunately, Siggi was not alone, he got some enthusiastic.

"There are some cultural differences between China and Iceland, in which I would say my colleagues truly helped me a lot teaching me the Chinese culture. As an example once my Chinese driver lost the keys of my car. My management suggested to withdraw RMB 500 from his salary to pay for new key. Due to the fact that we never 'dock' anyone's salary in Iceland, I said that we will not deduct anything from my driver′s salary despite my managers disagree with my decision. I can't judge whether the China incident is right or wrong based on Icelandic culture. Until now I still wonder if I was right, did I show too much 'leniency'? Would my workers think I was a 'weak' boss because of this? Was the management maybe correct and me wrong? Years passed, I am not sure who has a right. Now I probably listen more to managers and this which made me realize that there would be some differences in these rules. It's like the first page of your philosophy textbook, never look for the answer to a collective problem from your own perspective, and never judge another culture from your own culture. But now things are going well and I love the culture here."

The past obstacle was difficult to overcome, fortunately, it is already past. The current COVID-19 pandemic, by contrast, seems to be a more intractable problem.

"If you ask me about the biggest challenge right now, I would say it is COVID-19. First of all, Since December 2019, I have not been able to see my colleagues, and I even couldn't go back to China. We have to have meetings on Skype and WeChat, and a lot of things might get pushed to deadlines. Even in Iceland, almost 90% of us get two shots of vaccine, but that doesn't quite solve the problem. I still cannot go to China without admit to very difficult quarantine isolation for three weeks! It is no doubt a torment."

"Fortunately, the epidemic has had only a minimal impact on our management. Sales were down about 40% before, but by 2021 our profits have increased again, and we are glad that our work ability has not been further affected."

The COVID-19 pandemic has disrupted the dreams of many young people to start their own businesses. The closure of factories, the shutdown of enterprises and the rupture of capital chain have brought many problems to entrepreneurs in all walks of life. Who would have thought that in the 21st century, when technology is changing so fast, people would miss the free life without masks before?

Accepting Mistakes and Being the Lead Sheepdog

Siggi used an interesting analogy when it came to management: "Shepherds usually have two types of sheepdogs, some of which like to walk behind the sheep (even by biting the last sheep's leg) and drive the last sheep to make them go faster; the other always goes ahead of the flock, using their good judgment to guide and lead the flock. I prefer the second type, for I like to be the one to be followed but not the one that is biting."

It takes courage to be a decision maker and pioneer, and Siggi seems to have it in his blood. For Green Diamond that is on the verge of collapse, the way forward seems to be shrouded in mist. Then the first type of sheepdog would urge it on, sinking deeper and deeper into the fog, with only the dying end waiting for it. What it needed was a decisive guide, a pioneer, to show it the way, and Siggi was clearly the latter.

Green Diamond provided Siggi with meaning to move forward and rekindled his inner spark. As the leader, Siggi and the lost Green Diamond found their way back to rebirth. The courage of a pioneer enabled him to take on the responsibility of continually sharpening the knowledge foundations of life. He made the impossible possible.

In addition to his managerial role at work, Siggi is also a racing driver and pilot in his spare time. In racing, people have to quickly make decisions under pressure and it is difficult to handle every road corner very well, and mistakes are inevitable. However, when Siggi makes a mistake, he immediately forgets the incident and focuses on the next turn. "The person who is still thinking about the mistakes in his last turn will also likely mess up the next turn." It's hard to do something perfectly without regret, and the same goes for running a company. Accept your mistakes, and then think about the next step. Make small decisions quickly and make big ones slowly. Be pessimistic when things are going well, and optimistic when things are going badly. The lessons Siggi learned in these races have inspired him a lot in life.

Conclusion

Until now, Green Diamond has become one of the world's leading manufacturers of insoles and non-slip outsoles. In the past, it faced financing failures and the companies fell apart, but Siggi's arrival brought it new hope. Now it have reached a new peak of the world's non-slip technology, over the mountain of despair, a bright new future awaits it.

As a courtesy midway through the interview, we mentioned to Siggi our offer of a souvenir. Siggi unexpectedly asked us to send him some Chinese food, especially Hunan cuisine. During the interview of nearly an hour and a half, Siggi emphasized his love for China, Zhongshan and Green Diamond for more than ten times. Siggi said: "I just want to emphasize, you know, how much I love China. I can't wait to go back to China. I miss the lakes and blue sky there. I especially miss my colleagues in Green Diamond right now. They are some of the most effective and wonderful people I have ever met and worked with. Working with these Chinese people is the best thing that has ever happened to me."

It is rare to meet such an international friend who loves China so much. He had the courage to stretch two weeks to twelve years, it was his courage and perseverance that given him twelve glorious years in China. This is really admirable. May the epidemic recede soon, so Siggi can come back and many more Icelanders can fulfill their wishes.

(Huang Zijie He Jingxuan)

04

认真实干，平凡不凡

——访北京华迅国际客运服务有限公司董事长田香莲

“做人、做事、做企业都要讲究诚信，只要用心去做事，每项工作都能做出成绩。”这是在采访中田香莲多次提到的，坚持与诚信贯穿于她的工作和生活。

认真对待一件事情并不难，难的是几十年如一日地坚持认真对待每一件事。在事业初期认真打拼并不难，难的是在事业有所积累时依然全心投入。田香莲在航空服务行业工作至今已 30 年，历经了中国民航行业的波澜起伏，虽已年过花甲，却依然精力充沛。她亲切热情地与我们分享她的人生经历，从中我们深切体会到了她所坚持的企业精神。

陪伴航空十余载，与冰岛结缘

生于新中国成立初期，田香莲亲历了国家的发展历程，年轻时就梦想可以为国家的成长和强大做出努力。她 16 岁选择参军，成为通信技术人员，忠诚可靠地传达每一条指令，见证了一个个惊心动魄的历史瞬间。就是这样看似简单却十分重要的工作，她兢兢业业地坚守岗位 20 年，参与了中越自卫反击战和南海保卫战，坚定地履行了一名军人的职责。20 年的军旅生涯给她的人生打下了深刻的烙印。无论情况如何变化，她坚持爱岗敬业，吃苦耐劳，认真负责，军旅生涯铸就了她过硬的军人品质作风，沉淀了为人诚实守信、做事认真严谨的人生准则。这段独有的经历也为她之后的企业经营管理奠定了坚实的基础，塑造了脚踏实地、诚实守信的企业文化。

20 世纪 80 年代末，中国正朝着新时代蓄势待发，各行各业都面临着前所未有的机遇和挑战，田香莲也重新思考起自己的人生之路，她也想在变革的大潮中感受新时代的挑战，因此，她去戎从商，为自己开启了人生的第二篇章。

初入航空业，田香莲从航空货运起步。两年后，将工作重心转向客运，创办了北京华迅国际客运服务有限公司（以下简称华迅公司），从此开始了航空客运服务代理公司的工作，至今已有 28 年。当时，购买飞机票极为烦琐，并且只有一定职务级别的人才可以凭借单位介绍信预订机票；签发机票并不像现在这样便捷，而是靠工作人员手工填写旅客姓名、航班号、座位号和行李重量等所有信息。随着中国经济的发展，乘坐飞机的旅客日益增多，手工登机牌逐渐被高效率的印刷登机牌所取代。2000 年，推出了电子客票，旅客凭借身份证就可直接兑换登机牌。2017 年，推出了全国首张航空旅客运输电子发票。航空机票的每一次迭代都蕴藏着航空服务行业的辛勤努力，而每一个具有重大转折意义的事件，田香莲都亲身经历和参与。

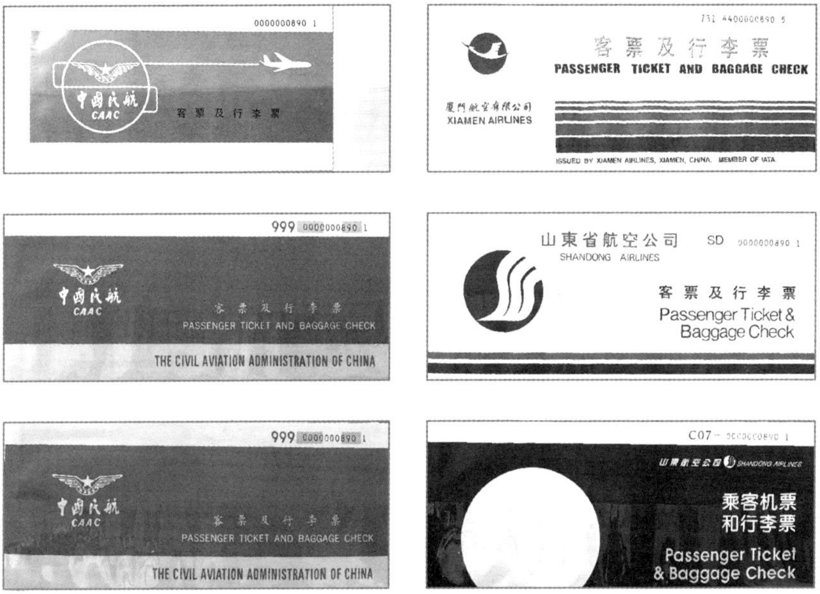

曾经使用的机票

在互联网普及之前，销售机票采用的是传统模式，航空公司指定航空服务代理商来提供服务和销售机票，如此形成航空服务产业链；代理商根据客户需求提供面对面的个性化服务。进入移动互联网时代后，更多旅客通过互联网在线购票。在谈及传统方式与现代科技的融合与冲突时，田香莲坚信，传统的代理服务的生命力会继续下去。互联网购票固然高效便利，受人青睐，但传统的代理服务也有自己的独特优势，那是机器替代不了的人性化服务，它的存在是航空服务业不可或缺的一部分。

2003 年，田香莲与冰岛航空相识结缘。冰岛航空亚太区总经理 Steinn

Larusson 来中国考察，他听闻田香莲所在的华迅公司在机票代理行业中成绩斐然，承接的业务量可观，于是他独自一人来到华迅公司柜台，想要具体了解公司。在人来人往的大厅中，田香莲注意到他一直没有办理业务，于是上前询问他是否需要帮助，在了解到对方身份和来意后，向他介绍了公司的经营情况。在得知对方来到中国后一直在工作，还不了解北京，便建议他可以去了解一下中国的历史和文化，如长城、故宫等有历史底蕴的地方。她还派公司员工和司机专门带他去游览这些名胜古迹，体验中国美食。Steinn Larusson 总经理亲眼看到华迅每位员工的积极忙碌的工作，更在交流中感受到了田香莲为人的热忱与诚信，当下就拍板决定让她做冰岛航空在中国地区的总代理业务。2003 年，他们签署了冰岛航空与华迅公司在中国的总代理合作协议。这是华迅公司签下的首家国际航空公司在中国的总代理合作协议，尽管之后也和其他外国航空公司进行合作，但对田香莲来说，和冰岛航空的合作是独一无二的，这拉开了她与冰岛航空近 20 年合作的帷幕，她对冰岛航空的情感是无可替代的。

田香莲（左二）与冰岛航空签约

感受冰岛魅力，结下深厚情谊

冰岛位于极北之地，是北大西洋中的一个岛国，岛上火山和冰川并存，自然奇观丰富多变，每年都吸引了成千上万的冒险爱好者和游客，旅游业在冰岛经济中占据了至关重要的地位。

冰岛首都雷克雅未克最具代表性的景点必定是蓝湖，也是冰岛最受欢迎的景点之一，地热水与海水的混合使湖水透出幽幽的蓝绿色，湖水中富含对人体有益的矿物质。当人们浸泡在温泉中时，还可以观赏周围白雪皑皑的冰川，褪去一身疲惫。田香莲曾多次到冰岛感受过冰岛的神秘与迷人，蓝湖最值得推荐，泡温泉时仿佛置身于天堂，可以让人暂时忘却一切烦恼。她在冰岛时常有奇妙际遇，曾结识到优秀的摄影师，专程前往冰岛进行婚纱摄影。一望无际的黑沙滩，随风飘扬的白色纱裙，不远处是奔腾的海浪，无一处不迷人。冰岛特有的绝美极光、全球唯一的冰洞探索、火山与寒冰的交相辉映，吸引了众多的自然爱好者和专业摄影师。

在亲身体验冰岛的魅力后，田香莲希望可以让中国游客最大限度地享受冰岛的自然之美。她最先提出“冰岛深度旅游”的概念，提倡根据景点的独有特点并结合游客本人喜好和兴趣，制定最符合游客期望、获得最大舒适度的沉浸式旅游产品。反观现在很多旅游产品都是为了旅游而旅游，为了打卡而拍照，这种走马观花式的旅游，不仅忽略了景色本身的韵味，还使游客身心疲惫，与旅游最初的放松愉悦的目的背道而驰。为此，华迅公司在中国市场首推了冰岛深度旅游产品，探索冰岛尚且不被大众所熟知的旅游景点，依照中国人对于摄影、探险的偏好来规划行程安排，力求让旅行变成真正的沉浸式放松体验。

田香莲认为，除了在冰岛旅游项目的深度挖掘外，作为冰岛航空在中国的代表，也要发力协助冰岛本地品牌的宣传。游客来到冰岛，不仅可以充分感受美景，还可以近距离接触当地特色产品，尤其是冰岛独有的自然原生态产品。冰岛全球闻名的雁鸭绒羽绒被采用的是冰岛雌雁鸭胸前和腋下的最柔软最温暖的绒毛，是世界上最珍稀的一种顶级羽绒。冰岛雁鸭有着超强的抗寒能力，但是数量却极为稀少，全球仅有 20 万只左右。这种鸭绒的收集也十分困难，采集者必须在冰岛雁鸭孵化期过后，爬上几千米的悬崖峭壁，在遗弃的育巢中收集一朵朵绒毛。羽绒被的原料采用纯天然的鸭绒，制作过程几乎全部由技工手工制成，可谓是一件最贴近自然的产品。相信游客可以在冰岛美景和卓越的特色产品中感受到冰岛多方面的魅力。

正是因为田香莲始终坚持诚信做人、亲切待人，她在与冰岛航空负责人初遇时，才有了坦诚而有效的交流，进而凭借公司的实力和人格魅力赢得了他的信任，成为冰岛航空在中国的总代理。随着合作的深入开展，田香莲也与时任冰岛驻华大使古士贤成了好友。古士贤大使非常重视宣传冰岛，为冰岛航空的工作提供了相当多的支持。自合作以来，田香莲带古士贤大使领略了中国的大好河山，两人经常交流两国文化。在古士贤大使离任之际，田香莲赠予他李纯博的书法作品，其上书“福寿康宁”以表身体康健、万事如意的祝愿，古士贤大使则是亲笔签署友谊长存，希望中冰友谊永久长存。田香莲正是把诚信和亲切作为对自己的要求，诚信做人，赢得他人的尊重与信任；亲切待人，一颗真心换来别人的真心。

为中冰航行努力，为中冰经贸出谋献策

田香莲自 2003 年开始从事冰岛航空总代理业务以来，已经与其合作了 18 年之久，为了让中国旅客更好地了解冰岛，更便利地出行冰岛，她做了很多努力。俗话说“要想富先修路”，这句话在航空业同样适用。随着中国和冰岛签署自由贸易协定，越来越多的商务客户前往冰岛。若要发展两国间的合作和贸易，首要解决两国间交通往来的障碍。华迅公司一直在为此努力。由于中国和冰岛两国间距离较远，对于飞机机型要求较高，且中国赴冰岛的旅游旺季主要在夏季，而冰岛来中国旅游的游客非常少，往返航班的飞行成本极高，很多原本打算去冰岛的旅客又会因为价格因素而改变出行计划。所以，中国和冰岛两地间的直飞航班就成为大家关注的焦点。冰岛航空在销售和市场方面做了很多投入，为未来实现两国直航做准备。田香莲带领团队积极向中国游客宣传冰岛，让国人对冰岛有更加细致具象化的了解，让冰岛从一个只在地图和国家报道中出现的模糊概念变得更触手可及，为旅客的出行及游玩提供便利，让向往冰岛的中国旅客更真切地感受冰岛之美。

2019 年，田香莲代表华迅公司和吉祥航空签订了协议，负责吉祥航空飞往冰岛的业务，尽管短期内还不能实现直飞航班，但可以实现便利套飞，缩短飞行时间。虽然这一计划因为突如其来的新冠肺炎疫情而暂时搁浅，待未来出行环境安全后开启实施，必将让冰岛成为充满魅力且便捷出行的旅游胜地。

旅游业在冰岛占据了第一大产业的地位，2019 年，飞往冰岛的国际游客近 200 万人次，其中中国游客约占 5%。在旺季，冰岛的住宿资源和服务业资源紧缺。因此，在谈到与冰岛的贸易合作时，田香莲也提出，青年

企业家可以更多地考虑服务贸易方面的机会。在旅游旺季，冰岛气候适宜，景色宜人，游客们更偏爱于感受温泉或湖泊这些自然景观。所以，可以考虑在旅游旺季时，针对露营地的住宿需求或日常需求进行投资。这样游客能获得更多舒适的方式与自然亲密接触，同时这也与“深度旅游”的概念不谋而合。

促进中冰交流，坚守诚信做人

在中国和冰岛的多年合作贸易中，华迅公司一直致力于让中国人更多地了解冰岛和冰岛产品，同时也希望把好的中国产品带到冰岛。田香莲的家乡位于河北省清河县，经过40多年的发展，清河已成为全国最大的羊绒产业集聚地，被誉为“世界羊绒之都”。田香莲在家乡建设了一座国际羊绒艺术展览中心，并且计划未来将清河羊绒产业的美名传播到冰岛，助力“世界羊绒看中国，中国羊绒看清河”，让冰岛人感受来自中国清河的羊绒衫的暖意。这不仅是两国贸易的拓展，更是中冰友谊的延伸。

济南大学冰岛研究中心在开展针对冰岛的国别研究工作方面在国内处于领先地位，致力于不断提升智库服务国家战略和社会需求的能力及水平。在谈到政府和济南大学冰岛研究中心等对中冰两国企业的发展支持时，田香莲认为，要发展中冰双方企业的合作，首先要进行全方位的宣传，邀请相关行业的专业人士或行业领头人物开展宣传讲座或论坛。合作共赢一定是建立在互相了解的基础上的，她希望政府能在媒体宣传和财政方面增加一些支持。就航空旅游服务业而言，应该弘扬航空服务、旅游服务的精神，拓展到社会各行各业，贯彻服务企业的理念，整合各个行业的发展过程，在总结走访调研过程中，真正了解并协助解决企业发展中的问题，进一步促进中冰企业的合作与发展。

田香莲在工作之余也有很多兴趣爱好，她尤其喜爱中国传统文化，醉心于戏曲，在空闲时常常听戏学戏唱戏，还曾经和马德华老师在中央电视台戏剧频道登台表演京剧《赤桑镇》选段，配合默契，惊艳全场。戏曲是我国传统文化中的瑰宝和典型代表，田香莲也希望可以在新冠肺炎疫情过去后去冰岛进行戏曲表演，把我国经典传统文化带到冰岛，让冰岛人民可以亲身感受中国传统文化。

田香莲曾参军工作20年，并坚守岗位，后在航空业工作至今已有30

年，其资历与成就足可让后来人称一声前辈。回首过往，她感慨于坚持诚信做人、踏实做事给自己和企业带来的机遇与成就。她说："一切做大事的人都是从小事做起，不要怕工作简单，如果你把每件小事做好，做一个守规矩的人，你会在每项工作都能做出成就。"

受全球新冠肺炎疫情影响，航空业是受到冲击最严重的行业之一，华迅公司也受到了很大影响。疫情初期，回国机票曾一票难求，但是田香莲坚持不会因为现在的困境而炒高机票价钱。她说："做企业就要由做服务来赚钱才安心，工作没有高低贵贱之分，只有对待工作的态度不同罢了。"诚信是她坚持并贯穿的人生理念，脚踏实地做好每一件事是她一直以来的守则。

如今时代在进步，社会在发展，各行各业的企业如雨后春笋般涌现。面对大千世界，年轻人需要学习一种精益创新的企业家精神，传承坚守诚信，用心钻研，脚踏实地，一定会有出色的成就。

（杨坤　朱昱茹）

Perfection from Ordinariness Through Serious and Diligent Work

— Interview with Tian Xianglian, Chairman of Beijing China Express International Air Service Co., Ltd.

"Be honest for life, work and enterprise, and do everything attentively, so that you can have accomplishments in every field." Persistence and integrity run throughout her work and life, this is what Tian Xianglian mentioned many times in the interview.

It's not hard to take something seriously. It's hard to take everything seriously for decades. It's not difficult to work hard at the beginning of career. It's difficult to remain committed to the career while having accumulated something. Tian Xianglian has been working in the air service industry for 30 years. She has gone through the ups and downs of China's civil aviation industry, and she is still energetic even though she is over 60. She kindly and warmly shared her life experience with us, from which we deeply felt her adherence to the spirit of enterprise.

Decades Careers in Aviation and Special Attachments with Iceland

Born in the early days of the founding of New China, Tian Xianglian experienced the development of the country. When she was young, she dreamed of making efforts for the growth and strength of the country. She joined the army at the age of 16 and became a communication professional technician who faithfully delivered every instruction and witnessed many soul-stirring moments in history. For such a seemingly simple but very important job, she remained faithfully to her post for 20 years. She participated in the Sino-Vietnamese Self-defensive Counterattack and the South China Sea Defense, and firmly performed her duties as a soldier. 20 years in the military left deep marks in her life. No matter how the situation changes, she insists on being devoted to her job, holding the serious and responsible spirits. Her military career has cast her excellent soldier quality style and gathered the rules for life of being honest and trustworthy and working seriously. This unique experience also laid a solid foundation for her business management. It helps to shapes a down-to-earth, honest and trustworthy enterprise culture.

At the end of the 1980s, China was poised for a new era, with all walks of life facing unprecedented opportunities and challenges. Tian Xianglian also rethought the road of her life, she wanted to feel the new challenge in the new era, so she shifted from military to business track, and started a new career in her life.

Tian Xianglian started her aviation career from air freight services. Two years later, she changed her focus to passenger transport and founded Beijing China Express International Air Service Co., Ltd. (hereinafter referred to as China Express). Since then, she has been working as an air passenger service agency for 28 years. At that time, buying an air ticket was extremely complicated, and only people of certain ranks could book air tickets with reference letters from their employers. Issuing an air ticket is not as convenient as now, instead, it required the staff to write all kinds of information, including passenger names, flight numbers, seat numbers, baggage weight and so on. With the development of China's economy and the increase of air passengers, manual boarding passes were gradually replaced by efficient printed boarding passes. In 2000, the newly introduced e-tickets allowed passengers to obtain boarding passes directly with their ID cards. In 2017, the country's first e-invoice for air passenger transport was introduced. All those upgrades in air tickets involve the hard work of the air service industry, and Tian Xianglian has personally experienced and participated in every major turning points.

Before the popularization of Internet, air tickets were sold with traditional mode. The airlines designated air service agents to provide services and sell air tickets, thus forming an air service industrial chain; and agents can provide face-to-face personalized services according to customer's demand. Entering the era of mobile Internet, more passengers buy tickets online through the Internet. When talking about the fusion and conflicts between traditional methods and modern technology, Tian Xianglian believed that traditional agency service will keep vitality. Though the Internet ticket buying has advantages in efficiency and convenience, the traditional agency service also keeps its unique advantages. It's a human-based service that cannot be replaced by machine, and its existence is an indispensable part of the air service industry.

In 2003, Tian Xianglian became acquainted with Icelandair. Steinn Larusson, the general manager of Asia Pacific Region of Icelandair, came to China to investigate Icelandair. He heard that Tian's China Express had achieved great achievements in the air ticket agent industry and good business performance, so he stepped into China Express' front desk by himself to learn more about it. In the busy hall, Tian noticed that he was not handling business, so she came forward to ask if he needed help. After learning his job and purpose, she introduced to him the company. Knowing that he had been working since he came to China and had not yet known Beijing, she suggested that he could learn about China's history and culture, such as the Great Wall, the Forbidden City and other places with historical heritage. She also sent employees and drivers to take him to visit these places of interests and experience Chinese food. Steinn Larusson saw the active and busy work of each employee in China Express, and felt Tian's enthusiasm and integrity in the conversation. He immediately decided to appoint her as the General Sales Agent of Icelandair in China. In 2003, they signed the general agency cooperation agreement between Icelandair and China Express in China. This is the first international airline that signed the general Chinese agent cooperation agreement with China Express. For Tian Xianglian, the partnership with Icelandair was a start point for her future cooperation with other airlines. It was unique and marked the beginning of her nearly 20-year partnership with Icelandair. Her connection with Icelandair is irreplaceable.

Experiencing the Charm of Iceland and Forming a Deep Friendship

Iceland lies in the far north and is surrounded by the Atlantic Ocean. The country is full of volcanoes and glaciers, Iceland's rich and varied natural wonders attract thousands of adventure lovers and tourists every year, and tourism is a vital part of Iceland's economy.

The capital of Iceland, Reykjavik's most iconic attraction must be the Blue Lake, one of Iceland's most popular attractions. The mixing of geothermal water and sea water makes the lake blue-green, which is reflected by naturally growing seaweed. It is rich in minerals that are good for human body. While soaking in the hot spring, people can also watch the surrounding snow-covered glaciers and relieve their fatigue. Tian Xianglian has been to Iceland many times to experience its mystery and charm, and the Blue Lake is the most recommended. Bathing in a hot spring feels like being in heaven and can make people forget all their troubles for a while. She often had wonderful encounters in Iceland. She met excellent photographers and made a special trip to Iceland for wedding photography. The endless black sand beach, the white gauze skirt fluttering in the wind, as well as the rolling waves not far away, are all charming. Iceland has attracted many nature lovers and professional photographers for its unique aurora, the only ice cave exploration in the world, and the combination of volcanoes and ice.

Wonderful landscapes in Iceland

After the first-hand experience of Iceland's charm, Tian Xianglian hoped to enable Chinese tourists to maximize their enjoyment of the natural beauty there. She put forward the concept of "in-depth travel to Iceland" first, advocating the development of immersive tourism products that best meet tourists' expectations and achieve maximum comfort according to the unique characteristics of scenic spots and tourists' preferences and interests. In contrast, with many travel products now, the travel is just for the sake of travel, and taking photos is only for posting the moment. Within such cursory tourism, not only the charm of the scenery itself is ignored, but also the tourists can get tired, which run against the original purpose of relaxation and pleasure of tourism. For this purpose, China Express is the first company to introduce the in-depth Iceland travel products in the Chinese market, advertising Iceland's tourist attractions that are not well known to the public, and planning the itinerary according to Chinese people's preference for photography and adventure, striving to make the travel a truly immersive and relaxing experience.

Tian Xianglian believes that in addition to in-depth exploration of tourism projects in Iceland, as the representative of Icelandair in China, she should also help promote the local brands in Iceland. When visitors come to Iceland, they can not only fully experience the beautiful scenery, but also get close to the local characteristic products, especially the unique natural and original ecological products of Iceland. Iceland's anseriformes duvet is famous around the world. It is made of the Icelandic female anseriformes' the softest and warmest down on the chest and armpits, which is the rarest top down in the world. Icelandic anseriformes is extremely cold-resistant, but its population is extremely rare, with only about 200,000 in the world. Their down is also difficult to collect. After the Icelandic anseriformes has hatched, collectors have to climb thousands of meters of cliff walls to collect the down from abandoned brood nests. The down duvet is made of pure natural down, and almost all of the process is made by hand. It can be described as a product closest to the nature. It is believed that visitors can experience the charm of Iceland in many aspects in its beautiful scenery and outstanding featured products.

Tian Xianglian (first from the left) presented Mr.Gunnar S.Gunnarsson (first from the right), former ambassador of Iceland to China, a calligraphy work

Because of Tian Xianglian's insistence on being honest and kind, when she first met the person in charge of Icelandair, she made candid and effective communication whth him. Then she won his trust by virtue of her company's strength and her personality charm became the general agent of Icelandair in China. With the deepening of cooperation, Tian Xianglian and Gunnar S. Gunnarsson, the former ambassador of Iceland to China, build deep friendship. Gunnarsson is very serious about promoting Iceland and provided considerable support for Icelandair's work. Since the cooperation, Tian has taken Gunnarsson to enjoy the beautiful mountains and rivers of China, and the two often exchanged views of two cultures. On the occasion of his departure, Tian gave him a calligraphy work by Li Chunbo, on which writing "Happiness, Longevity, Health, Peace" to express her wishes for good health and all the best. Gunnarsson wrote the friendship forever and hoped that the friendship between China and

Iceland would last forever. It is because of the integrity, honesty and kindness as Tian always sticks to, can she win the respect and trust of others. She treats people cordially and sincerely, and then they treat her sincerely in return.

Devoting for Sino-Iceland Aviation and Offering Ideas on Sino-Iceland Business Cooperation

Tian Xianglian has worked with Icelandair for 18 years since she started her general agency business in 2003. In order to let Chinese tourists better understand Iceland and facilitate air travel to Iceland, she has made a lot of efforts. As the saying goes, "Build roads before you get rich". It applies to the aviation industry as well. With the signing of a free trade agreement between China and Iceland, more and more business customers travel to Iceland. To develop the cooperation and trade between the two countries, the priority is to solve the traffic barriers between them. China Express has been working hard for this. Due to the long distance between China and Iceland, it requires bigger aircraft types. On the other hand, the tourist season of China to Iceland is mainly in summer, but there are very few Iceland tourists visiting China, so the round-trip flights cost highly. Many passengers who originally planned to go to Iceland will change their travel plans due to the price factor. Therefore, the direct flight between China and Iceland has become the focus. Icelandair has invested a lot in sales and marketing to prepare for direct flights between the two countries in the future. Tian Xianglian leads the team to actively promote Iceland to Chinese tourists, and makes Chinese people have better understanding of Iceland. She helps to give a clear picture of Iceland instead of that shown in maps and reports; she provides convenience for tourists, and makes Chinese tourists yearning for traveling to Iceland to enjoy its beauty.

In 2019, Tian Xianglian signed an agreement on behalf of the company with Juneyao Airlines for services to Iceland. Although direct flights cannot be realized in the near future, they can achieve stop-over flights with shortened traveling time. Although the plan has been temporarily suspended due to the sudden outbreak of COVID-19, it will be implemented when the travel environment is safe in the future, which will make Iceland a charming and convenient tourist attraction.

Tourism is the number one industry in Iceland. Nearly 2 million international passengers flew to Iceland in 2019, of which Chinese passengers accounted for about 5%. During the peak season, Iceland is even short of accommodation and service industry resources. Therefore, when talking about trade cooperation with Iceland, Tian Xianglian also proposed that young entrepreneurs could seize more opportunities in service trade. During peak tourist season, Iceland has a pleasant climate and beautiful scenery, and tourists prefer to experience natural attractions such as hot springs and lakes, so the investment in the accommodation or daily needs of camps during peak tourist season can be considered. By doing this, tourists can get more comfortable ways to get close to the nature, which exactly coincides with the concept of "in-depth travel".

Promoting China - Iceland Communication and Being Honest as Belief

In the trade cooperation between China and Iceland over years, China Express has been committed to making Chinese people know more about Iceland and its products, and also hoping to bring good Chinese products to Iceland. Tian Xianglian's hometown is located in Qinghe County, Hebei Province. Through more than forty years of development, Qinghe has become the biggest center of cashmere industry in China and is called "World Cashmere Capital". Tian Xianglian builds an international cashmere art exhibition center in her hometown and plans to spread the reputation of Qinghe cashmere industry to Iceland in the future. She tries her best to realize "the best cashmere in the world is from China, and the best cashmere in China is from Qinghe", so that Icelanders can feel the warmth of cashmere sweater from Qinghe, China. This is not only the expansion of China-Iceland trade but also the extension of China-Iceland friendship.

Icelandic Research Center of Jinan University takes the leading position in China in the nationality research on Iceland, and it is committed to continuously promoting the ability and level of think-tank service national strategy and social demands. In terms of the development support of the government and Icelandic Research Center of Jinan University on China-Iceland enterprises, Tian Xianglian thinks that, to develop the cooperation of China-Iceland enterprises, it is required to conduct the all-round publicity first and invite relevant professionals or industry leaders of relevant industries to attend publicity lectures or forums. The win-win cooperation must be established on the basis of mutual understanding, and she hopes that the government can increase some supports on media publicity and finance. In terms of air travel services, it is required to promote the spirit of air services and tourism services, expand them to all walks of life, implement the idea of service enterprise and integrate the development process of all industries. By researching and summarizing, thoroughly understand and assist to solve the problems in the development of enterprises, and further promote the cooperation and development between China-Iceland enterprises.

Tian Xianglian has many hobbies and interests at leisure, she especially enjoys the Chinese traditional culture and loves traditional opera. She often listens

Tian Xianglian (first from the left) and Ma Dehua perform excerpts from Beijing Opera *Chisang Town*

to, learns and performs the traditional opera in her spare time. She performed *Chisang Town* on the Central Drama Channel with Mr. Ma Dehua, which was tacit and wowed the audience. The traditional opera is the treasure of Chinese traditional culture. Tian Xianglian also hopes to perform the traditional opera in Iceland after the epidemic and brings Chinese traditional culture to Iceland, so that Icelanders can personally experience the Chinese traditional culture.

Tian Xianglian was the army for 20 years when she was young and stuck to her post. Now she has been working in the aviation industry for 30 years. The latecomers shall regard her as the senior for her qualifications and achievements. Looking back, she is impressed by the opportunity and achievements brought by being honest with people and working hard to herself and the enterprise. She said: "All people having bigger things start from the small. Do not be afraid that the work is simple, and if you are the person following the rules, you will make achievements in each task." Affected by COVID-19, the aviation industry is one of the industries most seriously affected, and China Express has also been greatly impacted. It is difficult to get a return ticket in the early stage of the epidemic; however, Tian Xianglian did not raise the ticket price for the current dilemma. She said, "We shall make money through services in the enterprise, and no job is noble or humble, the only difference is the attitude towards the work." Integrity is the concept that Tian Xianglian persists through her life, and doing everything step by step is the principle she observes all the time.

Now with the advancement of the era and the development of the society, enterprises in all walks of life spring up. When facing the world, the young shall learn the entrepreneurship of innovation, adhere to integrity and work hard step by step, and they will make excellent achievements.

(Yang Kun　Zhu Yuru)

05

为肢残者拼出完整的人生

——访奥索假肢矫形康复器材（上海）有限公司市场部经理

李迪琛

李迪琛

当我们问起为什么会关注到奥索假肢矫形康复器材（上海）有限公司（以下简称奥索）并且加入这个团体时，李迪琛说："奥索带给肢残人再生的机会，让他们可以和健全人一样奔跑。所以，我加入这家公司，希望帮助更多的残疾人突破生活和工作中的'局限'。"

正是因为对自己的工作怀有坚定的信念，在采访过程中，李迪琛的热情和专业态度深深地感染了我们。

自加入奥索这个大家庭以来，李迪琛接触了很多以前不曾接触过的残障人士。因为亲眼所见他人的伤痛，即使无法感同身受，她也深感庆幸自己能加入奥索，因为这份工作能帮助更多人"完整"自己的人生。

李迪琛作为奥索中国区市场部经理，不仅领导团队通过自媒体平台和各种市场活动向人们推广奥索的假肢和矫形器等产品，还积极组织线上线下活动，向消费者传递奥索的企业文化——"生活无局限"。

奥索假肢的大使们在展会大放异彩

李迪琛（前排右三）在奥索暴风飞毛腿试穿活动中

千里之行，始于足下

1971 年，在冰岛的雷克雅未克，一位截肢患者通过自己的研究和努力建立了一家工作室。这家工作室经过不断地发展，后来成了假肢矫形器领域唯一的上市公司，即冰岛奥索的前身。自成立以来，奥索通过不断地创新和发展，现在全球约 25 个国家设立了办事处，拥有 4000 多名员工。50 多年里，无数的截肢患者和骨性关节炎患者在奥索的帮助下，不仅重新站起来了，甚至跑得更快，跳得更高。哪怕有残缺的局限，也能拥有无局限的人生！

奥索是一家全球性的假肢矫形器材公司，致力于研究开发假肢、矫形器及其相关配件，并提供相应的技术咨询和技术服务，同时致力于将仿生学技术运用到该领域。李迪琛很高兴地向我们解释道："奥索所从事的事业就是为了提高人们的行动能力，在追求生活无局限的过程中，它不断地利用先进的技术和材料，并勇于将之与自己的产品相结合。"奥索是一家给肢残人带来重生机会的企业，如果有一天，穿戴假肢的人可以和健全的人一样能够奔跑跳跃，那么社会投射在残肢者身上的歧视会不会少一点？这也是让李迪琛最动容的一点，加入奥索，使她在工作的同时，还能帮助肢残人士获得生命的全新希望。

作为一家全球性的假肢矫形器材公司，奥索寻找来自世界各地的医疗专业人士，共同研发出有技术性突破的假肢和矫形器，不断提高奥索品牌的质量性能标准。

在我们谈及奥索品牌在中国的知名度时，李迪琛告诉我们，“假肢、矫形器，对于大部分人来说，是比较陌生的东西，所以普通人对奥索更是闻所未闻。”然而，统计数据显示，我国残疾人数量占全国人口总数的6.34%，其中肢体残缺的残疾人达到2412万人。对于奥索而言，这部分群体的存在意味着市场拥有很大的发展潜力。即便是受众领域较小，奥索也一直秉承对患者专业负责的态度，致力于提供最优质的服务和辅具保障。目前，奥索已经是行业内有名、在患者中享有良好口碑的企业，成为世界上最大的假肢矫形器公司之一。

李迪琛认为，在全球诸多的假肢集团和品牌中，奥索的产品能够脱颖而出，最重要的原因就是产品一直在创新和进步。

奥索身为假肢行业里的佼佼者，是一家充满高科技含量的公司，在智能假肢、碳纤运动储能假肢及硅胶套产品上都有很深的造诣，是世界上第一家开发假肢专用硅胶内衬套技术的公司。李迪琛告诉我们：“奥索正在研发大脑思维控制仿生假肢技术（意念控制假肢）。此项技术一旦研发成功，奥索将会成为创造历史的集团，甚至于在未来都会彻底改变假肢技术领域的发展。”

这便是奥索“生活无局限”企业文化的现实写照，勇于创新，敢于超越，旨在让肢残人士找到完整的自己，实现无局限的生活。奥索一直保持长远发展的眼光，用实力说话，依靠产品的科技含量和舒适度打造品牌影响力。

像假肢这类产品是十分精密的仪器，如果产品和使用者的适配性不达标，就会给患者带来糟糕的使用体验，甚至对患者的身体造成不可逆的损伤。因此，对产品零件的精细化分工是十分必要的。“奥索在广东惠州成立了一个专门的生产团队，专门负责配件产品的研发和制造，在制造完成之后再运到欧洲进行装配。因为我们最专业的技师团队在欧洲，各国生产的零配件都要运送至欧洲，整个产品在欧洲装配好了之后再运到中国来销售。”在李迪琛的介绍中，我们了解到了奥索的研发团队十分庞大，主要技术和研发中心都在冰岛和美国。

如果说，艺术家对自己的作品总是抱有挑剔的心，那么人们在奥索也能感受到一样严谨的态度。奥索每年都会有至少 5% 的营业额收入投入研发当中，因此奥索的产品也是一直占有中高端市场，保持着自己独有的竞争力。

在李迪琛看来：“不断地进行创新是奥索具有行业核心竞争力的主要原因。”像鸟儿爱惜自己的羽翼一样珍惜自己的品牌价值，李迪琛向我们表达了这样的企业价值观。

立足上海，引领亚太市场

无论是经济实力还是文化创新，中国的发展日新月异。世界已经看到中国市场的巨大发展潜力，奥索亦然。

2019 年，奥索参加了第二届中国国际进口博览会，并且奥索是唯一拥有特装独立展台的冰岛品牌。当我们问及关于奥索在亚太区的发展时，李迪琛向我们介绍说：“经过一段时间的深入考察和市场调研后，2006 年，奥索成立了相当于外企办事处的奥索假肢矫形康复器材（上海）有限公司。为了发展亚太市场，此后奥索分别在日本、韩国、新加坡、马来西亚等国家和中国香港地区建立了分公司。从 2019 年开始，奥索总部决定将上海作为亚太市场的中心。”

中国市场同样没有让奥索失望，“我们总部非常重视中国市场，为什么要把亚洲的总部选在上海？其实就是看中了中国，首先人口数量庞大，经济较为发达。”李迪琛告诉我们，“奥索在全球每年销售额在 7 亿 ~ 8 亿美元，其中亚太区销售额占全球销售额的 9%，中国占比为

奥索作为唯一有特装独立展台的冰岛品牌参加
2019 年第二届中国国际进口博览会

1% ~ 2%，约 1200 万美元。”由于奥索在亚太区的发展还处于成长阶段，故销售额占比远低于欧洲市场。当问起奥索在全球最大的销售市场时，李迪琛提到了很多人对奥索的误解，由于奥索基本一半的销售量都来自美国，导致行业里面很多人误以为奥索是一个美国公司。

前任冰岛驻华大使古士贤先生（右三）与李迪琛（右一）

目前，随着人们消费观念的转变，奥索在中国各省政府的支持下不断深入中国市场，奥索的产品也越来越受到中国消费者青睐。李迪琛说：“由于大众对假肢矫形概念非常模糊，不愿意把过多的钱花在假肢上，患者更愿意去买一辆 10 万块钱的代步车，而不是花几万块钱去买中高端假肢。现在奥索通过大力宣传，致力于让患者改变对传统假肢的看法，选择奥索假肢。”因为，奥索的追求并不止步于让患者站起来，而是可以让患者实现无局限的生活。

奥索之所以受到消费者的青睐，主要原因在于它不仅仅尊重各类患者不同层次的需求，更重要的是把残疾人也可以拥抱生活的理念和关怀传递给了患者。

李迪琛还为我们详细介绍了传统假肢和奥索假肢的区别。“传统的一些普通假肢虽然能满足患者日常生活和行走的普遍需求，但是存在稳定性不高的问题，甚至有些低端产品，比如脚板，因为弹性太差，行走时导致重心完全移至健侧。长时间的重心不稳，会使患者拖着假肢内侧行走，患者非常容易受到二次伤害，导致骨性关节炎。而奥索的假肢不仅使患者日常行走的稳定性、安全性有保障，且在性能和舒适度上也远远超过普通假肢产品。除了患者穿戴体验感会大大提升，奥索假肢还能满足患者跑步、跳跃，甚至登山的需求，对穿戴条件的局限更小。”

奥索定位中高端产品市场，选择高端材料，投入研发具有科技性突破的产品，不断引导患者进行产品升级。这一系列做法均离不开其品牌理念的影响。

疫情之下，扩渠求新

李迪琛作为奥索中国区的市场部经理，她的主要工作内容就是负责假肢和矫形器两大业务线的品牌宣传和产品推广工作。她告诉我们，奥索的产品大致可以分为两类：假肢和矫形器。“其中，假肢产品主要通过中国的经销商和代理商进行销售。截肢患者根据医院的推荐和介绍，到当地的假肢公司装配产品。”经过李迪琛介绍，我们了解到假肢的销售方式和我们以往接触到的产品销售方式有很大的不同。

“除了假肢和矫形器这类医疗产品，对于一些软护具，比如护膝、护踝、护腰，患者通过主流的线上销售渠道就可以购买。”软护具属于较大众的产品，因此需要这些软护具产品的消费者数量较硬护具而言翻了几倍，并且由于人们的健康意识的不断提高，所以对这类产品的需求也在不断增加。

新冠肺炎疫情给全球经济带来了冲击，对全球的供应链造成了较大的影响，各种贸易活动受到了不同程度的制约和影响。“奥索在全球疫情暴发初期，采取了一系列行之有效的应对措施，保证奥索强大的供应链和物流体系能正常运转。但是无法避免的是隔离措施的实施导致消费者数量下降，产品更换的需求减少，但是在通过直播、内容营销等多种数字营销策略，以及与重点经销商的战略合作，最终奥索中国区在 2020 年的销售额同比 2019 年还是上涨了 20%。”李迪琛说。

伴随着互联网、电商行业的兴起和繁荣，奥索也在借助各种媒体平台向终端患者和大众宣传奥索品牌。

奥索联合中国肢残人协会举办“公益无限，行走无疆”步态训练营

“显然全球疫情还会持续很长一段时间，但是中国的疫情还是相对比较稳定可控的。接下来，我们还需要通过在各种自媒体平台上的宣传来提升我们品牌和产品的知名度，让现有客户自愿进行产品的升级，从而来减少产品需求下降带来的损失。”李迪琛说，“其实做假肢这一类的产品，不仅仅是产品的销售，还需要给患者进行充分的心理建设，包括之后一系列后续产品知识和患者教育的工作都是需要我们去完成的。因此，在疫情期间，我们主要通过直播的方式给大家介绍产品的使用情况，并开展患者心理疏导等一系列在线心理咨询活动。”

同时，奥索还在自媒体上用心经营和传播着自身的文化和理念，鼓励人们通过锻炼身体来增强身体素质，使得电商业务在疫情期间有了很大的增长，奥索的品牌知名度也得到了很大的提升。奥索借助在短视频和直播中的宣传，让更多的人了解了这样一个来自冰岛的高质量假肢矫形器产品。

值得一提的是，就在 2020 年东京残奥会的赛场上，许多穿戴着奥索脚板的运动员频频亮相颁奖台。这些奥运健儿们都来自奥索之队，在奥索产品和技术的支持下，他们展示了自己的奥运精神，最终创下了 28 枚奖牌的辉煌历史！

奥索之队合影

中冰合作，友谊绵长

2019年，李迪琛协同四川省副省长及其代表团一行参观了位于冰岛的奥索总部。在双方进行了深入洽谈以及实地考察之后，最终在王一宏副省长的见证下，奥索与四川省人民医院签订了重大战略合作协议，从而推动了奥索在中国西部地区的发展。四川省代表团的此次到访，大大加强了中国政府与奥索的交流与合作，未来奥索有望服务于中国西南地区乃至全国人民，让世界领先的技术和康复辅具产业服务更多的中国人民。

这次冰岛之旅，既是奥索和四川省政府的跨国拜访交流之旅，也是李迪琛的成长之旅。“通过参观冰岛的社会福利中心和冰岛残疾人联合会后，我感受到了冰岛对残疾人良好的生活关怀，比如说，他们的残疾人通道以及残疾人就业保障方面，都给了我们很多的借鉴和启发。”

身在这样一个岗位，李迪琛接触了不一样的人群，看到了不一样的世界，这让李迪琛对实现个人价值也有了清晰的认识。她认为，在这份工作中，依靠科技的力量去帮助残疾人，是她实现个人价值、为社会做贡献的热情所在。这对患者和李迪琛来说，都有着非常深远的意义。

李迪琛（右一）协同四川省代表团一行参观冰岛奥索总部

面对在这个行业里时刻接触到的截肢患者，李迪琛除了提供专业的帮助，也有许多个人的想法。“例如在中国的某些省份，截肢的患者每隔 3 年便可以去残联免费领取一个价格大约四五千元的假肢，但是假肢的质量比较差，无法满足肢残人士正常走路的需要。”

在采访的最后，李迪琛表达了个人愿望。一方面，她希望未来中国能像欧洲国家一样将假肢纳入医疗保险，可以让更多的肢残者使用到高端假肢，体验到高科技假肢带来生活无局限的体验；另一方面，她希望残联能改变现有的运行模式，给患者提供更多的选择。例如，患者不需要 3 年换一次假肢，而是可以选择 6 年更换一次，这样可以提供给患者质量稍好一点的假肢，或者对自由选择假肢的直接补贴。

除了医疗保险制度的完善，李迪琛还提到了对残障人群的个人关怀问题。目前，中国的残疾人约有 8000 万，其中肢残人大概也有 2412 万，而我们在现实生活中却很少见到这部分人，他们在哪里呢？由此可见，我国政府对这部分人群的关注远远不够。一些残疾人的基础设施建设没有达到标准，比如盲道被机动车占用、没有专用的残疾人通道，以及不允许导盲犬进入公共场所等，都给他们出行带来不便。

与此同时，社会通过心理、物理、结构三方面将残疾人拦在了就业市场之外。由于刻板印象的存在，人们理所当然地默认一些群体具有某些特质，大部分情况下残疾人无法摆脱社会在人文关怀角度之外加在他们身上的“弱势群体”标签。因此，在公共场合大家总会对他们投来探究甚至异样的眼光，同时在就业市场上也受到了歧视。

“奥索的仿生技术致力于改变人们对残疾人的刻板印象。我们可以看到，戴着仿生假肢的人几乎和健全人一模一样。因此，仿生技术在功能和心理上都具有很高的价值。奥索的高科技产品不仅可以改变社会对残疾人的看法，同时可以让患者获得重生。”奥索和李迪琛的团队也在试图通过自己的努力，改变残疾人在正常生活和工作中存在的问题，让众多的肢残者实现肢残心不残的理念，撕掉有色标签，最大限度地回到普通人的生活。

奥索认为就业机会是平等的，公司致力于打造多元化的员工群体，求职者不会因为种族、国籍以及残障而在求职过程中受到歧视。

李迪琛在客户大会中发表演讲《拥抱数字营销》

“奥索为年轻人提供了很多平台和资源，让年轻的力量可以去发挥，去创造，所以我希望社会上的年轻人一定要坚信，很多公司都有这样的平台和资源，然后只要我们脚踏实地，一步一个脚印，都可以实现自己的人生梦想！”李迪琛的这段话激励了我们，同样也送给像她一样在自己岗位上发光发热的年轻人。相信新生力量一定会给社会带来更美好的未来！

（麻中怡　牛晓梦）

Going All Out in Work for the Complete Life of the Disabled

— Interview with Lee Dichen, Marketing Manager of Össur Shanghai

When talking about the reason why she paid attention to Össur and joined the team, Lee Dichen said, "Össur brings the rebirth opportunity to the physically disabled, so that they can be able to run like us. Therefore, I want to join this company to help more disabled people walk out of the limitations of life and work."

Work photo of Lee Dichen

Because of her firm faith in what she is doing, her enthusiastic and professional attitude left a deep impression on us during the interview.

Since joined the big family of Össur, Lee Dichen has come into contact with many mutilated people she had never contacted before. Though she cannot feel indebted as if it were received in person, she was so grateful to join Össur where she can help more people "complete" their lives after seeing the pain of others.

As the marketing manager of Össur in

China, Lee Dichen not only led the team to popularize prosthetics, orthoses, and other products to people by WeMedia platforms and various marketing activities and also actively organized on-line and off-line activities to transmit the enterprise culture concept of Össur — "Life Without Limitations"!

Friendship of Lee Dichen (the middle) and ambassadors

Lee Dichen (front row, first from the right) fitting activity of intelligent bionic hand of Össur

A Journey of a Thousand *li* Begins with a Single Step

In Reykjavik, Iceland in 1971, a patient suffering leg amputation established a studio by his own research and efforts. This studio becomes the only listed company in the field of prosthesis and orthosis through unremitting development, which is the prodecessor of Össur. Since the establishment, Össur has set up offices in about 25 countries around the world, with more than 4000 employees owing to their continuous innovation and development. In the last fifty years, many amputees and patients suffering osteoarthritis have stood up again and even run faster and jumped higher under the help of Össur. A person with limitations of disability can have the life without limitations!

Össur is a global prosthesis and orthosis company. It is committed to the research on the development of prosthesis, orthosis, and relevant accessories, and provides relevant technical consultation and services. Meanwhile, they bend themselves to applying bionics techniques to this field. Lee Dichen was very happy to explain that, "The business that Össur does is to improve people's mobility and it will continuously take advantages of advanced technologies and materials and combine them with its products in the process of pursuing the realization of enterprise logos." Össur is an enterprise that can bring the rebirth opportunity to the physically disabled. If one day the disabled wearing prosthesis can run and jump as same as the healthy people, then would there be less discrimination against them? This is the point that impressed Lee Dichen most. She can bring fresh hope of life to the physically disabled while working after joining Össur.

As a global prosthesis and orthosis company, Össur seeks the medical professionals from all over the world to jointly research and develop the prosthesis and orthosis with technological breakthrough and continuously improve the quality performance standards of its brand.

When talking about the popularity of Össur brand in China, Lee Dichen told us that, "For most people, prosthesis, orthosis and foot plate are very unfamiliar;

therefore, the ordinary people have never heard of Össur before." However, the statistical data shows that the number of the disabled people in China accounts for 6.34% of the national population, of which the number of lower limb amputations have a large population, exceeding more than 24.12 millions. As for Össur, this group means a great development potential of the market, and it also represents the population that requires help and concerns most at present. Even though the audience field is small, Össur always adheres to the professional and responsible attitude towards patients, and is committed to providing the high-quality services and equipment support. For now, Össur has been the famous enterprise in the industry and the enterprise with public praise among patients, and become one of the biggest prosthesis and orthosis companies around the world.

Lee Dichen believes that the reason why the products of Össur can stand out in many prosthesis groups and brands around the world is that its products are continuously innovated and improved.

As a leader in the prosthesis industry, Össur is full of high-tech content. It has profound deep attainments in intelligent prosthesis, carbon fiber moving energy storage prosthesis and silicone products. And it is the first company around the world to develop the special silicone lining technology for prosthesis. Lee Dichen explained to us, "Össur is researching and developing the technology of brain-controlled bionic prosthesis technology (idea-controlled prosthetic). Once the technology is researched and developed successfully, Össur will make history and even completely change the development of prosthesis technology in the future."

This is a realistic portrayal of Össur's "Life Without Limitations" corporate culture, dare to innovate and surpass, aiming to let the disabled find a complete self and realize an unlimited life. Össur always keeps the perspective of long-term development, focuses on the strength and creates the brand influence by technology contents and comfort level of products.

Because medical apparatus like prosthesis are highly precise instruments, if the adaptability of the products and the users is not up to standard, it will bring a terrible experience feeling, even irreversible damages to patients' bodies. Therefore, the fine division of product parts is particularly essential. "Össur established a special work team in Huizhou, Guangdong to take charge of R&D and manufacturing of accessories. The semi-manufactured goods will be transported to Europe after manufacturing for the subsequent assembly. Because our most professional technician team is in Europe, the spare parts manufactured in each country will be transported to Europe, and then the whole products will be transported to China after assembly in Europe for sales." By the introduction from Lee Dichen, we can understand that the R&D team of Össur is very large, and its main technology and R&D centers are now in Iceland and America.

Like the case that artists are critical about their works, people can feel the same rigorous attitude in Össur. Össur puts at least 5% of the operating income into R&D each year; therefore, the products of Össur have always occupies the middle and high-end market and maintain their own unique competitiveness.

In Lee Dichen's opinion: "The continuous innovation is the main reason to make Össur have the core competitiveness in the industry." Cherishing the own brand value like a bird cherishing its wings, Lee Dichen expressed the corporate values to us. Cherishing the own brand value like a bird cherishing its wings, Lee Dichen expressed the corporate values to us.

Being Located in Shanghai and Leading the Asia-Pacific Market

China's development is changing with each passing day whether in economic strength or cultural innovation. The world has seen the huge development potential of Chinese market, so has Össur.

In 2019, Össur participated in the 2nd China International Import Expo and it was the only Iceland brand with a specially decorated and independent exhibition stand. When we asked about the development history of Össur in the Asia-Pacific region, Lee Dichen introduced that "After a long-time in-depth investigation and market research, Össur established the Össur Shanghai in 2006, which is equivalent to the foreign enterprise office. In order to better develop the Asia-Pacific market, Össur has set up several branches in Hong Kong (China), Japan, the Republic of Korea, Singapore, Malaysia and others later. Since 2019, Össur has decided to take Shanghai as the hub of the Asia-Pacific market."

Chinese market has not let Össur down, "Our headquarters really put emphasis on Chinese market, and the reason why we chose Shanghai as the Asian headquarter is that the head office is sure that the Chinese market, whose population is very large and the economy is relatively developed, has a great future." said by Lee Dichen, "The global sales amount of Össur is about USD 700 million–800 million each year, of which that in the Asia–Pacific region accounts for 9%, and China accounts for 1%–2%, about USD 12 million." Because the development of Össur in the Asia–Pacific region is still in the growing stage, the proportion of its sales amount is far less than that of European market. When it came to the biggest sales market of Össur around the world, Lee Dichen mentioned the misunderstanding of lots of people on Össur. Because basically half of the sales amount of Össur is from America, many people in the industry mistakenly believe that Össur is an American company.

Nowadays, with the change of people's consumption concept, Össur continuously and deeply enters the Chinese market under the help of each Chinese provincial government, and the products of Össur are more and more favored by Chinese consumers. Lee Dichen said, "Because the public has a very vague concept on prosthetic orthosis and is not willing to spend too much money on prosthesis, and patients would rather spend ¥100,000 buying a scooter than spend tens of thousands buying the middle and high-end prosthesis. At present, Ossur is committed to changing patients' opinion on the traditional prosthesis by vigorous publicity and choosing the Össur prosthesis." Because the pursuit of Össur is not only ended with the condition that patients can stand up but also to make patients realize the life without limitations.

The main reason why Össur is favored by consumers is not only its respect on the demands of various patients at different levels, but more important that it transmits the concept and care that the disabled people can also embrace life to patients.

Lee Dichen introduced the differences between the traditional prosthesis and the Össur prosthesis in detail. "Although some traditional ordinary prosthesis can meet the general demands of patients in daily life and walking, there is the problem of low stability. Even some ordinary products, such as foot plate, lack elasticity, causing the center of gravity move completely to the tendon side while walking due to poor elasticity. The long-time unstable center of gravity will make patients drag the inner side of prosthesis to walk, and patients are vulnerable to the secondary injury, resulting in osteoarthritis. While the Össur prosthesis can not only have certain guarantee on the stability and safety in daily walking of patients but also provide the performance and comfort level which is far more than these provided by ordinary prosthesis. In addition to the great improvement of wearing experience feeling of patients, the Össur prosthesis can meet patients' demands on running, jumping even climbing mountains, with fewer limitations on wearing conditions."

Össur positions the middle and high-end product market, chooses high-end materials, researches and develops products with the scientific and technological breakthrough and continuously guides patients to insist on the product upgrade. This series of practices cannot be realized without the influence of its brand concept.

Channel Expansion and Innovation Under the Effect of COVID-19

As the marketing manager of Össur in China, Lee Dichen is mainly in charge of brand publicity and product promotion of two business lines (prosthesis and orthosis).

She told us that Össur's products could be roughly divided into two categories:

prosthesis and orthosis. "The prosthesis products are mainly sold through dealers and agents in China. According to the recommendation and introduction of the hospital, patients will go to the local prosthetic company to assemble products." After Lee Dichen's introduction, we learned that prosthesis was sold in a way quite different from products we have been exposed to in the past.

"Besides medical products such as prostheses and orthoses, some soft braces such as knee braces, ankle braces and waist braces can be purchased by patients through mainstream online sales channels." Soft braces are popular, so the number of consumers in need of these soft braces is several times higher than that of hard braces, and the demand for such products is also increasing because people's health awareness is constantly improving.

The COVID-19 gave a strong dash on the global economy and had a great influence on the global supply chain. Various trade activities have been restricted and influenced in varying degrees. Lee Dichen said, "At the beginning of the global outbreak of COVID-19, Össur took a series of effective countermeasures, to ensure normal operation of Össur's strong supply chain and logistics system. However, it was inevitable that the implementation of quarantine measures caused a decrease in the number of patients and the demand for product replacement. But through a series of marketing strategies such as Live Streaming and content marketing as well as the strategic cooperation with key dealers, the sales of Össur in 2020 increased by about 20% compared with 2019."

Lee Dichen (first from the left) in the live streaming studio at Tik Tok & Kuaishou

With the rise and prosperity of the Internet and e-commerce industry, Össur is also promoting the Össur brand to terminal patients and the public through various media platforms.

"Obviously, the global outbreak will continue for a long time, but the situation in China is relatively stable and controllable. Next, we still need to improve the popularity of our brands and products through our publicity on various WeMedia platforms, so that existing customers voluntarily upgrade products, thus mitigating the loss caused by the decline in product demand." Lee Dichen said, "Actually, engagement in prosthetic products involves not only the sales of products but also full psychological construction of patients, including a series of follow-up product induction patient education that we need to complete. Hence, during the outbreak, we mainly introduced the use of products through live broadcast and organized a series of online psychological counseling activities."

At the same time, Össur also manages and spreads its own culture and ideas with concentrated attention through WeMedia and encourages people to strengthen their physical fitness by exercising, so that the e-commerce business grow greatly during the outbreak and the brand popularity of Össur is greatly improved. With the help of the publicity in short video and live broadcast, Össur has made more people understand such a high-quality prosthesis and orthosis product from Iceland.

It is worth mentioning that, at the 2020 Tokyo Paralympic Games, many athletes wearing Össur prosthesis frequently appeared on the podium. These Olympic athletes are all from the Team of Össur. With the support of Össur's products and technologies, they showed their Olympic spirit and finally made a glorious history of 28 medals!

China-Iceland Cooperation and Long Friendship

In 2019, Lee Dichen, together with the Vice Governor of Sichuan Province and his delegation, visited the headquarters of Össur in Iceland. After in-depth negotiations and field visits, Össur Group signed a major strategic cooperation agreement with Sichuan Provincial People's Hospital under the witness of the Vice Governor Wang Yihong, which promoted the development of Össur Group in western China.

The visit of the delegation from Sichuan Province has greatly strengthened the exchanges and cooperation between the Chinese government and Össur. It is expected to serve the people in southwest China, even the whole country in the future, so that the world-leading technology and rehabilitation appliance industry can serve more Chinese people.

The trip to Iceland is a cross-border visit and exchange trip between Össur and Sichuan Provincial Government. It is a growth trip for Lee Dichen as well. "After paying a visit to Iceland's social welfare center and Disabled Persons' Federation, I felt Iceland's considerate care for the disabled, such as access for the disabled and employment security for the disabled, where we could get enlightenments and references."

Lee Dichen (first from the right) visited the headquarters of Össur in Iceland together with the delegation of Sichuan Province

Lee Dichen has met a different group and seen a different world in such position, which prompted her to have a clear understanding of fulfilling personal value. She believes that assisting the disabled depending on the power of science and technology in this job is her passion to achieve her personal value and make contributions to society. This is far-reaching significance for both the patient and Lee Dichen.

As for amputees always in contact with her, Lee Dichen has many personal ideas in addition to offering professional help. "For example, in some province of China, amputees can go to the China Disabled Persons' Federation (CDPF) to get a prosthesis (at a price of about RMB 4,000 to 5,000) free of charge every three years, but the quality of the prosthesis is too poor to meet the needs of the physically disabled for normal walking."

At the end of the interview, Lee Dichen expressed her personal wishes. On the one hand, she hoped that in the future China would include prostheses into medical insurance like European countries, so that more disabled people could use high-end prostheses and experience the unlimited life brought by high-tech prostheses. On the other hand, she hoped that CDPF could change the existing operation mode and offer patients more choices. For example, patients can choose to replace prostheses every six years instead of three years, so as to get prostheses of slightly better quality or direct subsidies for free choices of prostheses.

In addition to the improvement of the medical insurance system, Lee Dichen mentioned the humanistic concern for the disabled. At present, the number of the disabled in China is about 80 million, including 24.12 millions of the physically disabled. However, we rarely see them in real life. Where are they? This shows that our government's attention to the group of people is largely insufficient. It is inconvenient for them to go out because the infrastructure construction of some disabled people fails to meet the standards. For example, the blind tracks are occupied by motor vehicles, there is no special passage for the disabled in public places, and guide dogs are not allowed to enter public places, and so on.

At the same time, society keeps the disabled out of the employment market through psychological, physical and structural aspects. Due to stereotyped images, people naturally acquiesce that some groups have certain characteristics. In most cases, the disabled cannot get rid of the label of "vulnerable groups" attached to them by society outside the perspective of humanistic care. Therefore, people always take an exploratory or even strange glance of them in public. Meanwhile, they are discriminated against in the employment market.

"Össur's bionic technology is dedicated to changing people's stereotyped images of the disabled. We can see that people wearing bionic prostheses are almost identical to other people. For this reason, bionic technology is of high value in function and psychology. Össur's high-tech products can not only improve the society's view on the disabled but also make the patients reborn." Össur and Lee Dichen's team are also attempting to change the existing problems during normal life and work of the disabled through their own efforts, so that many persons with physical disability can have a strong will, remove labels and return to the lives of ordinary people to the greatest extent. Similarly.

Össur believes that employment opportunities are equal. It is devoted to building a diverse group of employees, and job seekers will not be discriminated against during job hunting because of race, nationality and disability.

"Össur has provided the young with a lot of platforms and resources, for development and creation, so I hope that the young in the society must firmly believe that many companies also have such platforms and resources, and then we can realize our life dreams as long as we come down to earth step by step!"

Lee Dichen's words do encourage us. They are also given to the young like her shining in their posts. I believe that fresh power is bound to bring a better future to the society!

(Ma Zhongyi Niu Xiaomeng)

06

慎始敬终，行稳致远

——访冰岛酒店集团中国区代表张士涛

张士涛

2006年，对现任冰岛酒店集团中国区代表张士涛来说，是一个特殊的年份。他从海尔的海外公司辞职后，在这一年加入了冰岛酒店集团，一直工作到今天。张士涛说，过去15年，他做得最正确的事情就是一直坚守在本行业，充分利用冰岛和中国的资源禀赋，打造自身的竞争优势，为客户提供优质的服务。

见微知著，睹始知终

作为一名英语专业学生，张士涛毕业入职海尔后，便被外派到欧洲开拓海外市场，开始了他与冰岛的不解之缘。

在派驻欧洲的近三年时间里，张士涛主要负责北欧和西欧的业务，这让他有很多机会接触、认识和熟悉冰岛。“冰岛是地球上地貌最像月球的一个国家，景色优美，每年都有大量的游客前去观光。”张士涛如是说，“但是冰岛地广人稀，当地酒店数量难以满足众多游客的住宿需求。”在发现这一市场机遇后，张士涛心动了。与在酒店行业打拼的冰岛好友商议后，张士涛决定加入这个团队，与合伙人携手打造属于他们的酒店王国。

酒店房间内部家具及床上用品

既然要做酒店，建材等相关产品从哪里购买呢？从冰岛本地购买吗？还是回中国采购物美价廉的“中国制造”呢？凭借对中国市场的了解，张士涛提出了回国考察的想法。相比于高收入高税收高福利的冰岛，中国的人口红利明显，产品价格优势显著。“大到建材、家具和床上用品，小到餐盘、刀叉和圆珠笔，都是我们在国内采购的。”在这样的模式下，张士涛加入集团后的首家酒店建成了，这也是冰岛酒店集团的第四家酒店。第二年，经过翻新改造的 Grand Hotel 也顺利开业了，现在成为冰岛规模最大、年头最久的四星级酒店。

Grand Hotel

此后，冰岛酒店集团几乎每年都在推进新酒店的建设业务，2021 年正在筹备它的第 18 家酒店。“我认为这是一项正确的决定，特别是我们选择在郊外建设酒店。”张士涛在谈到这件事时滔滔不绝，“这些年去冰岛旅游的游客数量急剧增加，冰岛的支柱产业也由原来的渔业转变为现在的旅游业，2019 年国际旅客数量近 200 万人次，与当地 30 多万的人口形成了鲜明对比，酒店供不应求。同时，冰岛的大多数酒店集中在首都雷克雅未克，位于郊外的酒店数量很少，规模也比较小。”得益于张士涛敏锐的市场嗅觉，冰岛酒店集团先后在郊外建立了 11 家酒店，抢占了市场先机，一跃成为冰岛最大的酒店集团。

作为一名在冰岛奋斗的中国人，张士涛身在冰岛，却时刻关注着中国的情况。他发现冰岛游客很多，但却很少看到中国人的身影。2010 年，到冰岛旅游的中国游客只有 5000 人左右，相比于中国人口，这个数字未免太过渺小。张士涛独见独知，洞察了中国市场的空白。张士涛依托冰岛强大的酒店资源，从 2010 年开始涉足中国到冰岛的旅游业务，成立了冰岛北极旅游集团。与位于北京、上海、广州、深圳、香港等拥有国际空港城市的大型旅行社合作，接待国内前往冰岛和北极的团队游客。

张士涛从未止步。身处互联网和大数据时代，知识和信息共享已成为常态，张士涛深知越来越多的消费者选择在线上获取旅游资讯、制作旅游攻略。自由行这一旅行方式因为能够满足旅客的个性化需求而备受青睐，这是大势所趋。于是，他紧跟旅游行业的发展态势，在 2019 年成立了冰岛土著旅行网，开展线上散客接待服务。利用便捷、即时的互联网，冰岛土著旅行网为有意前往冰岛的国内散客提供专业化、个性化的服务。这种灵活化的运作模式不仅需要领导者见微知著的能力和准确的判断，也离不开企业的长期积累与沉淀。行稳方能致远，正是张士涛的脚踏实地和稳扎稳打，为冰岛酒店集团开拓旅游业务奠定了坚实基础，为灵活的运作模式保驾护航。

见微知著，睹始知终。正如苏格拉底所言：“最有希望的成功者，并不是才干出众的人，而是那些最善于利用时机去努力开创的人。”选择在酒店行业创业，抓住中国—冰岛旅游市场的空白，运营在线旅游服务模式，张士涛凭借敏锐的市场嗅觉，抓住了重大市场机遇，带领冰岛酒店集团走过了 15 年。当然，一个成功的企业家仅有把握市场机遇的能力还远远不够。15 年来，张士涛兢兢业业、慎始敬终，打好酒店业务这一“地基”，加筑旅游业务这一“高楼”，始终保持脚踏实地的精神，一步一个脚印走到今天。

处变不惊，处逆不乱

苏轼在《晁错论》中写道：“古之立大事者，不惟有超世之才，亦必有坚忍不拔之志。”创业从来不是一帆风顺的，有多少企业没能跨过上升期 3 年这道坎，有多少企业能够存活 10 年以上，真实比例可能让人难以接受。“很多困难是你无法想象的，可能你看到了都会很惊讶，觉得世界上还有这样的事情吗？”张士涛在讲到这个问题时面带笑意，“面对困难，我们要学会坦然和坚持，要能做到处变不惊，遇事不乱。在顺境中不沾沾自喜，在逆境中也不垂头丧气。”

2008 年，金融危机席卷全球，冰岛首当其冲，经济陷入困境。彼时的冰岛酒店集团才刚刚成立 2 年，一时间风雨飘摇。“冰岛当地人基本上都是有贷款的，金融危机后，人们的负债相当于翻了 1 倍。金融危机前，冰岛克朗兑人民币大概是 1 元人民币兑换 8 冰岛克朗，但在金融危机后，1 元人民币兑换 18 冰岛克朗。当地人的生活压力确实比较大，而国内消费能力很低。”面对这种情况，张士涛坦诚道：“我们也没有什么好的办法，只能开源节流。我们当时没有开展其他业务，与中国的贸易活动也停止了，全身心地按照计划推进酒店业务。”在冰岛经济如此不景气的情况下，张士涛和他的合伙人并未被吓倒，而是乘风破浪，一举收购了 Fosshotel 这一品牌，从此冰岛酒店集团拥有了 Reykjavik 和 Foss 两个品牌。

Fosshotel

作为一名英语专业毕业生和酒店行业从业者，张士涛先前从未系统接触、了解过旅游行业，一切都要从零开始。“当时也是一路摸爬滚打，慢慢摸索过来的。”刚开始接触旅游行业，张士涛团队对旅游一无所知，“那时候，我们以为能够直接上手做，游客团来了我们直接接待就可以。”然而，这一切并不像张士涛团队最初设想的那样，真正做起来要复杂得多，这也让他们刚入行就跌了一个跟头。如果你问一个善于溜冰的人怎样获得成功时，他会告诉你“跌倒了，爬起来”，这就是成功。“每年大概什么时候开始设计线路，每年什么时候推出何种产品，这些计划要至少提前半年制定。”张士涛用了一年多的时间慢慢总结出了这个规律，旅游业务渐入佳境，逐步与中国的旅行社建立起了深入合作关系。2019 年，中国前往冰岛的旅客将近 10 万人次，冰岛酒店集团旗下的冰岛北极旅游集团成为中国游客在冰岛最大的地方旅行社。

然而 2020 年新冠肺炎疫情席卷全球，全球经济受到严重冲击，旅游业和国际贸易更是首当其冲。“由于新冠肺炎疫情，将近两年的时间，旅游业务一直没有复工，和 2008 年冰岛经济危机挺像的，一切都停滞了。”虽然旅游业务没能复工，但是冰岛酒店集团一直在推进贸易和酒店建设业务。

“我们正在建第 18 家酒店，使用的瓷砖就是从中国广东采购的。”当我们问到采购成本时，张士涛依然面带微笑：“采购和运输成本都提高了。产品原材料相比疫情前涨了百分之二三十，产品价格高了。海运费也涨了 1 倍多，几乎是我们协议价的 3 倍。而且，疫情之后基本只有中国在出口，集装箱无法返回到中国，我们订不到舱位。”明明是一件严肃而又棘手的事情，张士涛脸上却不见分毫焦虑与忧愁，真正印证了他的精神追求——不以物喜，不以己悲。

创业道阻且长，张士涛筚路蓝缕，栉风沐雨。短暂的采访时间无法让他将经历的种种困难一一道来，但窥一斑可知全貌，张士涛真正做到了“处变不惊，处逆不乱”。“我们应该用辩证的思维来处理问题，要学习更多的中国哲学思想。相比于工作，人生更加艰难。如果能真正做到坦然处之，那你就能够应付人生了。”人生不如意事十之八九，谁的人生也不可能一帆风顺。正是这种宠辱不惊的态度，张士涛才能做到面对困难不退缩、面对失败不气馁、面对成功不自满，不卑不亢，将冰岛酒店集团发展壮大。

争做中冰交往桥梁，展现企业责任担当

冰岛酒店集团作为一家国际公司，涉及中国和冰岛两国之间的贸易和旅游业务往来，积极参与到中国和冰岛之间的官方交往之中；作为冰岛最大的酒店集团，冰岛酒店集团也一直承担企业责任，致力于规范行业标准，合理控制行业服务价格，营造和谐的竞争氛围。

1971 年，中国与冰岛建交，此后，两国政府一直保持着友好合作关系。从 2006 年开始，中国与冰岛就自由贸易区相关事宜进行了谈判。2013 年，两国签订自由贸易协定，这是中国与欧洲国家的第一个自由贸易协定。“2011 年，我和我的冰岛合伙人都参加了中国与冰岛就自贸区进行谈判的活动。2013 年，国务院总理李克强与到访的冰岛总理约翰娜·西于尔扎多蒂在北京举行会谈。会谈后，中冰两国签署了自由贸易协定。我们也在现场见证了这个过程。”张士涛去往冰岛开展业务后，积极参与中国与冰岛的官方和民间活动，致力于为中国和冰岛两国的友好交往添砖加瓦。2018 年，冰岛外交部长索尔达松访华，张士涛作为冰岛酒店集团驻华酒店代表受邀出席，参加了驻华企业家交流会。2021 年，值中冰建交 50 周年之际，张士涛参加了中冰建交 50 周年暨冰岛国庆招待会。友好的两国关系对从事国际

贸易的企业来说大有裨益，“不论是经贸往来，还是出入境办理，我们都获益良多。”

“作为一名中国人，我们前去冰岛开展业务，实际上是起到桥梁和纽带的作用，但是我们的作用还是比较微小的，做起来也比较吃力。”当我们问到张士涛对中国与冰岛政府合作的建议时，他坦言道：“我认为中国这些年对世界的认识、对发达国家的认识是很清晰的。但是冰岛对中国的了解相对欠缺。如果说有何希望的话，那我希望冰岛政府能够更多地了解我们中国的实际情况，包括产品市场前景、中国的相关政策以及文化等方面，这样才能真正进入中国市场。”

张士涛对于国内旅游业的乱象痛心疾首。“我认为，我们国内旅游行业存在一定的恶性竞争，有些旅行社通过降低服务质量来压低价格，劣币驱逐良币，导致旅游行业的不良风气愈演愈烈，消费者对旅行社的观感也越来越差。”张士涛认为，这是一种不正确、不可持续的发展模式，终将会被市场所淘汰。只有走正当、合理、符合市场规律的道路，才能长足发展下去。张士涛是这样建议他人的，也是这样要求自己的。“在冰岛，商人的规则性其实很强。我们公司作为行业中的支柱企业之一，在维持冰岛旅游服务价格这方面是起了一定作用的。我不敢说得太大，但如果不是我们坚守着，那我们的同行们会很难做。”虽然张士涛表现得十分谦虚，但我们也可以从中体会到他们在中间发挥的作用、做出的贡献。一个行业，只有像张士涛这样的企业家在，像冰岛酒店集团这样的领头羊在，带领同行坚守行业规则、遵循市场规律，才能茁壮成长、健康发展。

做好做大一家企业不容易，带领好一个行业更不容易。而像张士涛这样坚守行业标准多年、承担社会责任、不局限于眼前的蝇头小利，尤为难能可贵。张士涛在旅游行业工作了 15 年，不仅成就了自己，也为冰岛的旅游行业营造了一个良性的竞争环境、为中国与冰岛的友好关系贡献了自己的力量。

扬帆正遇东风来，远征万里纵青骢。张士涛在谈到企业未来的发展时，眼神中依然透着对坚守行业规则、引领行业发展特有的执着。慎始敬终、行稳致远，是张士涛的精神追求，也是他的做事原则。

（孟伟　刘旻璞）

Being Careful in the Beginning for Long-Term Stability

— Interview with Zhang Shitao, Representative of Hotels of Iceland in China

---

2006 is a special year for Zhang Shitao, the current Representative of Hotels of Iceland in China. After resigning from Haier's overseas company, he joined the Hotels of Iceland at the same year and has been working for it until today. Zhang Shitao said that the best thing he has done in the past 15 years is staying in the industry, creating their own competitive advantage and providing high-quality services to customers by making full use of the resource endowment of Iceland and China.

Learning About What Is Forthcoming by Observing Tiny Clues

As a graduate of English major, Zhang Shitao was sent to Europe to explore overseas markets after he had joined Haier Group and made his indissoluble bond with Iceland.

During nearly three years when he was dispatched to stay in Europe, Zhang

Shitao was mainly responsible for the businesses of Northern and Western Europe continues, which gave him a lot of opportunities to contact, know and get familiar with Iceland. "Iceland is a country on the earth which possesses the landform same as that on the moon. A large number of tourists go there to visit the beautiful scenery every year." Zhang Shitao said. "But Iceland is vast and sparsely-populated, and the number of local hotels is difficult to meet the accommodation needs of so many tourists." After discovering the market opportunity, Zhang Shitao was intrigued. Through discussing with his Icelandic friends who worked in the hotel industry, Zhang Shitao decided to join the team and work with his partners to build their Hotel Kingdom.

Since he wants to be engaged in the hotel industry, where can he purchase building materials and other related products? Does he purchase them locally in Iceland or go back to China to buy the beautiful and cheap products "made in China"? With his understanding of the Chinese market, Zhang Shitao put forward the idea of going back to China for investigation. Compared with Iceland, a high-welfare country with high income and high taxes, China has a significant demographic dividend and product price superiority. "We purchased everything in China, including building materials, furniture, bedding, dinner plates, knives and forks and ball-point pens." In this mode, the first hotel after Zhang Shitao joined the Group was completed, which is also the fourth hotel of Hotels of Iceland. The next year, the renovated Grand Hotel also opened successfully, which becomes the largest and oldest four-star hotel in Iceland.

Since then, Hotels of Iceland has been promoting the construction business of new hotels almost every year, and was preparing its 18th hotel in 2021. "I think it is my correct decision, especially when we choose to build a hotel in the suburbs." Zhang Shitao talked eloquently about the matter, "the number of tourists to Iceland has increased sharply in recent years, and Iceland's pillar industry has also changed to current tourism from the original fishery. In 2019, the number of international passengers was nearly 2 million, in sharp contrast to the local population of more than 300,000, thus the supply of hotels was in short supply. At the same time, most hotels are gathered in Reykjavik, the capital of Iceland. The number of hotels in the suburbs was small and their scale was relatively small." Thanks to Zhang Shitao's sharp sense market, Hotels of Iceland has successively established 11 hotels in the suburbs, seizing the market opportunity and becoming the largest hotel group in Iceland.

A suburban hotel of Hotels of Iceland

As a Chinese struggling in Iceland, Zhang Shitao always pays attention to the situation in China although he was in Iceland. He found that there were few Chinese people in so many tourists to Iceland. In 2010, there were only about 5,000 Chinese tourists to Iceland, which is too small compared with the Chinese population. Zhang Shitao is discerning and has insight into the gap in the Chinese market. Relying on their great hotel resources in Iceland, Zhang Shitao began to set foot in the tourism business from China to Iceland in 2010 and established the Iceland Arctic Travel Group. The Company cooperates with large travel agencies in Beijing, Shanghai, Guangzhou, Shenzhen and Hong Kong and other cities with international airports in China, to receive Chinese group tourists to Iceland and the Arctic.

Zhang Shitao never stopped his business. In the era of Internet and big data, knowledge and information sharing has become regular things. Zhang Shitao knows that more and more consumers choose to obtain tourism information and make tourism strategies on line. Independent travel is favored by tourists because it can meet the personalized needs of tourists, which is the general trend. Therefore, following the development trend of the tourism industry, he established the Iceland's Indigenous Tourism Network in 2019 to offer online reception services for individual tourists. Using the convenient and instant Internet, Iceland's Indigenous Tourism Network provides professional and personalized services for domestic individual tourists who intend to go to Iceland. This flexible operation mode not only requires the leaders' ability of recognizing the whole through observation of the part and judging accurately but also is inseparable from the long-term accumulation and precipitation of the Enterprise. Stable growth can make the enterprise develop for a long term. It is Zhang Shitao's down-to-earth and steady work that makes Hotels of Iceland lay a solid foundation for developing tourism business and keeping the flexible operation mode on course.

Learning about what is forthcoming by observing tiny clues. As Socrates said, "The most promising achievers are not those with outstanding talents, but those who are the best at using the opportunity to create." By choosing to start a business in the hotel industry, seizing the gap in the China-Iceland tourism market and running the mode of online tourism services, Zhang Shitao grasped the major market opportunities with his sharp market sense and led Hotels of Iceland for 15 years. Of course, it is far from enough that a successful entrepreneur only has the ability to grasp market opportunities. Over the past 15 years, Zhang Shitao has been working hard and carefully, thus laying the "foundation" of hotel business and building a "high-rise building" of tourism business. With a down-to-earth spirit, he gets to where he is now one step at a time.

Keeping Calm in the Face of Disasters and Adversity

Su Shi wrote in *Treatise on Chao Cuo*: "Those who made great achievements in ancient times must not only have extraordinary talents, but also have the ambition of perseverance." Starting a business isn't all plain sailing. Many enterprises have failed to cross the three-year rising period and survive for more than ten years. The number of the enterprises which has survived may be unacceptable. "Many difficulties are unimaginable. Maybe you will be surprised when you see them or you will say, 'Is there such a thing in the world?'" Zhang Shitao smiled when talking about this problem. "In the face of difficulties, we should learn to keep calm and persist in the principle so as to proceed in an orderly manner. We shall neither be complacent in prosperity nor lose heart in adversity."

In 2008, the financial crisis swept the globe. Iceland bore the brunt of economic plight. At that time, the Hotels of Iceland had just been established for two years, and it was in precarious situation for a time. "Almost every Icelandic local has loans, so their liabilities doubled after the financial crisis. Before the financial crisis, the exchange rate was that RMB 1 could be converted to about 8 Icelandic Krona, while after the financial crisis, the exchange rate was that RMB 1 could be converted to 18 Iceland Krona. The living pressure of the locals is really high, and the domestic consumption power is very low." Faced with this situation, Zhang Shitao said frankly: "we don't find any better way, we can only increase revenues and reduce expenditure. We didn't carry out other business at that time, our trade activities with China ceased as well. We were fully devoted to promoting the hotel business according to our plan." In the case of such a stagnant economy of Iceland, Zhang Shitao and his partners were not frightened. Instead, they rode the waves forward and acquired the brand of Fosshotel at one fell swoop. Since then, the Hotels of Iceland has owned two brands, Reykjavik and Foss.

As a graduate of English major and a practitioner in the hotel industry, Zhang Shitao has never systematically contacted and knew about the tourism industry before. Thus he has to start from scratch. "At that time, I went through hard work and then slowly groped for it." At the beginning of exposure to the tourism industry, Zhang Shitao's team knew nothing about tourism. "At that time, we thought we could get the hang of it directly. When the tourist group came, it's no trouble in giving a reception to it." However, all those are not like what Zhang Shitao's team initially assumed. It is much more difficult to carry out, which also makes them meet with a setback when they first entered the industry. If you ask a person who is good at skating how to succeed, he will tell you: "fall and pick yourself up". This is success. "The plans for the time to start designing tourist lines and launching tourism products every year shall be made at least half a year in advance." It took more than a year for Zhang Shitao to slowly sum up this law. His tourism business got better and better, and he gradually established in-depth cooperative relations with Chinese travel agencies. In 2019, the number of Chinese passengers to Iceland was nearly 100,000. The Iceland Arctic Travel Group became the largest local travel agency of Chinese tourists in Iceland.

However, in 2020, COVID-19 epidemic swept the globe and caused a serious impact on the global economy. Tourism and international trade were the first to bear the brunt. "As a result of COVID-19 epidemic, the tourism business has not been resumed for nearly two years, everything is stagnant just like 2008 Global Financial Crisis in Iceland." Although the tourism business failed to resume, the Hotels of Iceland has been promoting the business in trade and hotel construction. "We are building the 18th hotel. The ceramic tiles for it are purchased from Guangdong, China." When we asked about the purchasing cost, Zhang Shitao was still smiling: "The purchasing and transportation costs have increased. The raw materials of the products have increased by 20% or 30% compared with that before COVID-19 epidemic, and the product price is even higher. The ocean freight has also more than doubled, nearly three times our agreement price. After COVID-19 epidemic, basically only China can export such products. The containers can't be returned to China for we can't book shipping spaces." Obviously, it is a serious and troublesome thing, but there is no anxiety and sadness on Zhang Shitao's face, which really confirms his spiritual pursuit — not pleased by external gains, not saddened by personal losses.

The road to start a business is long and difficult. Zhang Shitao endured great hardships in pioneer work and went through a lot of difficulties. The short interview time can't allow him to describe all the details of the difficulties he has experienced.

A peck knows the whole sack. Zhang Shitao is really the man who can "keep calm in the face of disasters and adversity". "We should deal with problems with dialectical thinking and learn more Chinese philosophy. Life is more difficult than work. If we can really take things calmly, we can cope with the changes in life." Eight or nine out of ten things in life are not as we wish. No one's life can be plain sailing. Zhang Shitao remains indifferent whether granted favours or subjected to humiliation that enables Zhang Shitao to be succeed and make the Hotels of Iceland boom.

To Be a Bridge Between China and Iceland, to Demonstrate the Responsibility of Enterprises

As an international company, the Hotels of Iceland is involved in trade and tourism between China and Iceland, and actively participates in the official exchanges between China and Iceland. As the largest hotel group in Iceland, the Hotels of Iceland has also been undertaking its corporate responsibility, committed to standardizing industry standards, reasonably controlling the service prices of the industry and creating a harmonious competitive atmosphere.

In 1971, China established diplomatic ties with Iceland. The two governments have always maintained friendly and cooperative relations since then. From 2006, China and Iceland negotiated about the matters related to the free trade zone. In 2013, the two countries signed a Free Trade Agreement (FTA), which is the first FTA between China and European countries. "In 2011, my Icelandic partner and I participated in the negotiation on the free trade zone between China and Iceland. In 2013, Chinese Premier Li Keqiang and Icelandic Prime Minister Johanna Sigurdardottir held talks in Beijing in 2013. After the talks, the two countries signed a free trade agreement. We were there to witness the process." After Zhang Shitao went to Iceland for business, he actively participated in the official and non-governmental activities between China and Iceland and was committed to contributing to the friendly communication between China and Iceland. In 2018, Icelandic Foreign Minister Soldarsson visited China. Zhang Shitao, as the representative of the Hotels of Iceland in China, was invited to attend the exchange conference of entrepreneurs in China. In 2021, Zhang Shitao attended the reception for the 50th anniversary of the establishment of diplomatic relations between China and Iceland and Iceland's National Day. The friendly relations between the two countries are of great benefit to enterprises engaged in international trade. "We have benefited a lot from both trade practice and entry-exit application."

"As a Chinese, when we go to Iceland to do business, we actually play a role of bridges and bonds, but our role is still relatively small and there is some difficulty." When we asked Zhang Shitao about his suggestions on cooperation between Chinese and Icelandic governments, he said frankly: "I think that China has well known about the world and developed countries in recent years. Relatively speaking, Iceland, however, know little about China. If there is any hope, I hope the Icelandic government can know more about the actual situation of China, including the market prospects of products, China's relevant policies and culture to truly enter the Chinese market."

Zhang Shitao is very distressed about the chaos of domestic tourism. "I think there is some malignant competition in our domestic tourism industry. Some travel agencies drive down prices by reducing service quality. Bad money drives out good, which results in an increasingly bad practice in the tourism industry and consumers' perception of travel agencies." Zhang Shitao believes that it is an incorrect and unsustainable development mode and will be eliminated by the market at last. Only by taking a proper, reasonable and market-oriented approach can we gain substantial development. Zhang Shitao suggests others doing so and disciplines himself as well. "In Iceland, businessmen strictly adhere to the rules. As one of the pillar enterprises in the industry, our company has played a certain role in maintaining the price of tourism services in Iceland. I dare not throw the hatchet, but if we don't stick to it, it will be difficult for our peers to do business." Although Zhang Shitao is very modest, we can also realize their role and contribution in the aspect. An industry can thrive and develop sustainably only when entrepreneurs like Zhang Shitao and leaders like the Hotels of Iceland lead their peers to adhere to the rules of industry and market.

Photo taken by Zhang Shitao, representative of the Hotels of Iceland in China, during his trip

It is not easy to make an enterprise expand and grow in a smooth manner. It is even more difficult to keep an industry on good course. It is very precious that Zhang Shitao sticks to the industry standards, undertakes social responsibility but doesn't seek for trifling advantages for many years. Zhang Shitao has worked in the tourism industry for 15 years. He has not only become what he wants to be but also created a benign competitive environment for Iceland's tourism industry and contributed to the friendly relations between China and Iceland.

Just as people set sail in the east wind, so the explorer goes on an expedition for thousands of miles. When Zhang Shitao talked about the future development of his enterprise, his unique persistence in adhering to the industry rules and leading the development of the industry still can be seen in his eyes. It is Zhang Shitao's spiritual pursuit and his working principle to be careful in the beginning for long-term stability.

(Meng Wei Liu Minpu)

07

兼收并蓄，保持底色

——访冰岛护肤品牌 BIOEFFECT 蓓欧菲大中华区总裁山月

山 月

“守其初心，始终不变”，这是采访过程中山月传递给我们最深刻的道理。在她将 BIOEFFECT 蓓欧菲带到中国的 10 年里，始终坚持和明确的一点是，要以做品牌的理念去做产品。

山月于 2000 年至 2007 年就读于奥地利维也纳大学生物医学工程专业，2008 年后移民到冰岛，后在北京大学国家发展研究院攻读 EMBA。作为中国侨联青年委员、冰岛知名护肤品牌 BIOEFFECT 蓓欧菲大中华区总裁，她常年往返于中国和冰岛，希望把真正有效的优质商品带给中国女性，成为价值品牌的传递者。

慎始而敬终，终以不困

山月作为冰岛的华商代表，最早是以消费者的身份了解到 BIOEFFECT 蓓欧菲这个品牌。当时 BIOEFFECT 蓓欧菲已经在欧洲市场取得了良好的口碑，创始人之一 Dr. Bjorn Ovar 联系到她，计划将品牌推广至遥远的中国市场，特意向她了解市场情况。在冰岛生活的经历，使得山月非常清楚冰岛人对于追求高品质的态度，所以，她对 BIOEFFECT 蓓欧菲品牌进行了深入的调研。“我对 BIOEFFECT 蓓欧菲品牌的母公司——ORF 在生物基因学的行业地位有了清晰的认知，他们主要专注于生物原料、再生医学行业领域，凭借北欧人的专注、过硬的研发成果，获得了瞩目的成绩。”在她看来，BIOEFFECT 蓓欧菲有很高的研发储备和品牌技术势能，正在用生物医学技术降维来生产护肤品，这在目前的市场中是不多见的。此外，BIOEFFECT 蓓欧菲的产品在推出之后，依靠真实可见的有力的效果取得了巨大的市场认可。经过多维度的了解和调研，山月与 BIOEFFECT 蓓欧菲团队就产品在中国市场的销售前景和发展策略达成一致共识，开启了进入中国市场的篇章。

位于英国伦敦的 Harrods 百货公司 BIOEFFECT 蓓欧菲橱窗展示

与此同时，山月也对中国市场做了非常详细的调研。在政府层面，《中冰自由贸易协定》的签署使得 BIOEFFECT 蓓欧菲所属的品类能够获得很好的支持和优惠政策；在市场层面，2013 年之前，中国对进口商品并没有细分，也没有形成利基市场①，中国的消费者对于护肤品更多的是追求一些奢侈品牌或者国际大牌。2013 年之后，中国消费市场迅速发展，消费升级日趋明显。中国消费者开始自发地分辨和挖掘优质的、小众产品。从最初对大品牌的追求，逐渐转变为对小众品牌的追求和认同，从被广告引导转变为从自身需求出发，开始追求与众不同和高品质的生活，使得像 BIOEFFECT 蓓欧菲这样具有产品优势的海外的小众品牌有了更大的发展空间。山月表示，2013 年是一个关键的时间点，也让 BIOEFFECT 蓓欧菲品牌从进入中国市场开始就出现了第一个小的爆发期。

“慎始而敬终，终以不困”，任何市场都存在泡沫，在发现商机之后还能够谨慎调研、沉着冷静，这是作为企业家非常难得的品质。从品牌价值、研发能力、产品功效，到中国和冰岛的政策、中国市场的特点和消费者心

① 利基市场是在较大的细分市场中，具有相似兴趣或需求的一小群顾客所占有的市场空间。大多数成功的创业型企业一开始并不在大市场开展业务，而是通过识别较大市场中新兴的或未被发现的市场而发展业务。

理，山月的每一步都做到了行稳踏实，认真谨慎。在纷繁复杂的市场中，她始终坚守初衷，用她的行为为我们展示了何为“慎始敬终”。

求同存异，君子和而不同

与海外企业合作最不可避免的问题就是差异，针对这一点，山月在采访中举了很多浅显易懂的例子。与中国不同，冰岛国土面积仅 10.3 万平方公里，人口约 36.6 万，但却是一个人均 GDP 高达 6 万美元的国家（2020 年数据）。国家内部丰富的能源储备、美丽的自然景色以及稳定的国家收入，带给了冰岛人民高收入、高福利和不可避免的高价格的产品。除了地域差距，两国的文化也有很大差异。冰岛人是维京人的后代，性格勇敢、富有开拓精神。另外，由于历史原因，美军曾驻守冰岛，使得冰岛人受到冰岛古典文化和美国文化的双重影响。山月告诉我们，冰岛有一个专门的 App，输入社会保障号之后可以找到包括总统在内的任意一个冰岛人的关系网络。在这样信息透明、安全感强的环境下，冰岛人也形成一种对内信任、对外谨慎的性格。在中华五千年传统文化的熏陶之下，“和”已经根植于每个中国人，勤劳勇敢、自强不息也是冰岛人对中国人最深的印象。正是由于地域、文化等方面的差异，导致在对待同一个问题上有完全不同的认知。“我们的差异在于看待同一件事物的角度不同，导致处理方式不同。”但是在双方合作多年之后，她也认为，虽有差异但仍然存在很多相似之处，并且这个交集在不断扩大。也正是因为这种差异，团队在协作中才更容易摩擦出不一样的火花。

在互相尊重的前提下，求同存异是跨越差异的最佳方法。对于 BIOEFFECT 蓓欧菲来说，正是由于山月的经历和对冰岛的认知，让他们愿意交付信任。同样，山月作为冰岛的华商代表，在 BIOEFFECT 蓓欧菲给予足够的支持和理解之下，也愿意站在对方的角度考虑问题，共同建设品牌、维护品牌的形象。

“君子和而不同”，山月秉承互相尊重、互相理解的原则，与冰岛方进行积极沟通，为 BIOEFFECT 蓓欧菲的品牌发展献计献策。山月表示，“我们与蓓欧菲总部的共同理念是，将品牌做长做美，而不是一味地做大做强。”沟通是最好的桥梁，山月的经历值得每一位跨国企业家学习。

博采众长，坚守传递十载

随着时间的推移，中外市场也发生了巨大的变化。为了让冰岛总部更加了解中国市场，山月团队一直在密切关注中国市场以及中国消费者的细微变化。随着越来越多的中国人走出国门，中国消费者的消费观念和生活追求发生了很大的改变。同时，中国的媒体渠道也从最初的报纸、杂志、网络等传统媒体迅速转变为微博、微信、小红书、抖音等社交和视频平台，而且日流量逐渐超过传统媒体。媒介和技术的发展导致消费者的心态和认知得到了整体的提升，对于产品的需求也逐渐转向高品质的产品。后疫情时代的到来，使得电商平台成为主要的销售渠道，使用电商平台购物的消费者年龄层逐渐扩大，与此同时，由于消费者的国货情节，国潮的兴起和迭代，让整体竞争变得更加激烈。

针对如此多的差异与变化，在山月的协调下，BIOEFFECT 蓓欧菲品牌总部及时做出调整，加快新产品推出的速度，尤其是在疫情期间，中国的电商平台的快速发展发挥了重要作用。在疫情影响下，各个品牌都受到了不同程度的影响，BIOEFFECT 蓓欧菲品牌也不例外。很多不确定性的因素，除了增加备货量保证货源外，还加大了线上销售渠道的比重，逐渐向线上转型。对 BIOEFFECT 蓓欧菲品牌来说，中国市场的电商平台发展迅速。冰岛企业对电商不太了解，在冰岛，当地线下销售渠道比重最大，他们注重与客人面对面交流和购物的体验等，电商只是作为一个补充渠道。经过山月的沟通与推动，BIOEFFECT 蓓欧菲品牌包括市场、产品、设计、生产等部门协同合作以快速适应中国市场的变化。从品牌策划到产品生产都在积极适应新的变化。例如，创始人之一 Dr. Bjorn Ovar 在拍摄电商视频时，从最开始的迷茫到现在的手到擒来，他知道如何处理拍摄环境、拍摄内容、服装配合，甚至是简单的中文表达，完全知道如何最好地展示产品。山月和她的团队为这样的变化付出了很多的努力，她们不断向总部传递信息，积极沟通，使得研发团队充分理解并完全接受这些变化，最终实现海外品牌和中国市场相互适应的局面。在品牌原则与规划基础之上，融入中国市场的需求，双方相互沟通理解，才能将品牌与市场打通，形成良性循环。

2020 年，BIOEFFECT 蓓欧菲品牌成立 10 周年，推出了周年限量版产品。然而在全球疫情影响之下，品牌信心被严重打击，此时总部与山月及时沟通，并当机立断决定将中国作为全球首发市场。山月和她的团队临危上阵，迅速反应，结合中国市场的情况以及产品的特点，制订营销方案并快速执行。这一切的努力都是值得的，中国市场也不负众望地带动了全球销量，海外消费者纷纷求购。在山月的运作下，中国市场俨然成为BIOEFFECT蓓欧菲销售范围的最重要的部分。在管理方面，作为一个海外小众高端品牌，BIOEFFECT蓓欧菲也逐步由偏责任制转变为更注重协同性。在多项目、多交叉的情况下，小组灵活协调的重要性就更为凸显，因此BIOEFFECT蓓欧菲当下还积极致力于建立内部信息系统，力争做到公开、透明、快速、灵活。

时任冰岛驻华大使古士贤先生（右三）及BIOEFFECT
蓓欧菲高层携手徐慧主任（右二）共同出席EBE系列的首发活动

在国际化大环境下，博采众长，包容和开放已经成为BIOEFFECT蓓欧菲大中华区以及山月团队最重要的文化。大家都会积极适应多国、多地、多团队的差异，密切关注外界环境的变化。与此同时，也尊重员工的自主权。

坚持初心，拒绝随波逐流

近年来，BIOEFFECT蓓欧菲在中国市场的发展稳步提升。2019年下半年，中国最大的电商平台——天猫国际挖掘和扶持小众品牌的发展，山月团队了解到这个情况之后，迅速与冰岛驻华大使馆商务处联络，并通过与品牌总部密切交流，使得 BIOEFFECT 蓓欧菲作为众多小众品牌里中国消费者接受度最高的品牌，成为当年的一匹黑马。同时，冰岛贸促局与天猫国际在冰岛雷克雅未克的中国驻冰岛大使馆共同签署战略合作备忘录。同年 11 月，天猫国际与冰岛贸促局在第二届中国国际进口博览会现场签署战略合作协议。

十年的中国市场经历，山月帮助 BIOEFFECT 蓓欧菲迅速成长并持续发展。在谈到经验与建议时，她提到了“初心”一词，“可能听起来有点虚，但有一些东西是需要坚持的”，山月说。中国市场变化迅速，追逐的热点很多，消费者的变化也很多，如果随波逐流，很容易被营销热点牵着鼻子走，是无法集中力量做好自身领域的。核心资源要用在核心优势上，ORF 历经了十余年的沉淀，将品牌的核心成果投入护肤品市场，打造出 BIOEFFECT 蓓欧菲品牌。这是一个厚积薄发的品牌，也是引领未来科技和成分的结晶。作为差异化品牌，BIOEFFECT 蓓欧菲肯定是要将自己品牌独有的小而美的优势放大，不追求做大做强，只追求做得美而长久，稳定自己在该领域的地位。对于来自冰岛的小众品牌，坚守品牌一致性、不断建设品牌是非常重要的，不能轻易改变。对内进行内部信息化建设，以内容为王，而不单是销售，将围绕产品所产生的内容以及客户产生的内容收集起来，形成产品上的内容闭环。在流量昂贵的现状下，坚持用产品来说话。最后，山月说道，希望能把大家对冰岛的美好的认知反映到品牌上，让我们深刻感受到她作为一个传递者对品牌和消费者的责任心。

对于品牌未来的发展以及偏旅游性质的产品如何在国内激活这一问题，山月分享了自己的见解。首先，对于品牌本身的国际化发展，BIOEFFECT 蓓欧菲将自己定位为国际领先的生物科技品牌。在这个前提下，会将自己的销售渠道拓宽到世界各地，并且特别关注航空免税市场。专注旅游市场对品牌加分很多，并且全球渠道布局会使消费者认可它是一个国际化的品牌。其次，在中国，由于 BIOEFFECT 蓓欧菲的主线产品的新原料只能通过跨境电商进行销售，这对品牌来说是非常困难的。随着近几年中国数据挖掘的快速发展，目前也会利用大数据在投放方面进行一些筛选，做简单的优化，因而渠道就成为未来打通的重点，只有拓宽渠道才能尽可能多地触达消费者。BIOEFFECT 蓓欧菲未来工作的重点将放在新原料审批以及拓宽全渠道方面，在专注发展本品牌优势的前提下，灵活解决当下的问题。

坚持初心，拒绝随波逐流，这个道理并不难懂，但真正能坚持做到的人并不多。在大数据的技术发展背景下，从“用心做产品”到“用心做营销”，流量与营销似乎成了弥补产品不足的一剂速效药，越来越多的品牌追随营销热点，以流量为王。山月能够认识到这一点难能可贵，她坚信，无论市场与经济环境如何变化，品牌都要有自己的高质量的产品，这永远是抵御风险的信心。

理解支持，共促中冰友好

2013 年 4 月 15 日，中国和冰岛签署自由贸易协定，这是我国与欧洲国家签署的第一个自由贸易协定，关税大幅降低。在中国国际进口博览会的合作以及与电商的合作中，两国使馆以及商务处都对 BIOEFFECT 蓓欧菲鼎力协助。

关于政府对于中冰两国企业经贸往来的支持，山月提到 BIOEFFECT 蓓欧菲作为基因研发的公司，其新原料在中国的审批有特殊监管，比较谨慎，申报备案预计至少一年才能通过，所以产品与国外的版本相比在进度上有些滞后。山月表示，她完全理解中国政府的考虑，严格的监管是对消费者的负责。现在国家逐步开放市场，鼓励引入创新材料和新原料，大使馆和商务处也积极为企业提供帮助。推进成分引入，能够打开更大的市场增量，也会带来更大的新产品世界，为中国消费者带来更好的产品。

采访中，济南大学冰岛研究中心就新冠肺炎疫情的影响展开提问，得到的回答还是比较明朗的。疫情初期，运输处于相对停滞的状态，从冰岛到中国，再到中国国内运输，只能依靠囤货来缓解运输问题。随着中国疫情的迅速控制，在国内除了物流方面有些影响以外，其他方面并无大碍。

最后，山月对想要参与中冰贸易的年轻企业家提出了以下建议：冰岛本土市场规模有限，物流成本昂贵，在冰岛做投资或者想在冰岛投资项目需要非常谨慎。大的环境背景，还是要看核心资源优势。比如冰岛地广人稀，有额外增长需要的话可以投入，劳动密集型的行业不太适合。冰岛有一些“独角兽”的公司，拥有稀缺的资源，中国市场有需求，但也要充分了解两国的情况。

BIOEFFECT 蓓欧菲品牌代表与现任冰岛驻华大使易卜雷先生（Thorir Ibsen）（左一）及夫人易卜芝女士（Dominique Ambroise Ibsen）（左三）共同出席第四届中国国际进口博览会

2021 年恰逢中冰两国建交 50 周年，近年来两国相互尊重，双边关系稳步发展。济南大学冰岛研究中心在采访中直观地体会到，中冰企业的经贸往来得到了来自两国政府的大力支持。中冰友好深入人心，希望两国继续深化不同领域的合作，增强互信，推动中冰关系进一步发展，为两国和两国人民带来更多福祉。

（王楚　刘昊蓉）

Seeking the Original Color Through Inclusive Learning

— Interview with Shanyue, President of Greater China of BIOEFFECT

"Stay true to the original self" is the most profound truth that Ms. Shanyue transmits to us during the interview. In the years since she brought BIOEFFECT to China, the thing she always insisted on and clarified was to manufacture products based on brand concept.

Ms. Shanyue majored in Biomedical Engineering at the University of Vienna, Austria from 2000 to 2007, immigrated to Iceland after 2008, and studied EMBA at the National School of Development at Peking University later. As a young member of All-China Federation of Returned Overseas Chinese and president of Greater China of BIOEFFECT, an Iceland nationally-renowned skincare brand, she travels back and forth between China and Iceland all year round, hoping to bring real and effective high-quality products to Chinese females and becomes a transmitter of the valuable brand.

Being Careful in the Beginning and Ending for Avoiding Risk of Going Bogged Down

As one of the Chinese merchant representatives of Iceland, Ms. Shanyue understood the brand of BIOEFFECT as a consumer first. At that time, BIOEFFECT had gained great public praise in the European market. Dr. Bjorn Ovar, one of the founders, planned to promote the brand to the remote Chinese market and contacted her to know more about the conditions of the market. The experience of living in Iceland makes Shanyue deeply know the attitude of Icelanders on pursuing high quality; therefore, she made an in-depth investigation on the BIOEFFECT brand. "I have a clear comprehension of the industry position of the parent company of BIOEFFECT — ORF on bio-genetics, they mainly focus on biomass and regenerative medicine industry, and obtain remarkable achievements by their concentration and excellent research as well as development results." In her opinion, BIOEFFECT has good research and development reserves and brand technology potential, and it manufactures skincare products with biomedical technology in a dimensionality reduction manner, which is rare in the current market. In addition, after launching its products, BIOEFFECT obtained huge market recognition by its true, visible, and powerful effects. After multi-dimensional comprehension and investigation, Shanyue and BIOEFFECT team reached an agreement on the sales prospects and development strategies of the products in the Chinese market, opening the chapter of entering the Chinese market.

At the same time, Shanyue made a very detailed investigation of the Chinese market. At the government level, the signing of the China-Iceland Free Trade Agreement enables the categories of BIOEFFECT product to receive good support, and preferential policies; at the market level, before 2013, China did not do the market segmentation of import goods and had no formed niche market[①], Chinese consumers mostly pursued some luxury brands or international brands for skin care products. After 2013, the Chinese consumer market has rapidly developed and the consumption upgrades were obviously increased. Chinese consumers began to spontaneously distinguish and search high-quality niche products. The gradual

① Niche market is the market space occupied by a small group of customers who have similar interests or demands in the bigger market segment. Most successful entrepreneurial enterprises do not carry out businesses in big markets at the beginning but by identifying the emerging or undiscovered market in the bigger market.

transformation from the pursuit of big brands initially to the pursuit and recognition of niche brands and from advertising guidance to self-demand and the pursuit to different and high-quality life made overseas niche brands with advantages, for example, BIOEFFECT, have larger development space. Shanyue said, the year 2013 was a key time point and it made the BIOEFFECT brand encounter the first small upsurge period from entering the Chinese market.

"Being careful in the beginning and ending for avoiding risk of going bogged down", there may be bubbles in any market, and it is a rare quality for entrepreneurs to carefully conduct the investigation and stay calm after discovering business opportunities. From brand value, R&D capability, and product efficacy to China and Iceland policy, the characteristics of the Chinese market and consumer psychology, Shanyue has done every step of the way steadily and cautiously. In the complex market, she can always insist on her original intention and show "being careful in the beginning and ending" with her behavior.

Seeking Common Ground While Reserving Differences, and Seeking Harmony but Not Uniformity

The difference between countries is an inevitable problem in the cooperation with overseas enterprises, and Shanyue lists lots of easy-to-understand examples in the interview for this point. Different from China, the land area of Iceland is only 103,000 km^2 and the population is about 366,000, but Iceland's GDP per capita can be up to USD 60,000 (Data in 2020). This country has rich energy reserves, beautiful natural scene, and stable national revenues, which bring high income, high welfare and inevitably high price of products to Icelanders. In addition to the regional differences, the cultures of two countries are quite different. Icelanders are the descendants of Vikings, and they are brave and have the pioneering spirit. In addition, due to historical reasons, the US military stationed in Iceland due to historical reasons, which made Icelanders being influenced by both Icelandic classical culture and American culture. Shanyue told us that there is a special App in Iceland, you can find the relationship network of any Icelander including the president after entering the social security number. Under such an environment with transparent information and a strong sense of security, Icelanders form a personality of being trustworthy internally and cautious externally. Under the influence of Chinese traditional culture with a history of 5,000 years, "harmony" has been rooted in each Chinese. Hardworking, bravery and perseverance are the deepest impression that Icelanders have on Chinese people. The differences in territory, culture and others result in different perceptions on the same thing. "The difference between us is the different perspectives, resulting in different handling methods." However, after many years of cooperation between both parties, she also thinks that there are differences but there are still many similarities, and this same part is constantly expanding. It is precise because of such differences that the team can more easily have diverse sparks during cooperation.

On the basis of mutual respect, seeking common points while reserving differences is the optimal method to handle differences. As for BIOEFFECT, the experience of Shanyue and the perception of Iceland make them be willing to give the trust. Similarly, as the Chinese merchant representative of Iceland, Shanyue is also willing to consider things in the role of the Iceland's side under enough support and understanding given by BIOEFFECT to jointly construct the brand and maintain the brand image.

"Seeking harmony but not uniformity", Shanyue adheres to the principle of mutual respect and understanding to actively communicate with Iceland and provide suggestions for the development of the BIOEFFECT brand. Shanyue said that "The common concept between us and BIOEFFECT headquarters is to develop the brand instead of expanding it only." Communication is the best bridge. Shanyue's experience is worth learning for every multi-national entrepreneur.

Learning from Others' Strong Points and Insisting on the Transmission for Ten Years

Over time, Chinese and foreign markets have also undergone tremendous changes. To make the headquarters in Iceland better know about the Chinese market, Shanyue's team always pays close attention to the subtle changes of the Chinese market and consumers. As more and more Chinese people go abroad, the consumption concept and life pursuit of Chinese consumers have greatly changed. At the same time, the media channels in China have rapidly changed from the newspaper, magazine, network and other traditional media to Weibo, WeChat, Xiaohongshu, TikTok and other social and video platforms, and its daily flow gradually exceeds the traditional media. The development of media and technology leads to the overall improvement of the attitude and perception of consumers, and the demand of consumers has gradually turned to high-quality products. The arrival of the post-epidemic era makes the e-commerce platform be the main sales channel, the age group of consumers using e-commerce platform for shopping gradually expands. At the same time, due to domestic products, the rise and iteration of the shopping trend of domestic products has made the overall competition more intense.

As for so many differences and changes, under the coordination of Shanyue, BIOEFFECT brand headquarters made adjustments in time and accelerated the launch of new products. The rapid development of the e-commerce platform in China played an important role, especially during the epidemic. Affected by the epidemic, all brands were affected in different degrees, so was the BIOEFFECT brand. There were many uncertain factors. In addition to increasing the stocking volume to ensure the supply of goods, the company has also increased the proportion of online channels and gradually transformed to online. As for the BIOEFFECT brand, the e-commerce platform in the Chinese market develops rapidly. Iceland enterprises do not know much about e-commerce, the offline channel has the biggest proportion in Iceland. They pay more attention to face-to-face communication with customers and improve the shopping experience, so the e-commerce is just a supplementary channel. Through the communication and promotion of Shanyue, BIOEFFECT brands, including the marketing, product, design, production and other departments collaborated quickly to adapt to the changes in the Chinese market. From brand planning to product production, they actively adapted to the new changes. For example, when shooting the e-commerce video, Dr. Bjorn Ovar, one of the founders, from the initial confusion to now very familiar, he knows how to deal with the shooting environment and shooting content, clothing coordination, even speak simple expressions in Chinese. He could fully know how to best display products. Shanyue and her team have made lots of efforts for such changes. They continuously transmitted information to headquarters and made active communication, so that the R&D team can fully understand and accept such changes and finally realize the mutual adaptation between the oversea brand and the Chinese market. The demand of integrating into the Chinese market is based on the brand principle and planning, and only through mutual communication and understanding of both parties, the brand and the market can be connected, forming a virtuous cycle.

In 2020, the 10th anniversary of the brand, BIOEFFECT launched the anniversary limited-edition products. However, affected by the global outbreak, the brand confidence was seriously hit, and at this time, the headquarters communicated with Shanyue in time and promptly decided to take China as the first launching market of the products around the world. Shanyue and her team responded quickly. Combining the situation of the Chinese market and the characteristics of the product, they formulated a marketing plan and implemented it quickly. All these efforts were worthy, and the Chinese market lived up to the expectation and drove global sales, making overseas consumers look for products. Under the operation of Shanyue, the Chinese market has become the most important part of the BIOEFFECT's sales range. In terms of management, as an overseas niche high-end brand, BIOEFFECT gradually transmits from accountability orientation towards paying more attention to cooperativity. Under the condition of multiple projects and intersections, the flexible coordination of the team is very important; therefore, BIOEFFECT is also actively committed to building an internal information system to strive for brand's publicity, transparency, rapidness and flexibility.

In the international environment, learning others' strong points, tolerance and openness have become the most important cultures of BIOEFFECT Greater China and Shanyue's team. Everyone will actively adapt to the differences of many countries, places and teams, and pay close attention to changes in the external environment. At the same time, it also respects the autonomy of employees.

Keeping the Original Intention and Refusing Going with the Flow

In recent years, the development of BIOEFFECT in the Chinese market improves steadily. In the second half of 2019, the biggest e-commerce platform in China — Tmall Global dug and supported the development of niche brands, Shanyue's team quickly communicated with the Commercial Office of the Iceland Embassy in China after knowing the information, and through close communication with the brand headquarters, BIOEFFECT can be the brand highly accepted by Chinese consumers among many niche brands and be the surprise winner in the same year. At the same time, Iceland Trade Promotion Bureau and Tmall Global jointly signed the strategic cooperation memorandum in the Embassy of the People's Republic of China in The Republic of Iceland, Reykjavik, Iceland. In November of that year, Tmall Global and Iceland Trade Promotion Bureau signed the strategic cooperation in the site of the 2nd China International Import Expo.

BIOEFFECT and Tmall Global senior leaders attended the 2nd China International Import Expo together

With ten years of experience in the Chinese market, Shanyue helps BIOEFFECT rapidly grow and continuously develop. When talking about experience and suggestions, she mentioned the words "original intention" and said, "It sounds a bit illusory, but there shall be something required to insist on." Chinese market changes rapidly, with many hotspots pursuing and the consumers also changing a lot. If we go with the flow, it will be easy to be led by the marketing hotspot and hard to concentrate on our own field. The core resources shall be concentrated on the core advantages. ORF has experienced more than 10 years of accumulation and put the core achievements of the brand to the skin care product market, creating the BIOEFFECT brand. This is a brand with rich accumulation, which can also guide for future science and technologies. As a differentiated brand, BIOEFFECT is certainly to amplify the unique advantages of its brand, pursue the development instead of expanding only, and stabilize its position in the domain. It is very important for the niche brand from Iceland to insist on the consistency of the brand and continuously construct the brand, and not change it easily. It focuses on the internal informatization construction, with contents as the main part instead of sales only, and collects the contents generated by products and customers to form the closed loop of contents on the products, and insists on manufacturing high-quality products under the condition of expensive flow. Finally, Ms. Shanyue said that she hoped to reflect everyone's beautiful perception of Iceland to the brand, which made us deeply feel her sense of responsibility for the brand and consumers as a transmitter.

Shanyue shared her own opinion on the future development of the brand and how to activate products with tourism nature in China. First, as for the international development of the brand itself, BIOEFFECT positions itself as the international leading brand on biotechnology. In this premise, it will broaden its sales channels around the world and pay special attention to the aviation duty-free market. Focusing on the tourism market is a bonus point for the brand, and the global channel layout will make consumers recognize the brand as an international brand. Secondly, in China, since new raw materials of the main products of BIOEFFECT can only be sold by cross-border e-commerce, it is very difficult for the brand to develop. With the rapid development of Chinese data operation in recent years, it is available to screen inputting by big data at present to realize simple optimization; therefore, channels will be the key point to get through in the future, and only the broadening of the channel can reach consumers as many as possible. The future key point in the work of BIOEFFECT will be the approval of new raw materials and the broadening of all channels, and it is required to flexibly solve current problems on the premise of focusing on the development of the brand advantages.

Keeping the original intention and refusing leading by the flow is not hard to understand but only a few people can truly insist on that. Under the technical development background of big data, it changes from "attentive product manufacturing" to "attentive marketing", data flow and marketing seem like the active remedy to make up deficiencies of products, more and more brands pursue the marketing hotspot and regard the data flow as the main. It is very precious that Ms. Shanyue can realize the importance of the original, and she believes that no matter how the market and economic environment change, the brand shall have its high-quality products, and this is always the confidence to fight against risks.

Mutual Understanding and Support, Promoting Friendly Relations Between China and Iceland

On April 15, 2013, China and Iceland signed the free trade agreement, the first free trade agreement signed by China with European countries. The tariff has been greatly reduced. During the cooperation in China International Import Expo and with the e-commerce, the embassies and commercial offices of both countries made every effort to assist the sales of BIOEFFECT brand.

As for the support provided by the government for economic and trade exchanges of China-Iceland enterprises, Shanyue mentioned that as a genetic research and development company, the approval of new raw materials of BIOEFFECT in China was specially supervised, which was very cautious, and the report for records was planned to be one year at least; therefore, the schedule of products in China was later than that in foreign countries. Shanyue said that she fully understood the consideration of the Chinese government, and the strict supervision was a kind of responsibility for consumers. At present, China opens its market gradually and encourages to introduce innovative materials and new raw materials, the embassy and commercial office will also provide help for enterprises. The promotion of ingredient introduction can open the bigger market increment, bring a bigger new product world and bring better products for Chinese consumers.

Ms. Shanyue (first from the right) of BIOEFFECT was invited to attend the 50th anniversary reception of establishment of diplomatic relations between China and Iceland

We can get a clear answer for the questions of the impact of the epidemic when making an interview with the Icelandic Research Center of Jinan University. Transportation was in a relatively stagnated state in the early stage of the epidemic, which was from Iceland to China and then the internal transportation in China, and it can be solved only by stocking. With the rapid control of the epidemic in China, there is almost no serious problem except for some impact on logistics in China.

Lastly, Ms. Shanyue gave the following suggestion for all young entrepreneurs who want to participate in the China-Iceland trade: The local market scale of Iceland is limited and the logistics cost is expensive, and it is required to be very cautious to have investment or investment projects in Iceland. It is necessary to see the core resource advantages under big environmental background, for example, Iceland owns vast and sparsely populated, the investment may be required in case of additional growth demands, and the labor-intensive industry is not suitable here. There are some "unicorn" companies in Iceland that have scarce resources. If there are demands in the Chinese market, you shall fully understand the conditions of both countries.

The year 2021 is the 50th anniversary of the establishment of diplomatic relations between China and Iceland, and the bilateral relationship develops steadily in recent years based on the principle of mutual respect. You can intuitively feel this in the interview with the Icelandic Research Center of Jinan University. The economic and trade exchanges of China-Iceland enterprises have been greatly supported by the government of both countries. The friendly relationship between China and Iceland is deeply rooted in the hearts of the people, and we hope that both countries can continuously deepen the cooperation in different fields, enhance the mutual trust, promote the further development of the relationship between China and Iceland, and bring more well-being for both countries and the people of both countries.

(Wang Chu　Liu Haorong)

08

从专家学者到卓越企业家

——冰岛碳循环国际公司市场与营销总监 Omar Sigurbjornsson 的探索之旅

Omar Sigurbjornsson

人们常说“隔行如隔山”，在现实生活中，也不乏一些专业学者在尝试转战商界时惨遭滑铁卢的实例。而冰岛碳循环国际公司的市场总监 Omar Sigurbjornsson 却用他独特的个人经历向我们展示了兼顾学术与商业的可能性。

作为一名碳循环领域的知名学者，Omar Sigurbjornsson 将研究所得付诸实践，积极推动冰岛碳循环国际公司的技术进步与市场拓展。同时，他在担任市场总监期间，促成了冰岛碳循环国际公司与中国政府以及中国民间企业的多次合作，为冰岛与中国的经济往来做出了贡献。

读万卷书，行万里路

Omar 本科就读于冰岛历史最悠久的大学——冰岛大学，学习化学。毕业之后，他选择前往加拿大不列颠哥伦比亚大学继续攻读硕士学位。在那里，他曾从事过物理化学方面的研究并发表多篇学术论文，这为其未来从事碳循环方面的工作打下了坚实的理论基础。在进行学术研究之余，Omar 也非常乐于参加学生组织。“在冰岛大学，我曾经担任过学生会财务主管，经常要做一些类似于账目管理和人员协调的工作，就像经营一个小企业一样。这也是我后来涉足商业管理的契机。”

在加拿大，Omar 也从事过一段时间的教师工作。采访中，他与我们分享了冰岛学生与中国学生之间一些有趣的不同点。“冰岛学生往往更具创造力，他们什么都想要尝试，而中国学生更加遵守纪律，也更尊敬老师，这一点我很喜欢。”

完成学业之后，Omar 回到冰岛，加入了一家研究机构，从事物理和化学方面的教育工作。这为他未来在碳循环国际公司的工作提供了丰厚的学术积累。提到这段经历时，Omar 的语气中饱含着怀念的情绪：“当我从事科研工作的时候，有时别人觉得这项研究不可行，但我依旧坚持了下来并发现它是可行的，那种喜悦感非常棒。”

纸上得来终觉浅，绝知此事要躬行

Omar 的成就并不止步于学术理论，凭借着扎实的科研实力和过人的商业素养，他加入了碳循环国际公司并担任了市场研究和发展总监一职。众所周知，将在学校所学到的理论知识应用于实践中是非常困难的。由于社会与学校的巨大差别，当学生们踌躇满志走出校园准备一展所长之时，总是会遇到各种各样的问题与困难。在谈到从研究机构到实业的环境转换时，Omar 也认为两者存在着很大的差异。在从事科学研究时，环境相对封闭，研究工作更强调独立思考。与之不同的是，企业更需要团队合作，需要将技术理论以一种更加简洁明了的方式解释给团队及其他同事。冰岛独特的研究环境帮助他更好地适应了这种转换。“冰岛是个人口基数较小的国家，因为独特的研究环境，冰岛人往往身兼多个职业角色。所以，在那里，你更容易找到为你提供各种专业帮助的人，像经济学家、地理学家等等，你会很容易找到他们。”Omar 如是说。

Omar 职业生涯的另一个转折是他由碳循环国际公司的市场研究和发展总监调任到了市场与营销总监这一职位，也是在此期间，他与中国结下了不解之缘。

君子藏器于身，待时而动

2020 年 9 月，中国政府在第七十五届联合国大会上提出：“中国将提高国家自主贡献力度，采取更加有力的政策和措施，二氧化碳排放力争于 2030 年前达到峰值，努力争取 2060 年前实现碳中和。”2021 年 3 月，中国国务院《政府工作报告》中指出，“扎实做好碳达峰、碳中和各项工作。制定 2030 年前碳排放达峰行动方案。优化产业结构和能源结构”。一时间，碳中和理念在中国风靡一时，促进了国内环保企业的快速发展。为了不被行政部门处以罚款，各工业企业开始使出浑身解数来降低自己的碳排放量。这给碳循环国际公司这样专精于碳元素再利用的企业带来了发展机会。

“中国的新能源产业是一个很大的市场，而我们只是这个市场中很小的一部分。除我们之外，这个市场中还有很多其他企业，未来我们希望能有机会与他们展开合作。”抱着这样的想法，Omar 多次来到中国，代表碳循环国际公司与浙江吉利控股集团、河南顺成集团及江苏斯尔邦化工有限公司开展了包括甲醇汽车燃料研发、工业废气再利用等方面的合作。

2021 年 6 月 22 日，上海环境能源交易所发布《关于全国碳排放权交易相关事项的公告》，决定建立全国碳排放权交易机构来负责组织开展全国碳排放权集中统一交易。被纳入交易体系的企业将获得初始碳排放权，这些企业可以在碳市场上买卖碳排放权。在这一政策下，企业需要将碳减排成本、超额碳排放成本、购买碳配额的成本与超额排放生产带来的收益进行比较，做出最优决策。Omar 表示，这一政策的颁布，使碳循环国际公司的技术可以帮助钢铁企业等减少碳排放，并将二氧化碳转化为清洁能源，可以有效降低企业的碳减排成本，对于碳循环国际公司来说，中国已成为一个具有巨大潜力的海外市场。

对于近年国际范围内备受关注的能源危机问题，Omar 也提出了他的观点。自 2021 年 9 月以来，欧美天然气、动力煤、原油等能源品价格纷纷升至历史高位。极端天气严重拖累绿色能源发电，2021 年年初以来的超高压天气给欧洲的风力发电体系带来重大损伤。Omar 认为，风力发电局限性较大，不仅易受天气等环境因素的影响，也同样面临着供需时间错位问题。然而，碳循环国际公司的清洁甲醇能源技术则能够完美摆脱这方面的束缚。由于甲醇具有耐低温、不易变质的特点，无论是在能源的便携性还是长期储存方面都具有很大优势，与传统清洁能源相比受气候因素影响很小。借助这项技术，碳循环国际公司能够为解决能源危机这个令各国政府束手无策的问题提供重要的解决方案。

在采访的最后，Omar 针对中冰两国的关系表示，虽然中冰两国相距万里，但两国人民心中有着紧密的友情纽带。相信在未来，中国与冰岛的友好关系将会进一步稳健发展，为两国人民带来更多福祉。

（毛雨　刘子涵）

Outstanding Entrepreneur from an Expert and Scholar

— The Journey of Exploration of Omar Sigurbjornsson, Sales and Marketing Director of Carbon Recycling International

Omar Sigurbjornsson

People often say that "difference in profession makes one feel worlds apart". In real life, there are many examples of some professional scholars who suffered a decisive defeat when trying to move to business. But Omar Sigurbjornsson, Sales and Marketing Director of Carbon Recycling International (CRI), shared experience of balancing academic and businesses with us.

As a well-known scholar in the field of carbon cycle, Omar Sigurbjornsson put the research results into practice and actively promoted the technological progress and market expansion of Carbon Recycling International. Meanwhile, when he held the post of Sales and Marketing Director, he helped to bring about a number of cooperation between Carbon Recycling International and the Chinese government as well as China non-government enterprises and contributed to the economic communication between Iceland and China.

Learn as Much as You Can and Do All You Can

Mr. Omar once studied in the University of Iceland (UI), the oldest university in Iceland. After graduation, he chose to continue his master's degree at University of British Columbia (UBC). There, he was engaged in research in physical chemistry. He published many academic essays, which have laid a solid theoretical foundation for his future work on carbon recycling. Besides his academic research, Mr. Omar was also very happy to join student organizations. "At University of Iceland, I served as the treasurer of the student union. I often had to do something like account management and personnel coordination, which seems as if I ran a small business. This is also an opportunity for me to get involved in business administration later."

In Canada, Mr. Omar also worked as a teacher for a while. In the interview, he shared with us some interesting differences between Icelandic students and Chinese students. "Icelandic students tend to be more creative and want to try everything, while Chinese students are more disciplined and respect their teachers, which I like it very much."

After completing his studies, Mr. Omar returned to Iceland and joined a research institution and was teaching chemistry and physics. That provides him with abundant academic experiences for his future work in Carbon Recycling International. At the time of referring to the experience, there was full of nostalgia in Mr. Omar's tone: "When I was engaged in scientific research, sometimes others thought the research was not feasible, but I still insisted on it and found that it practicable in the end. At that time, I was filled with joy."

Paper Will Sleep Shallow. You Never Know the Matter Without Practice

Mr. Omar's achievements aren't confined in academic theories. By means of solid scientific research strength and excellent business attainments, he joined Carbon Recycling International and served as Director of Research and Development. As is known to us, it is very difficult to apply the theoretical knowledge learned in school to practice. Due to the great differences between society and campuses, students will always encounter all kinds of problems and difficulties when they are complacent and ready to give full play to their strong points after graduation. When we talk about the environmental transformation from research institutions to industry, Mr. Omar said that there are great differences between them indeed. While he was doing scientific research, the environment is relatively closed, and the research work underlines independent thinking. In contrast, when he joined CRI, teamwork is more needed in the enterprise, and the technical theory needs to be explained to the team members and other colleagues in a more concise and clear way. Iceland's unique research environment helped him better adapt to the transformation. "Iceland is a country with a small population. So Icelanders often have several professional roles because of their unique research environment. Therefore, it's easier for you to find people who provide you with all kinds of professional help, such as economists, geographers and so on, and you'll find them easily." Mr. Omar said.

Another pivotal point in Mr. Omar's career is that he was transferred from the Director of R&D of CRI to the position of Sales and Marketing Director. During the period he served as Sales and Marketing Director, he formed an indissoluble bond with China.

Chance Favors Only the Prepared Mind

In September 2020, the Chinese government proposed this, at the 75th Session of the United Nations General Assembly: "China will scale up its Intended Nationally Determined Contributions by adopting more vigorous policies and measures. We aim to have CO_2 emissions peak before 2030 and achieve carbon neutrality before 2060." Then, it was pointed out in the *Report on the Work of the Government* of the State Council of China in March 2021 that China would take solid steps toward the goals of achieving peak carbon dioxide emissions and carbon neutrality, draw up an action plan for carbon emissions to peak by 2030, and improve China's industrial structure and energy mix. For a time, the concept of carbon neutrality was all the rage in China, which promoted the rapid development of domestic environmental protection enterprises. In order not to be fined by the administrations, industrial enterprises began to try their best to reduce their carbon emissions. Therefore, development opportunities are brought to enterprises specializing in carbon reuse like CRI.

"There is a huge market in China's new energy industry, but our company we are only a small part of the market. Besides us, there are many other enterprises in the market, we hope to have the opportunity to cooperate with them in the future." With this idea, Mr. Omar has been to China many times to carry out cooperation with Zhejiang Geely Holding Group, Henan Shuncheng Group and Jiangsu Sierbang Petrochemical Co., Ltd. in the fuel research and development for methanol-fueled automobiles, industrial waste gas recycling and others.

On June 22, 2021, Shanghai Environment and Energy Exchange issued the *Announcement on Matters Related to National Carbon Emission Trading*, and decided to establish a national carbon emissions trading institution which is responsible for organizing and carrying out centralized and unified the trading of national carbon emissions rights. The enterprises included in the trading system will receive initial carbon emission rights, which can be bought and sold in the carbon market. Under the policy, enterprises need to make the best decision by comparing the cost of carbon emission reduction, the cost of excess carbon emission and the cost of purchasing carbon emission quotas (CEA) with the benefits brought by excess emission/production. Mr. Omar said that the promulgation of the policy enables the technology of CRI to help iron and steel enterprises and others to reduce carbon emissions and convert CO_2 into clean energy, which can effectively reduce the cost of carbon emission reduction. For CRI, China has become an overseas market with great potential.

He also put forward his views on the recent international energy crisis. Since

September 2021, the prices of natural gas, thermal coal, crude oil and other energy products in Europe and the United States have risen to historic highs. Extreme weather has seriously dragged down the green energy power generation with green energy, and the ultra-high pressure weather since the beginning of 2021 has brought significant damage to the wind power generation system in Europe. Mr. Omar holds that wind power generation has great challenges. It is not only vulnerable to environmental factors like weather, but also faces the problem of time warp between supply and demand. However, the clean methanol energy technology of CRI can perfectly get rid of the constraints in this regard. Because methanol is characterized by low-temperature resistance and difficult deterioration, it has great advantages in energy portability and long-term storage. What's more, it is little affected by climate factors compared with traditional clean energy. With the help of the technology, CRI can provide important solutions to the energy crisis, which makes the governments of all the countries feel quite helpless.

At the end of the interview, Mr. Omar said that although China and Iceland are thousands of miles apart, there are close ties of friendship in the hearts of Icelandic and Chinese people, and he is convinced that in the future, the friendly relations between China and Iceland will further develop steadily and bring more benefits to Icelandic and the Chinese people.

(Mao Yu　Liu Zihan)

09

坚定方向，开拓未知

——访冰岛极地绿色能源集团中国区总经理赵鑫

“不给自己设限”“实践出真知”，这是赵鑫总经理在采访过程中分享给我们的最受益的成功经验。在这个飞速发展的时代，人们被万千世界五彩缤纷的事物环绕，对学习的钻研成了很多人难以静心完成的事情。而赵鑫总经理在忙碌的工作中，始终坚持学习，且学习的涉猎面很广。无论是本专业的还是非本专业的知识，她都能够认真钻研，精益求精，始终坚持自己内心所愿，意志坚定而泰然从容。

冰岛极地绿色能源集团是一家基于冰岛地热技术、在全球范围内进行清洁能源开发的专业化公司。在赵鑫总经理刚步入地热行业时，中国地热能应用尚未开展，她勇敢地迈出了第一步，毅然决然的努力促使这个行业在中国不断得以推进。正如赵鑫所说，“成功需要一些勇气”。赵鑫总经理不断进取、心系地热产业的热忱深深地感染着我们。

勇敢开拓，实践出真知

赵鑫本科就读于南开大学国际商学院，研究生就读于英国知名学府——兰卡斯特大学，之后深造于哈佛商学院。与精彩的求学之路相呼应，她的工作阅历同样丰富多彩。赵鑫曾就职于安永会计师事务所和冰岛银行，从事审计和管理工作，后加入了能源企业——冰岛极地绿色能源集团。

赵 鑫

在采访过程中，赵鑫叙述了一件对她来说印象深刻的事情。赵鑫最初加入这个行业时，曾去参加一个项目仪式，当天她穿了双高跟鞋和一条精致修身的裙子去了现场。然而，赵鑫发现，与之前她所从事过的白领、金领的工作相比，这是一份完全陌生的工作。在现场工作的合作伙伴同样是拥有优秀教育背景的专家，但他们整日在项目工地上工作。为了工程进度连续数日没有睡一个安稳觉，在工作的过程中，他们的衣服早已被汗水浸湿了。就是这样一个很细微的一点触动了赵鑫，她意识到，在这份工作中，亲力亲为、切身地融入项目是必不可少的。每个人，无论拥有怎样的教育背景，都必须亲力亲为地去做好每一件事情，而不是仅仅表面化，靠言语去指导他人应该如何完成工作。这件事给赵鑫带来了深刻的影响，也让我们感触颇多。赵鑫结合所见所闻进行了思考，如何才能做好这份工作，“亲力亲为，实践出真知”正是赵鑫得出的答案。“不驰于空想，不骛于虚声”。自加入冰岛极地绿色能源集团以来，赵鑫深入基层，深入项目，走访了很多乡村和城镇，不再囿于城市这个圈子。她的努力促使地热产业在中国的发展越来越普及，地热供暖成为令人关注的新能源落地项目。现如今，这个起初在中国几乎没有任何存在感的行业越做越大，更多的人了解到地热，甚至越来越多的百姓熟知地热。赵鑫鼓励当代年轻人应当到偏远的地方去，实地了解偏远地区的环境和生活，而不是仅仅坐在教室里，享受着优裕的生活，从书本、报纸、电视等各种媒介上了解外面的世界。年轻人需要走出去，通过自己的实践去看看外面的世界，将所学知识真正运用到需要知识的地方，勇敢地跳出自己的舒适圈，为社会做出一些贡献。

学习不止，不给自己设限

“吾生也有涯，而知也无涯”，这是赵鑫关于学习的态度。从求学到工作，无论处于哪个阶段，赵鑫都在不断地汲取新的知识。从银行、投行跨越到能源集团，她在工作中接触到的事物跨度极大。赵鑫在这个过程中，持之以恒地学习新的知识，从不给自己设限，并不会因为所涉及的知识非自己的专业领域就置之不理。赵鑫持有专业的态度，尽力去学习所有的知识，跳出舒适圈，精进自己，拓展知识面。对于自己的专业知识，赵鑫更是精益求精，力求将所有的事情做到完美。正是这样追求完美的态度，成就了她事业上的成功。赵鑫作为中国涉足地热开发和应用的商界领军者，将对地热这一清洁能源的热情融进财务管理专业知识，秉持初心，助力地热能源在中国的发展。赵鑫将自己事业成功经验主要归结于三点：第一，勤于学习。无论何时何地，学无止境，要不断汲取新的知识，增加生命的厚度，让知识储备变得更加渊博，同时在学习的过程中不限制专业范围，有意识地拓宽知识结构的广度。第二，深度思考。孔子曰：“学而不思则罔。”对于任何一件事应该有自己的观点，认真思考而不是随波逐流，一味地听从别人的观点。随大流是当今时代一个普遍现象，很多人失去了独立思考、判断是非的能力，这是不可取的。对任何事情应积极认真地思考，并能在思考后表达自己的观点是很重要的。第三，勇于探索。当赵鑫初入地热行业时，没有人能告诉她，她的选择是否正确，只有自身坚定了这个选择，并有勇气在这条路上坚持不懈地探索下去，敢于在关键问题上承担起责任，才能得到最终的成功。勇气对年轻人来说是很重要的品质，正是因为有勇气去做一件别人没有做过的事情，才促成了赵鑫在地热行业中的成功。《文化苦旅》一书中，余秋雨认为登山的意义在于留下属于自己的脚印，而并非快速登顶，心平气和慢慢地爬，最终总会到达巅峰。赵鑫就是在做这样一件事，她坚定目标，为了目标持之以恒，不断汲取新鲜的知识，一步一个脚印，在这片没人踩过的荒漠中记录下了自己的足迹，最终登上了冰山之巅。万里蹀躞，以此为归，这条路赵鑫会一直走下去，致力于地热清洁能源供暖，同时为促进中冰两国合作和双边关系的良好发展贡献力所能及的一份力量。

团队同心，投身清洁能源

作为冰岛极地绿色能源集团中国区总经理，赵鑫率领的团队一步步壮大起来。赵鑫刚刚踏入地热能行业时，中国在这一领域还没有开始正式起步，有的只是这一家公司的基本框架，一个中冰两国在地热能源发展上可以合作的契机。刚加入冰岛极地绿色能源集团的时候，公司的规模非常小，甚至在 2008 年的时候还是处于亏损状态，未来的发展道路上布满荆棘。赵鑫认为，首先，公司作为中国在这一领域内第一个吃螃蟹的人，面临的体制机制、政策环境、市场适应程度都是全新的。为了应对这些复杂的挑战，必须坚定方向——清洁供暖是服务民生的方向，同时在企业管理方面应进行创新，以符合中国国内的体制、政策和市场需求，这样才能保证地热这个对于中国来说新兴的行业能够从冰岛这么一个遥远的国度来到中国落地生根。其次，中国与冰岛在地热能开发上存在着一定的差距。两国的地热条件不一致，冰岛的地热资源禀赋是极佳的，地热温度较高，应用非常广泛，除了用于供暖，还包括融雪、渔业养殖、工业、温室等方面，间接用途则主要是地热发电。而中国的地热条件整体上没有冰岛那么好，主要还是以中低温供暖为主。从经验上看，冰岛从20世纪70年代就开始了地热的现代化开发与利用，积累了非常丰富的地热发展经验，并且还对外输出地热体系的各种行业标准。中国由于地热条件与冰岛不一样，并不能直接照搬冰岛的体系，需要探索出适合本国国情的发展方式。这一切都成为公司未来发展的严峻挑战。

不过，赵鑫也看到了中国地热发展的突破与创新。根据地热的特点，形成了我国独特的发展模式，那就是把地热资源提取出来后，再回灌到原来的地层上，实现地热的可持续发展。冰岛之前在这方面没有进行相应的发展，因此从可持续角度来讲，中国显然是走在了其他国家的前面。目前，冰岛在一些项目上也开始学习中国，尝试开展回灌实验。通过这些技术研发，赵鑫认为，两国地热领域之间的差距正在逐步缩小，中国已经清晰地意识到了自身的条件及如何在现有条件下做到因地制宜。

赵鑫主持北极圈论坛中国分论坛可持续发展议题

在此过程中，赵鑫也带领着她的团队收获了丰硕的成果。2010年，团队申请的“通过地热减少二氧化碳排放”的方法学在联合国获得了注册，是全球范围清洁能源领域方法学内唯一以中国项目为基础开发的方法学，填补了我国在这一领域的空白。

针对地热项目的投资，赵鑫慎之又慎，她认为需要考虑的因素众多。首先，要考虑的是宏观上投资领域的政策环境，比如税收政策。冰岛的税收政策并不利于投资。另外，本地的一些金融性保护也可能成为地热投资的阻碍。其次，要看项目是否具有长期性。一个项目不能只考虑当期利润，要看到较长阶段的投资回报，实现经济性是长期发展的保障。最后，更要关注社会效益和环保效益，这样的双边投资才有意义，合作才会更加长久。

积极交流，尊重促进合作

对于发展中冰两国关系，赵鑫进行了深刻的分析。中国和冰岛两国有着深厚的友谊，在经贸、旅游、教育、科研等诸多领域有广泛密切的合作。冰岛地处北美洲和欧洲板块的交界处。作为一个人口仅有三十余万的国家，冰岛深受地缘政治的影响，赵鑫深刻地认识到了这一点，也尊重这一特点。同时，冰岛也涌现出像前总统奥拉维尔·拉格纳·格里姆松阁下这样的全球政治领袖，积极发挥冰岛作为北极圈国家的优势。中冰两国虽相距遥远，国情不同，但是亲历了中冰地热合作 16 年的历程，赵鑫很高兴看到中冰两国关系一直保持健康稳定发展，希望两国加强在经贸、旅游、地热、应对气候变化、可持续发展等领域的交流与合作，更好造福两国和两国人民。从赵鑫个人所做的工作角度来讲，减少二氧化碳排放、应对气候变化，是极地绿色能源集团发展的契机，更是增进中冰两国人民了解和信任的桥梁。

对于中冰两国未来合作，赵鑫提出展望，面对未来日渐严峻的气候变化挑战，中国提出将力争 2030 年前实现碳达峰、2060 年前实现碳中和的目标，充分彰显了中国积极应对气候变化、走绿色低碳发展道路的坚定决心。中国前驻冰岛大使、国际问题研究院前院长苏格称赞此次地热合作是两国关系的“压舱石”，对稳固双边关系起到积极作用。地热和清洁能源领域的合作应当在新的历史时期发挥更大的作用。在共同应对气候变化方面加深合作将造福两国人民、增进人民福祉。更重要的是，将我们的合作带向包括“一带一路”沿线国家在内的第三国，将合作成果转变为全球性的示范。国际可再生能源机构在 2021 年 5 月将中冰合作中石化绿源在雄安新区的地热开发作为城市能源转型的成功案例进行了全球推广。2023 年 4 月，世界地热大会将在北京举行，这将是中国首次承办全球地热能行业世界级的盛会。这既是世界地热行业对于中国地热开发模式的认可，也是中冰两国双边合作成果应用于国际合作中，提升两国共同应对全球气候变化共同使命的宝贵机会。

中冰两国建交 50 年来，双方本着相互尊重、平等相待的原则，政治互信不断巩固，各领域务实合作，成果丰硕，两国人民友谊不断加深。2021 年，两国共同庆祝了建交 50 周年，并共同庆祝了两国地热合作 15 周年，作为亲历者，赵鑫期待同中冰各界人士共同努力，推进中冰友好关系以及在各领域的合作取得更大发展。

（张子豪　梁译文）

Exploring the Unknown in the Clear Direction

— Interview with Zhao Xin, China General Manager of Iceland, Arctic Green Energy Corporation

"Life has no limitations" and "Genuine knowledge comes from practice" are the most beneficial successful experiences shared by General Manager Zhao Xin during her interview. In the era of rapid development, people are surrounded by thousands of colorful things in the world, and the learning has become something that many people can't complete calmly. However, General Manager Zhao Xin always insists on learning in her busy work, and her learning is involved in a wide range of subjects. She can seriously study the knowledge, whether professional or non-professional, constantly strive for perfection, and always adhere to the desire grown inside her heart, firm and calm.

Iceland Arctic Green Energy Corporation is a professional company based on Icelandic geothermal technology to develop clean energy around the world. When General Manager Zhao Xin first entered the geothermal industry, the application of geothermal energy in China had not yet been carried out. She bravely took the first step and made decisive efforts to promote the industry in China. As Zhao Xin said, "Success requires some courage". We are deeply affected by General Manager Zhao Xin's enterprising spirit, enthusiasm for and devotion to geothermal industry.

Practice Bravely and Experience Is the Mother of Wisdom

Zhao Xin studied at the Business School of Nankai University as an undergraduate, at Lancaster University as a postgraduate, and then studied at Harvard Business School. Echoing the wonderful road to seek knowledge, her work experience is also rich and colorful. Zhao Xin was occupied with audit and management in Ernst & Young and Bank of Iceland, and later joined the energy enterprise — Iceland Arctic Green Energy Corporation.

During her interview, Zhao Xin described a thing that impressed her greatly. When Zhao Xin initially joined the industry, she, wearing a pair of high heels and a delicate slim skirt, attended a project ceremony. However, Zhao Xin found that compared with her previous white-collar and gold-collar work, the job is completely strange to her. The partners working on the site are also experts with excellent educational background, but they work on the project site all day. For the progress of the project, they haven't had a peaceful sleep for several days, and their clothes have been soaked with sweat in the process of work. It was such a subtle point that touched Zhao Xin. She realized that in the job, it is essential to do it herself and personally integrate into the project. Everyone, no matter what educational background they have, must do everything by themselves, rather than just superficialising and relying on words to guide others how to complete their work. This matter not only makes a profound impact on Zhao Xin but also brought us a lot of strong feelings. Zhao Xin thought about how to do the job well with what she saw and heard. "Do it yourself and practice makes perfect" are the answer Zhao Xin got. "I avoid the distractions of unsubstantial ideas and superficial fame". Since joining Iceland Arctic Green Energy Corporation, Zhao Xin has gone down to the grass roots and projects, visited many countrysides and towns, and is no longer confined to the circle of cities. Her efforts have made the development of geothermal industry more and more popular in China, and geothermal heating has become a new energy project of concern. Now, this industry, which initially had little sense of existence in China, is growing larger and larger. More people know about geothermal energy, and even more and more people are familiar with geothermal energy. Zhao Xin encouraged contemporary young people to go to remote places and learn about the actual environment and life in remote areas, rather than just sitting in the classroom, enjoying a good life and knowing about the outside world from books, newspapers, television and other media. Young people need to go out, look at personally the outside world, really apply the knowledge they have learned to the places where the knowledge is needed, bravely jump out of their comfort circle and make some contributions to the society.

Learn More and Never Limit Yourself

"Life is limited, but the knowledge is not." This is Zhao Xin's attitude about learning. From school to work, no matter what stage Zhao Xin is constantly learning new knowledge. She has been exposed to a wide range of things in her work from bank, investment bank to energy group. In the process, Zhao Xin keeps learning new knowledge, never sets limits on herself, and never ignores it just because the knowledge involved is outside her field of expertise. Zhao Xin has a professional attitude and tries her best to learn for all the knowledge. She gets out of her comfort zone, improves herself, and expands her width of knowledge. For her own professional knowledge, Zhao Xin is more excelsior and strives to do everything perfectly. It is this attitude of pursuing perfection that leads to the success of her career. As a business leader involved in geothermal development and application in China, Zhao Xin incorporates her passion for geothermal as a clean energy into her financial management expertise to help develop the geothermal energy in China. Zhao Xin mainly ascribes her successful career experience to three points. Firstly, study diligently. No matter when and where, the knowledge is boundless. Constantly acquiring new knowledge, increasing the life richness, and making the knowledge abundantly are very essential. At the same time, do not limit the scope of expertise in the process of learning, and consciously broaden the breadth of knowledge structure; Second, think deeply. Confucius said: "Learning without thought is useless." You should have your own opinion on everything and think carefully instead of following the general trend and blindly listening to the opinions of others. Following the general trend is a common phenomenon today. Many people have lost the ability to think independently and judge right and wrong, which is not desirable. It is important to think positively and seriously about anything and be able to express your opinion after thinking about it. Third, explore bravely. When Zhao Xin first entered the geothermal industry, no one could tell her whether she was making the right choice. Only by making the choice firmly, having the courage to explore unremittingly on the way, and having the courage to assume responsibility on key issues, could she achieve the final success. Courage is an important quality for young people, and it is the courage to do something that no one else has done that has contributed to Zhao Xin's success in the geothermal industry. It was written in *Cultural Perplexity in Agonized Travel* that, Yu Qiuyu believes the meaning of mountaineering lies in leaving the personnel footprints, rather than reaching the top quickly. So long as you climb slowly and calmly, eventually you will reach the top. That is what Zhao Xin is doing. She moves toward her goals perseveringly, constantly learns new knowledge, step by step, records her own footprints in this untrodden desert, and finally reaches the top of iceberg. Walking a thousand miles in small steps in order to gain success. Zhao Xin will keep going along this path and devote herself to geothermal clean energy heating, and make her own contribution to promoting Sino-Iceland cooperation and good development of bilateral relations.

Uniting as One and Committing to Clean Energy

As the China General Manager of Iceland Arctic Green Energy Corporation, the team led by Zhao Xin has grown gradually step by step. When she first entered the geothermal energy industry, China had not yet started in earnest in this field. There was only a basic framework of the company, and an opportunity for cooperation between China and Iceland in geothermal energy development. When she first joined Iceland Arctic Green Energy Corporation, the company was rather small. Even in 2008, the company was still in loss, and the future development path was full of thorns. According to Zhao Xin, first of all, as the first pioneer in this field in China, the company was faced with a new system and mechanism, policy environment and market adaptability. In order to deal with these complex challenges, a firm direction must be determined first — clean heating is to serve people's livelihood. At the same time, the management of enterprises should be innovated in accordance with China's domestic system, policy and market demand, so as to ensure that geothermal, an emerging industry for China, could take root in China from a faraway country like Iceland. Secondly, there was a gap in geothermal energy development between China and Iceland. The natural geothermal conditions in two countries are not consistent. Iceland has excellent natural geothermal resources with high temperature and a wide range of applications. In addition to heating, geothermal is also used for snow melting, fishery breeding, industry, greenhouse and other aspects. The indirect application is mainly the geothermal power generation. However, China's overall geothermal conditions are not as good as Iceland's, mainly with low and medium temperature heating. From the perspective of experience, Iceland has started the modern development and utilization of geothermal energy since the 1970s, accumulated rich experience in geothermal development, and exported various industry standards of geothermal system. However, China could not directly copy Iceland's system due to its different geothermal conditions, so it needed to explore a development way suitable for its national conditions. All these had become serious challenges for the future development of the company.

Nevertheless, Zhao Xin also saw the breakthroughs and innovations in China's geothermal development. According to the characteristics of geothermal, a unique development model for China has been formed, that is, to extract geothermal resources and recharge them into the original stratum to achieve sustainable development of geothermal. Iceland had not developed in this territory before, so China was clearly ahead of other countries in terms of sustainability. At present, Iceland also began to learn from China in some projects, trying to carry out the recharge experiment. Through these technologies, Zhao Xin believed that the gap between the geothermal fields of the two countries was gradually reduced, and China had a clear sense of its conditions and how to adjust measures to them.

In this process, Zhao Xin achieved plentiful achievements with her team as well. In 2010, the geothermal methodology applied by the team to reduce carbon dioxide emissions was registered at the United Nations, which was the only methodology developed based on a Chinese project in the field of clean energy worldwide, filling the gap in this field in China.

Zhao Xin was very cautious about the investment of geothermal project, she thought there were many factors that need to be considered. The first thing to consider is the macro investment policy environment. For example, the taxation policy. The taxation policy in Iceland is not good for investment. Besides, some local financial protections may also be a barrier to geothermal investment. Then, whether the project is long-lasting needs to be considered. Profitability of a certain period shall not be the only perspective, instead, investment return over life span of the project shall be the key. Finally, bilateral investment will only be long lasting and meaningful if it creates social and environment benefits.

Communicating Actively and Respecting the Cooperation Promotion

Zhao Xin made a profound analysis of the development of Sino-Iceland relationship. China and Iceland enjoy a profound friendship and have extensive and close cooperation in economy, trade, tourism, education, scientific research and many other fields. Iceland, with population of merely over 300,000, geographically located in between North America and Europe. Iceland is immensely influenced by geopolitics. Zhao Xin is deeply aware of it and she respects it. Meanwhile, there are also global leaders like H.E. Olafur Ragnar Grimsson, former President of Iceland, who is actively strengthen Iceland's role in Arctic affairs on global stage. China and Iceland are geographically far apart from each other and have so many differences. Having witnessed 16 years successful cooperation in geothermal, Zhao Xin is very glad to see China-Iceland relations have maintained a sound and sustained development. She hoped the two sides could strengthen the exchanges and cooperation in the fields of economy and trade, tourism, geothermal, climate change, sustainable development for the benefit of the two countries and two peoples. In terms of Zhao Xin's work, fighting against climate change on a global scale is an opportunity for Arctic Green to grow faster and is the best bridge for people of the two nations to strengthen understanding and trust.

Zhao Xin (first from the right) participated in the signing ceremony between Asian Development Bank and Iceland Arctic Green Energy Corporation

As for the Sino-Iceland cooperation in the future, Zhao Xin put forward a prospect that joint response to climate change is the major goal of bilateral cooperation. Facing the increasingly severe challenge of climate change in the future, China proposes to strive to achieve the goal of carbon peak by 2030 and carbon neutrality by 2060, which fully demonstrates China's firm determination to actively deal with climate change and take the path of green and low-carbon development. The geothermal cooperation was praised as a "ballast" for bilateral relations by Su Ge, the former Chinese Ambassador to Iceland and former President of China Institute of International Studies, which plays a positive role in stabilizing bilateral relations. The cooperation in fields of geothermal and clean energy should play a greater role in the new historical period. The joint action against climate change will bring benefit to people of the two nations. It is more importantly to take our cooperation to a third country, including countries along "the Belt and Road" Initiative, and turn the results of cooperation into a global demonstration. In May 2021, the International Renewable Energy Agency promoted the Sino-Iceland collaborated geothermal development in Xiong'an, China, as a successful global showcase of urban energy transformation. April 2023, World Geothermal Congress will be held in Beijing. It is the first time that China hosts international geothermal event. It is a recognition of China's geothermal development model, moreover, it will be a precious opportunity to present our Sino-Iceland cooperation to the international community and enhance our joint mission against climate change.

Since the establishment of diplomatic relations between China and Iceland 50 years ago, the two sides have, on the basis of the principle of equality and mutual respect, continuously consolidated the political mutual trust and witnessed fruitful outcomes in pragmatic cooperation across a wide range of areas. The traditional friendship between the two peoples has also been deepened. Last year, China and Iceland jointly celebrated the golden jubilee of the establishment of diplomatic relations and celebrated 15 year anniversary of geothermal collaboration. As witness of the development, Zhao Xin is looking forward to working with Chinese and Icelandic people from all walks of life to promote China-Iceland friendly relations as well as cooperation in various fields for further development.

(Zhang Zihao　Liang Yiwen)

10

知行合一，终身学习

——访马瑞奥中国区董事总经理吕勇

吕　勇

孔子曰："学而不已。"马瑞奥中国区董事总经理吕勇回顾自己的从业经历，最大的感触是"学习是一种常态"。

在这个知识与信息爆炸的时代，终身学习已经成为很多人的口号，但是能坚持下来的人却寥寥无几。吕勇在食品行业深耕近20年，主动学习相关知识，了解行业前沿动态已经成了他的工作习惯。这个时代瞬息万变，每一次的变革都充满新鲜感，吕勇在不断学习中看到了食品行业的未来。这大概就是为什么他能始终如一地保持着对食品加工的兴趣、对行业的热爱以及对食品行业创新技术的敏感性。恰逢中冰建交50周年之际，马瑞奥中国区董事总经理吕勇在百忙之中以书面形式接受了我们的采访，字里行间中，我们深深地感受到了他本人的严谨与认真。

嗜之越笃，技巧越工

卡耐基曾经说过，"你兴趣所在的地方，就是能力所在的地方。"能够投身于自己感兴趣的行业的人是幸运的。吕勇便是如此，虽然并非农业或食品专业出身，但他始终对植物的种植、动物的养殖，以及如何能够通过科技和工业的手段不断地将食品进行开发和创新保持着高昂的兴致。与此同时，为了做好每一份工作，他不忘在业余时间学习相关知识，提升专业能力，认真细致地完成每一项任务，这也为他之后的职业晋升奠定了坚实的基础。

马瑞奥（Marel Townsend Futher Processing B. V.）是总部位于冰岛的全球性肉制品高端加工设备制造企业，其设备和解决方案涵盖红肉、家禽和水产品等行业，应用范围覆盖从屠宰、加工到终端产品生产，并使用先进的数字化技术，确保生产流程效率可视，以及从源头到货架的可追溯性。

马瑞奥的业务范围和设备生产能力使得吕勇看到了迎合时代需求、推动产业升级需求、高效化满足顾客需求的产业链融合模式，这正是他感兴趣的方向。

要成为一个优秀的企业家，一定要有成熟的思维体系、高瞻远瞩的战略思维能力和果断的决策能力。吕勇在食品行业工作，对整个产业都充满了热情与好奇心，并借此机会学习和了解植物种植、动物养殖、农副产品加工等相关行业知识。他并没有将自己的视野局限于原材料的培育与加工方面，而是结合自己多年的经验，深入思考如何满足顾客需求，如何降低成本并提高效率，如何在生产加工过程中结合科技与工业的手段对生产线进行优化，等等。他越是深入思考，越是广泛了解，他对这个行业越是感兴趣。在加入马瑞奥之后，他的兴趣与马瑞奥的战略充分契合，于是吕勇开始在马瑞奥中国区推进自己的产业链融合模式。

在采访中，我们了解到吕勇所推进的产业链融合模式已经促使马瑞奥在设备生产方面实现了自动化、智能化与数字化。高科技的生产线以及先进的数字化平台已经融入其智能化食品加工解决方案之中。

马瑞奥北京办公室

兴趣与事业的抉择是现在很多人讨论的焦点话题，兴趣可以随心所欲，而事业却不能。吕勇将兴趣融入事业，带着好奇心，不给自己的能力设限，不断探索与突破，进行着深入的思考。他用自己的责任心、严谨、努力、规划等“砖瓦”构筑起自己事业的大厦。在这个过程中，他见证了中国食品加工行业从初级到高级、从去中心化到集中化、从手工到自动化、从劳动密集型到人工智能等变化的进程。与此同时，他也为食品行业的积极变化贡献出了自己的力量。

砥砺深耕，笃行致远

在一个行业深耕将近20年，并将继续下去，这样的坚持除了兴趣，也成了一种有始有终并不断提升和挑战自己的习惯。笃行致远，在食品行业不断深耕，从马铃薯种植到肉制品深加工，财务专业出身的吕勇告诉我们：这一路上，他收获了更多的经历和见识。

从基础的工作中开始学习，已经成为吕勇的工作惯例。对于一项工作，吕勇会深挖到这个工作中最基本的一个环节进行学习。进入食品行业之初，吕勇是在美国马铃薯加工龙头企业辛普劳集团工作。那时他工作的终极目标很简单，就是为客户提供优质高效的薯条和薯饼产品。这些问题看似不难，却需要将育种、种植、收获、储存、加工、库存等方面进行综合分析，同时结合客户开店速度、业务布局、新产品研发、市场行情波动等产业链条上的多重因素，最终帮助和指引公司及客户做出最佳决策，这需要极大的耐心和全产业链的综合分析和管理能力。吕勇在对工作内容进行分析后，意识到了加工前端环节——马铃薯种植的重要性后，专门抽出时间去学习和了解马铃薯从种植、收获、储存到加工的具体过程，以及工作中的痛点、难点，从最基础、最前端的内容开始学习和了解，进行深入分析，通过搭建财务和业务模型，对问题和决策过程进行了可量化的分析和支持。

此后，他在辛普劳集团的工作转移到了肉牛养殖项目，目标转变为从无到有建立肉牛规模养殖种群，并不断提高养殖效率和出成率。虽然是财务出身，他也毫不犹豫地投入对养殖的各个环节的学习了解和掌握当中。牛犊的遴选、初乳的重要性、饲料的配比、生物安全防护、疫病处置、一线的参与和学习等都成为他的日常管理工作。作为肉牛养殖的重要基础，他的工作重点也同时要兼顾确保优质饲草供应，并因此参与建设了一个 2 万亩优质饲草种植项目。在短短 3 年间，该肉牛项目便在行业内异军突起，达到肉牛存栏 3000 头、年产优质饲草 2 万吨的规模，并在次年开始盈利。谈到这段历史，吕勇对于在美国辛普劳集团中国区财务总监这样的位置上，能够与业务如此深度地融合参与，并与合作伙伴们共同创造了出色的成果感到很自豪。虽然非常辛苦，条件也非常艰苦，但吕勇说那是他职业生涯中最愉快的时光之一。

此后，他并没有停止自己前进的脚步，在辛普劳工作 10 年后，他加入了福喜集团，从此进入了白羽鸡养殖屠宰和加工领域，并投身到肉制品深加工行业。吕勇和我们分享了当时发生的一件非常巧合的事情。他在福喜工作期间，去福喜美国工厂参观，当地团队跟他分享了他们工厂的生产研发人员是如何与设备供应商团队密切合作，不断提升生产效率，并帮助他们实现了许多创新和改进的目标。了解到这点的吕勇特别兴奋，因为这个问题恰恰涉及他在中国面临的一个核心痛点，即食品企业在面临新产品研发或重大结构性效率提升等问题时往往是在单打独斗，而他认为这一问题必须通过产业链合作的方式加以解决。那时作为合作伙伴的设备厂商恰恰就是马瑞奥，但是当时的吕勇并不了解，也没想到不久的将来他会与马瑞奥有更加紧密的联系。

“砥砺深耕，笃行致远”，吕勇用他近 20 年的从业经历对这句名言做了近乎完善的阐释。即使是在忙碌的工作中，他仍然持续提升自己的专业知识与能力，坚持在干中学，并以所学指导实践、推动工作。采访中，对于自己工作上的成就吕勇并未强调，但不难发现，“知行合一，脚踏实地”是他成功的秘籍，也是他人生最宝贵的财富。

勇立潮头，实践改革

“万丈高楼平地起。”同建造高楼一样，公司的发展同样需要夯实基础。同他之前的工作一样，吕勇入职马瑞奥集团的第一步，并未着手自己最感兴趣的食品加工产业链融合相关事宜，而是在分析马瑞奥的具体情况后，选择推动马瑞奥全球本地化进程，对公司之前收购的品牌 MPS 与施托克（STORK）在中国完成品牌整合，随之成立马瑞奥中国区。

跨国公司在治理方式上与我国现有的国有企业和民营企业有很大的差别。随着中国市场的壮大，跨国公司如何突破在华生存发展瓶颈成为令众多企业家头痛的问题。作为一名在跨国公司工作了近 20 年的管理者，吕勇告诉我们，跨国公司在华发展和竞争当中会遇到一些独特的问题和挑战。如何确保公司整体战略和标准的贯彻实施，同时还能够让总部的同事及时了解和接受当地市场和客户的所需所想，并及时做出调整改变，从而形成发展战略和行动的合力，是多数外企成功的关键，也是制约许多企业发展的重要因素。

“九层之台，起于累土。”吕勇的每一步都为马瑞奥在中国扎根奠定了良好的基础。在吕勇入职之前，马瑞奥中国区从属于亚太区，中国在马瑞奥的全球组织结构中并不是单独的区域。随着中冰两国经贸合作的深入，中国广阔的市场机遇以及不断改善的营商环境，让马瑞奥决定将中国设立为一个单独的区域，从亚太地区脱离出来。吕勇作为专业的管理人才，加入之初便致力于推动马瑞奥中国的本地化进程。在工作过程中，他发现马瑞奥收购的各个业务单元之间还存在着一定的分散性，组织架构[1]还可以进一步优化。同时，他也发现，马瑞奥作为一个跨国企业，其全球统一的政策制度框架和业务流程要求是十分明确的。于是，他将工作首要重点放到了增强内部的理解互信和沟通协作方面。由于许多外企的组织架构和决策流程复杂而低效，建立起有效的沟通和信任就显得尤为关键。良好的沟通可以显著提升组织决策的效率和质量，且在内部流程等框架恒定的情况下，充分的沟通和信任至关重要。

为了建立有效的沟通和信任渠道，吕勇提出在中国设立开放创新中心。首先，类似的中心在马瑞奥欧洲和美洲等市场已经具备很成熟的经验，大家对于建立这样一个中心认同和接受度都很高。其次，由于新冠肺炎疫情的影响，不管是马瑞奥（中国）内部还是总部同事跟中国客户之间的交流都受到了很大的影响。在这种不利情况下，如何把客户和市场的需求以及马瑞奥提供的解决方案进行具象化的表达呈现成为当下一个重要的问题。在思考解决方案的过程中，吕勇想到开放创新中心将成为一个最佳的载体。在他的推动下，总部将中心落地中国的时间提前了两年。

马瑞奥在中国开放创新中心的作用正如吕勇所讲到的，“是为马瑞奥在食品深加工领域的下一步规模化发展做好充分的准备”。首先，在自动化、数字化、智能化的食品加工领域，特别是肉制品加工领域，马瑞奥将通过开放创新中心展示马瑞奥在食品加工领域的最先进的技术、多方面的解决方案和深入的行业知识。其次，在食品加工领域，不断创新对于食品企业的成功是至关重要的，马瑞奥希望成为食品加工企业在创新方面的合作伙伴，把这个中心发展成为一个共创平台。通过这个平台向客户展示马瑞奥在创新方面的成功故事，特别是在全球其他地区和市场的成功故事，帮助食品企业做好研发和创新。最后，在食品安全、可持续发展和供应链整合等方面，马瑞奥也希望能给客户带来益处，介绍马瑞奥以及行业领先的相关企业在这些方面的最佳实践，如马瑞奥的设备清洁设计理念、预防性维护保养的重要性、食品安全的过程控制、整个产业链的食品安全协作等。

---

① 组织架构（Organizational Structure）：是指一个组织整体的结构，是在企业管理要求、管控定位、管理模式及业务特征等多因素影响下，在企业内部组织资源、搭建流程、开展业务、落实管理的基本要素。就像人体有其基本骨架一样，任何组织都在相当程度上需要有某种架构形式来对组织任务加以分化和整合。有了清晰的组织架构，企业中的各个管理职能才能有效地发挥应有的作用。

2021年是中冰两国建交50周年，马瑞奥中国区在吕勇的推动下，于2021年5月底在上海闵行区莘庄工业区确认投资意向并启动注册事宜。2021年8月，马瑞奥食品科技（上海）有限公司成立。同年11月，马瑞奥中国开放创新中心在上海建成并开业。这意味着马瑞奥扎根中国，开始进入新的创新阶段。

现任冰岛驻华大使易卜雷先生（Thorir Ibsen）（左三）和马瑞奥高层共同出席马瑞奥中国开放创新中心启动仪式

马瑞奥中国区的成立进一步深化了中国与冰岛的合作。作为冰岛在华代表企业，马瑞奥在华跨世纪的发展历程见证了中国肉制品加工产业的变化，并在此过程中也发挥了其积极的作用。正如吕勇所说："马瑞奥在华的几十年，是中冰两国经贸关系发展的成果，也可以说是冰岛企业在华发展的成功典范。"

当吕勇被问到为何加入马瑞奥时，他回答："我在2019年加入马瑞奥，就是看准了马瑞奥清晰准确的战略，以及它支持和服务食品产业的这一定位。"马瑞奥是食品行业中的重要成员，而其所处的位置又非常独特。相较于其他经济体，冰岛位置、资源、文化等特点相对突出。中国和冰岛两国关系友好，近年来在人员、商务和投资往来方面蓬勃发展。作为冰岛重要企业的代表，马瑞奥集团主要生产和研发基地遍布欧洲大陆，自从1983年成立发展至今，已经成为全球食品加工设备制造及智能化系统应用领域的行业领导者。马瑞奥中国区也特别希望在业务不断发展进步的同时，也能够为中冰两国友好关系的发展积极贡献力量。

创新突破，未来可期

在新冠肺炎疫情全球暴发大环境下，人们的消费习惯和饮食习惯发生了改变，加速了产业链的变革，整个行业都面临巨大的挑战。吕勇曾在行业高峰论坛上的演讲中引用过管理学大师彼得·德鲁克的一句话——“预测未来的最好方式是创造它”。

创新是引领新时代发展的第一动力。由于疫情的原因，目前很多欧洲的服务工程师不能进入中国更好地为中国客户提供服务，在这种情况下，亟须加速培训本土工程师，提高本土工程师的技术能力，以及利用远程技术连线欧洲的专家，为中国客户提供实时的支持。这更加凸显了数字技术、大数据和人工智能在食品行业发展中的重要性。2021 年，在吕勇的推动下，在上海建立的马瑞奥中国开放创新中心配备了 VR 演示和模拟技术。该体验中心的设立，着眼点在于更加贴近中国快速发展的深加工行业，以中国开放创新中心为窗口，向业内企业展示马瑞奥的设备能力。通过 VR 演示，参观者可以身临其境地体验马瑞奥加工解决方案的各种应用场景。未来，为了向客户提供深度体验、合作研发等服务，开放创新体验中心还会引进一些先进的设备，面向中国的客户进行展示和演示，以及开展培训、交流和共同研发新品等工作。此外，创新体验中心将坚持以市场为导向的创新，为食品加工企业和餐饮零售企业的客户提供更好的服务。

易卜雷大使在马瑞奥中国开放创新中心启动仪式上发言

提高发展质量是新时代势所必然的。吕勇在充分认识到中国市场及中国加工行业规模不断扩大的同时，对发展质量的要求也在不断提升。中国市场对自动化、智能化和数字化的需求在不断深化，而这些变化也带来了一系列的具有历史意义的重大市场发展机遇。吕勇指出，目前马瑞奥的产品和解决方案大部分是基于欧洲客户的需求设计的，并不是100%适合中国市场，需要针对中国客户的需求进行调整，因此在推进本土化的方面还有待提高和加速。

虽然未来充满了不确定性，但在不确定中所蕴含的机遇也是清晰可见的。来自多方的因素与变化都会促使新的消费习惯与消费方式产生。这就要求行业中的企业家要准确地、迅速地在市场汹涌的浪潮中把握住航行的方向，通过产品、模式、加工方式等方面的创新，主动出击，迎接未来的挑战。

吕勇表示，马瑞奥在中国的规划将持续进行，深入了解市场，理解中国客户的需求，并为中国客户、中国市场提供更符合需求的解决方案。通过助力客户业务的增长，来实现马瑞奥自身业务的进步。对于吕勇的管理团队而言，他们将与马瑞奥一起，在相对复杂的环境中简化过程，提高沟通的质量和效率，把更多的时间和精力真正聚焦于客户和市场的需求，从而让整个企业能够迅速地对外部的需求和变化做出反应，提升客户体验和价值。在吕勇看来，中国是世界上最有活力的市场之一，广阔的市场机遇和不断改善的营商环境一直吸引着来自不同地区的投资。马瑞奥中国区的成立，可以让公司直观地感受到市场变化，便捷地和客户沟通，及时地响应客户的需求，从而让马瑞奥更高效地服务于中国市场。

吕勇（左五）携马瑞奥代表团与易卜雷大使（左六）共同出席2021中国国际渔业博览会

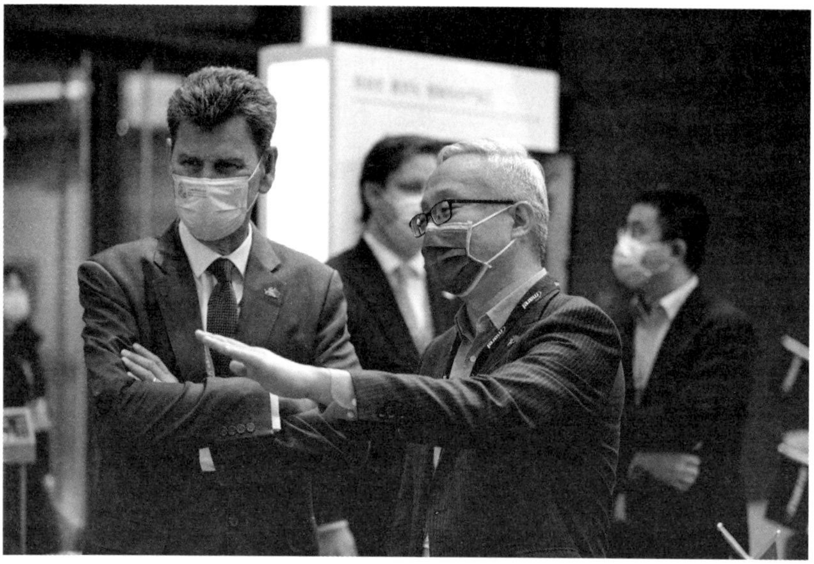

中国国际渔业博览会上吕勇（前排右一）为易卜雷大使（前排左一）做介绍

采访最后，吕勇简单分享了企业发展为中冰两国友好交往所提供的帮助。“时光飞逝，中国改革开放已经过了40多个年头，在华冰岛企业也再次面临着新的发展机遇和挑战。我们对中国市场充满信心！同时，我们坚信，像马瑞奥这样的企业，会随着在中国的投资发展不断成长壮大，并为中国经济发展和社会进步持续贡献不可或缺的力量。”

立足现在，放眼未来，在吕勇的心中，马瑞奥中国区的战略及未来的方向已然胸有成竹。

（刘昊蓉　王楚）

Lifelong Learning for the Unity of Knowledge and Practice

— Interview with Denver Lyu, Regional Managing Director of Marel China

Confucius said, "Learn and unceasingly." Denver Lyu, Regional Managing Director of Marel China, recalled his working experience, and what he felt the most is "Learning is normal."

In this era of knowledge and information explosion, lifelong learning has become the slogan of many people, but only few people can stick to it. Denver has been working in the food industry for nearly 20 years. Taking the initiative to learn relevant knowledge and understand the frontier of industry dynamic has become his working habit. In this era of rapid changes, every one of them is full of freshness, Denver saw the future of the food industry through continuous learning. This is probably why he has consistently maintained his interest in food processing, his love of the industry and his sensitivity to innovative technology in the food industry. On the occasion of the 50th anniversary of the establishment of diplomatic relations between China and Iceland, Denver, the Regional Managing Director of Marel China, accepted our interview in writing in his busy schedule. Between the lines, we deeply felt his preciseness and seriousness.

The More You Like It, the More Skillful You Are

Denver Lyu

Carnegie once said, "where are you interested in, that is, where you can." People who can devote themselves to the industries they are interested in are lucky. This is the case with Denver Lyu. Although he has not majored in agriculture or food, he is always interested in planting plants, breeding animals, and how food can be continuously developed and innovated through technological and industrial means. At the same time, he will learn relevant knowledge in his spare time, improve his professional ability, complete every task carefully and meticulously to do his jobs well, which also lays a solid foundation for his subsequent career promotion.

Marel Townsend Futher Processing B. V. is a global manufacturer of high-end processing equipment for meat products with headquarters in Iceland. Its equipment and solutions cover industries such as red meat, poultry and aquatic products. Applications cover primary processing, secondary processing, further processing and production of consumer end products; the advanced digital technology is used to ensure the transparency of the production process and efficiency and traceability from source to shelf. By understanding Marel's business scope and equipment production capacity, Denver sees the industrial chain integration mode that caters to the needs of the times, promotes the industry upgrading needs and efficiently meets the needs of customers, which is the direction he is exactly interested in.

To be an excellent entrepreneur, you must have a mature thinking system, a far-sighted strategic thinking ability and a decisive decision-making ability. Worked in the food industry, Denver is full of enthusiasm and curiosity for the whole industry, and has learned and understood the food industry knowledge such as plant cultivation, animal breeding, agricultural and sideline products processing, etc. He did not limit his vision to the cultivation and processing of raw materials, but thought deeply about how to meet the needs of customers. How to reduce costs and improve efficiency? How to optimize the production line by technological and industrial means in the process of production and processing, etc. combined with his years of experience. The more he thinks about it deeply and understands it widely, the more he is interested in this industry. After joining Marel, his interest fully matched with Marel's strategy, so Denver began to promote his industrial chain integration mode in Marel.

During the interview, we learned that the industrial chain integration mode promoted by Denver has already enabled Marel to realize automation, intellectualization and digitalization in equipment production. High-tech production lines and advanced digital platforms have been integrated into their intelligent food processing solutions.

The choice between interest and career is the focus topic among many people now. Interest can follow your heart, but a career can't. Denver combined his interest with his career, and was full of curiosity about the industry and did not put limits on what he can do, explored and broke through constantly and thought about the industry deeply. He laid a solid foundation for his career with his responsibility, preciseness, efforts, planning and other "bricks and tiles". In this process, he witnessed the changes of China's food processing industry from primary level to mature level, from decentralization to centralization, from manual to automation, from labor-intensive to artificial intelligence, etc. In addition, he also contributed to the positive changes in the food industry.

Strive Forward and Walk the Talk

In addition to the interest, working in an industry for nearly twenty years or more has also become a habit of finishing what you start, constantly improving and challenging himself. Denver, a financial professional, has striven forward and deeply explored in the food industry from potato planting to deep processing of meat products. He has gained more experience and insights in the whole process.

Learning from the most basic work has become a working practice of Denver. For any job, Denver will understand and learn the most basic link of the job first. At the beginning of entering the food industry, he worked in Simplot Group, the leading potato processing company in the United States. At that time, his ultimate work goal was very simple, that is, providing customers with high-quality and efficient potato chips and cakes. It seems that these problems are not hard, but it is necessary to comprehensively analyze breeding, planting, harvesting, storage, processing, inventory, etc. At the same time, he shall combine with multiple factors in the industrial chain, such as store opening speed of customers, business layout, new product research and development, market fluctuation and so on. Finally, he helps and guides companies and customers to make the best decisions, all of which requires great patience and comprehensive analysis and management ability of the whole industrial chain. After analyzing the work contents, Denver realized the importance of potato planting — the front processing link. Then he took time to learn and understand the specific process of potato planting, harvesting, storage and processing as well as the pains and difficulties. He began to learn and understand from the most basic and front-link contents, and then conducted deep analysis, finally quantitatively analyzed and supported the problems and decision-making process by building financial and business models.

Hereafter, his work in Simplot has been transferred to the beef cattle breeding project, with the goal of building a large-scale beef cattle breeding population from scratch, and constantly improving the breeding efficiency and output rate. Despite he is a financial professional, he did not hesitate to study, understand and master all links of cultivation. The selection of calves, the importance of colostrum, the proportion of fodder, biosafety protection, epidemic disease treatment, and learning in the front line have become his daily management work. As an important foundation of beef cattle breeding, he also focused on ensuring the supply of high-quality forage grass at the same time, so he participated in the construction of a 20,000 mu high-quality forage grass planting project. In just three years, the beef cattle project has risen suddenly in the industry, reaching the scale of 3,000 beef cattle with an annual output of 20,000 tons of high-quality forage grass, and began to make profits in the following year. Speaking of this period of history, Denver is still very proud of being fully participated with the business as the Chief Financial Director of Simplot Group, and creating outstanding achievements with his partners. Although it was very hard and the conditions were very difficult, Denver said that it was one of the enjoyable times in his career.

He hasn't stopped racing ahead. After working in Simplot for ten years, he joined OSI Group. Since then, he has engaged in the field of breeding, slaughtering and processing of white feather chickens and devoted himself to the deep processing of meat products. Denver shared with us a coincidence that happened at that time. When he worked at OSI, he visited OSI factory in the United States, and the local team shared with him how the R&D personnel in their factory worked closely with the equipment supplier team to continuously improve the production efficiency and help them achieve many innovation and improvement goals. After visiting and understanding, Denver was particularly excited, because this problem just related to a core pain point he faced in China, that is, when food enterprises faced with problems such as new product research and development or major structural efficiency improvement, they were always fighting alone; he thought that this problem must be solved through industrial chain cooperation mode. At that time, the equipment manufacturer as a partner was Marel, but Denver didn't know it at that time, and he didn't expect that he would have closer contact with Marel in the near future.

"Strive forward and walk the talk", Mr. Lyu fulfilled this famous saying perfectly with his nearly twenty years' working experience. Even if he is busy with work, he continued to improve his professional knowledge and ability, persisted in learning by doing, guided practice and promoted work with what he had learned. During the interview, Mr. Denver didn't emphasize his achievements in his work, but it's not difficult to find that "walk the talk, work hard step by step" is the secret of his success and the most precious wealth of his life.

Keep Pace with the Times and Fulfill the Reformation

Great oaks from little acorns grow. Just like building tall buildings, the development of the company shall also lay a solid foundation. As before, Denver did not focus on the integration of the food processing industry chain that he was most interested in after joining Marel. Instead, after analyzing the specific situation of Marel, he chose to promote the global localization process of Marel, completed the brand integration of MPS and STORK previously acquired in China, and then set up Marel China.

Transnational companies are quite different from the existing state-owned enterprises and private enterprises in China in governance way. With the growth of the Chinese market, how to break through the bottleneck of survival and development in China has become a bugbear for many entrepreneurs. As a manager who has worked in multinational companies for nearly 20 years, Denver told us that multinational companies will encounter some unique problems and challenges in development and competition in China. How to ensure the implementation of the company's overall strategy and standards, while also allowing the colleagues at headquarters to understand and accept the needs and thoughts of the local market and customers in a timely manner, and make timely adjustments and changes to form a synergy of development strategies and actions, it is the key to the success of most foreign companies and an important factor restricting the development of many companies.

A nine-story platform starts from the base soil. Each step of Denver has laid a solid foundation for Marel to take root in China. Before Denver joined Marel, Marel China belonged to the Asia-Pacific region and China was not a separate region in Marel's global organizational structure. With the deepening of China-Iceland economic and trade cooperation, broad market opportunities in China and the improvement of business environment, Marel decided to set up China as a separate region and separate from the Asia-Pacific region. Denver, as a professional management personnel, was committed to promoting the localization process of Marel China from the beginning of joining. In the course of his work, he found that the various business units acquired by Marel are still scattered to some extent, and the organizational structure can be further optimized. On the other hand, he also found that Marel, as a multinational enterprise, shall have a clear global unified policy system framework and business processes requirements. Therefore, he first focused on enhancing internal understanding, mutual trust and communication and cooperation. As the organizational structure[①] and decision-making process of many foreign enterprises are complex and inefficient, it is particularly critical to establish effective communication and trust. Good communication can significantly improve the efficiency and quality of organizational decision-making, and adequate communication and trust are crucial in conditions where frameworks such as internal process are constant.

In order to establish effective communication and trust channels, Denver proposed to set up Shanghai Progress Point in China. First of all, Marel has very mature experience in markets such as Europe and America in such aspect, so everyone has high recognition and acceptance for the establishment of Shanghai Progress Point. Secondly, due to the impact of COVID-19, the communication within Marel (China) and between colleagues in the headquarters and Chinese customers has been greatly affected. How to visualize the demands of customers and markets and the solutions provided by Marel in this unfavorable situation becomes an important issue at present. When considering the solution, Denver thought that

---

① Organizational structure: refers to the overall structure of an organization. It is the basic element for organizing resources, building processes, developing business and implementing management within an enterprise under the influence of many factors such as enterprise management requirements, management and control positioning, management mode and business characteristics. Just as the human body has its basic skeleton, any organization needs some kind of structure to differentiate and integrate organizational tasks to a considerable extent. With a clear organizational structure, each management function in an enterprise can effectively play its due role.

the Progress Point would be the best carrier. With Denver's unremitting efforts, the headquarters advanced the establishment time for the Progress Point in China by two years.

As Denver said, the role of Marel in Shanghai Progress Point is "to make full preparations for the next large-scale development of Marel in the food deep processing field". First of all, in automatic, digital and intelligent food processing, especially in the meat processing industry, through Progress Point, Marel will showcase its state-of-the-art technology, multi-faceted solutions and in-depth industry knowledge in food processing. Secondly, continuous innovation is crucial to the success of food enterprises in the field of food processing. Marel hopes to become a partner in innovation for food processing enterprises and develop the center into a co-creation platform. Through this platform, the success stories of Marel shown to the customers in innovation, especially those in other regions and markets around the world, can help food enterprises do a good job in R&D and innovation. Finally, in areas such as food safety, sustainable development and supply chain integration, Marel also wants to benefit customers. The best practices of Marel and industry-leading enterprises in these areas will be introduced, such as the design concept of Marel equipment cleaning, the importance of preventive maintenance, process control for food safety, and collaboration on food safety throughout the industrial chain.

The year 2021 marks the 50th anniversary of the establishment of diplomatic relations between China and Iceland. Driven by Denver, Marel Shanghai confirmed its investment intention and started registration at the end of May in Xinzhuang Industrial Park, Minhang District, Shanghai. In August 2021, Marel Food Technology (Shanghai) Co., Ltd. was established. In November of the same year, the Shanghai Progress Point was completed and launched in Shanghai. This means that Marel has taken root in China and started to enter a new stage of innovation.

The establishment of Marel China has further deepened the cooperation between China and Iceland. As Iceland's representative enterprise in China, Marel's cross-century development in China has witnessed the changes of China's meat processing industry and played an active role in this process. As Denver said, "The past decades in China are the fruit of the development of economic and trade relations between China and Iceland, which can also be considered a successful model for the development of Icelandic enterprises in China."

When Denver was asked about why he joined Marel, he answered, "I joined Marel in 2019 because of its clear and precise strategy and its position to support and serve the food industry." Marel is an important member in the food industry, and its position is very unique. Compared with other economies, Iceland's location, resources, culture and other characteristics are relatively prominent. China and Iceland enjoy friendly relations, with personnel, business and investment exchanges developing vigorously in recent years. As the representative of an important Icelandic enterprise, the main production and R&D bases of Marel are located throughout the European continent, and it has become a global industry leader in the field of food processing equipment manufacturing and intelligent system application since its establishment in 1983. Marel China also hopes to make more contributions to the development of friendly relations between China and Iceland while developing its business continuously.

Innovation Breakthroughs and Making New Future

In the context of the global outbreak of the COVID-19 epidemic, people's consumption habits and eating habits have changed, accelerating the transformation of the industrial chain, and the whole industry is facing enormous challenges. "The best way to predict the future is to create it", Mr. Denver once quoted Peter F. Drucker, a master of management, as saying in his speech at the industry summit.

Innovation is the first driving force to lead the development of a new era. Many European service engineers cannot come to China at present to serve Chinese customers due to the COVID-19 epidemic. In this case, it is urgent to train local engineers, improve their technical ability and take advantage of remote technology to contact European experts to assist Chinese customers in real-time. This highlights the importance of digital technology, big data and AI in the development of the food industry. In 2021, Shanghai Progress Point has been deployed with VR demonstration and simulation technology thanks to Denver's unremitting efforts. Shanghai Progress Point focuses on being closer to China's fast-growing deep processing industry and demonstrates the capabilities of Marel's equipment to the industry as a window. Visitors can experience various application scenarios of Marel processing solutions through VR demonstration. In the future, Shanghai Progress Point will also introduce some advanced equipment, show and demonstrate to Chinese customers, and carry out training, exchange and joint R&D of new products, so as to provide customers with in-depth experience, cooperative R&D and other services. In addition, Shanghai Progress Point will adhere to market-oriented innovation to provide better services for customers of food processing enterprises and catering retail enterprises.

Improving the quality of development is inevitable in the new era. Denver is fully aware of the continuous expansion of the Chinese market and the scale of China's processing industry. At the same time, the requirements for the development quality are constantly improving. The demand for automation, intelligence and digitization in the Chinese market is deepening, and these changes have also brought a series of historic and significant market development opportunities. Denver pointed out that most of Marel's products and solutions are designed based on the needs of European customers at present, not 100% suitable for the Chinese market; therefore, such products and solutions should be adjusted according to the needs of Chinese customers, and the localization should be improved in the future.

Although the future is full of uncertainty, the opportunities thereupon are also clearly visible. Various factors and changes will promote new consumption habits and consumption patterns. This requires entrepreneurs in the industry to accurately and quickly grasp the direction of navigation in the turbulent market, and take the initiative to meet future challenges through innovation in products, models, processing methods and other aspects.

Denver said that Marel's planning in China would continue to deeply understand the market and the needs of Chinese customers, and provide more suitable solutions for Chinese customers and the Chinese market. By helping the growth of customer business, Marel can realize the progress of its own business. Denver's management team will work with Marel to simplify the process in a relatively complicated environment, improve the quality and efficiency of communication, and focus more time and energy on the needs of customers and the market, so that the whole enterprise can quickly respond to external needs and changes and enhance customer experience and value. In Denver's opinion, China is one of the most dynamic markets in the world, and its broad market opportunities and improving business environment have always attracted investors from different regions. The establishment of Marel China enables us to intuitively feel the market changes, communicate with customers conveniently and respond to customers' needs in time, so as to make Marel serve the Chinese market more efficiently.

In the end, Denver briefly shared the benefits brought by enterprise development for the friendly exchanges between China and Iceland. "As time flies, China has been developed more than 40 years since the reform and opening-up, and Icelandic enterprises in China are once again facing new development opportunities and challenges. We have full confidence in the Chinese market! At the same time, we firmly believe that enterprises like Marel will continue to grow with the development of investment in China, and make indispensable contributions to economic development and social progress in China."

Based on the present and looking forward to the future, the strategy and future direction of Marel China are already well-planned in Denver's mind.

(Liu Haorong Wang Chu)

11

去了解，去信任，去尊重

——访威定海鲜贸易有限公司首席执行官 Biggi Stefansson

“海内存知己，天涯若比邻。”放眼世界，相信 Biggi 一定算得上是这样一位中国的知心好友。Biggi，全名 Biggi Stefansson，是一位来自北欧的杰出企业家。他是威定海鲜贸易公司的创始人兼首席执行官、中国冰岛企业家论坛首席负责人。

作为一位成功的海鲜贸易企业家，时至今日，Biggi 已经深耕中国市场十余年。多年来，他在掌管威定海鲜的相关贸易事务之余，还积极推动中冰民间友好往来，为中冰的民间外交发展发挥了独特作用，做出了积极贡献。Biggi 融合中冰文化，为自己设计了一个独特的中文名字——彭嘉锐。

从 8 岁那年的工作说起
（了解我们需要做什么）

Biggi 出生于冰岛最北端一个只有 1200 人的小渔镇。在 Biggi 年幼时，他的父亲就是一名船长，而他子承父业，在 20 岁时便取得了船长的资格认证。同时，他的祖父也曾掌管过中国渔船，三代人辛劳不辍，传承家业至今。

受家庭环境的影响，与我们大多数人不同，Biggi 的工作生涯开始得很早：“8 岁那年，我意识到我的父母有很重的经济压力，于是我开始向人们分发传单来赚钱，我不想成为他们的负担。所以他们不用担心我，也不用费心思讨论关于我的事。”

在 14 岁那年，年少的 Biggi 跟着他的父亲上了渔船，为他第一阶段的渔业生涯拉开了序幕。“你无法想象那是一个 14 岁小孩子正在做的事，那时候我每天工作 18 个小时，休息 6 个小时，这意味着我每天最多可以睡 5 个小时。”渔船上的工作强度是十分高的，不间断的工作几乎充满了当时仅 14 岁的 Biggi 的日常生活，他甚至几乎没有任何闲暇时间与精力去思考如何玩耍，但也带给了他一些独特的“财富”：“你会了解钱是怎么来的，你投入这么多精力去努力工作，就能得到这么多钱。所以，我认为它（工作）是一所很好的‘学校’，而且是极其重要的。”

也许这也正是现在很多年轻后辈所欠缺的。大多数 20 岁以下的中国年轻人除了上学几乎从未工作过，有的学生在寒暑假奔走于各处补习班。中国的年轻人应该去了解钱从何而来，他们需要去做些什么。

“也许你会问我是否后悔，我考虑了一下，也许我确实曾错失一个可以再多做一会儿天真无邪的孩子的机会，尽管如此，我想我仍然有一个美好的童年。”Biggi 说。

后来我决定做自己真正理解的事（了解自己真实的位置）

年轻的时候，也许我们每个人都说过“我想要干出一番大事业，向所有大人们证明，我是可以的！”“我想要做一个独一无二的创新，只有我自己能想到的，震惊所有人！”

初次创业时，Biggi 也曾意气风发：“我记得我之前告诉过你，我想做一些和我家人完全不同的事情，和我第一次来中国时完全不同的事情。但后来我了解到，由于我的家庭数代从事渔业并拥有自己的渔船，我在销售海鲜上拥有独特的比较优势。”Biggi 在工作中渐渐了解到，想在中国市场生存，仅仅靠着一时的意气风发是远远不够的，进入中国的市场太需要竞争力了。后来，他开始找寻自己真实的位置。“如果你想要开始创业，你需要明白：你在这个行业有发展的空间吗？是你的服务还是你的产品让你更具有竞争力？”“你会喜欢你所从事的行业吗？这是你热衷的事情吗？如果你没有去做这件事的热情，你为什么要去做？”

Biggi 与他的海鲜

《道德经》上说：“知人者智，自知者明；胜人者有力，自胜者强。”当下，创业在年轻一代中仍然颇为流行。“趁着年轻，有资本，去干出些属于我自己的事业”是一代代年轻创业人们心中不变的信念。然而，人们在决定创业、准备去了解并进入一个行业市场之前，必须认真去思考这些问题：我的核心竞争力从何而来？这就是我所热衷的事情吗？我真的喜欢这个行业吗？我了解自己在这里真实的位置吗？Biggi 在采访中提到：去思考我为什么要做？我有竞争力吗？我真的喜欢吗？这是他对年轻创业者的真切建议，对于每一个即将踏入社会的年轻人来说，也许都值得去认真思考。年少时，Biggi 思考了其真实的定位，他决定做他真正最擅长的事，也是他真正想做的事。

“我做得最好的决定是做一些我真正理解的事情，所以我最后选择回归了海鲜市场，但我并不后悔，中国是全世界竞争最激烈的市场，我想在这里生存下去。”

Biggi 眼中的人际关系（了解身边的人）

当我们讨论中国的商业市场时，总免不了涉及“关系”。长久以来，错综复杂的人际关系成了中国经贸的一大关键词。Biggi 在采访中不例外地也提到了这一点。“你知道，在中国，有一件事很重要，叫作关系，你需要与人建立人际关系。我们公司曾经有一个美国销售人员，他每天都要参加 20 个会议。在美国，他是一个非常好的销售员，但在中国，他却是一个非常糟糕的销售员。”

中国人总是在贸易双方有了一定了解之后，才会讨论商务合作，这与国外的商人有些不同。一些外国商务人士会认为建立关系费时费力，枯燥而又低效。“我告诉那个美国销售员：放轻松，尝试去与他们沟通，去了解他们，和他们一起喝茶、聊天，建立关系，这需要很长时间。”“我们在做生意之前总要相互了解一下，大家都不喜欢过来打个招呼然后就直接谈生意，那样我们对彼此都没有了解。”为了相互了解，在中国有时需要花上几个小时喝茶、聊天，然后再花一点时间来决定是否合作。诚然，这看上去似乎十分不合理，但这又是十分值得的。在中国，合作关系往往不仅仅是合作关系。

中国社会是一个集体社会，是一个互帮互助的社会，“有什么能帮助的，不用客气”“多个朋友多条路”是不少中国人常挂在嘴边的话。中国人相信，团结就是力量，整体大于部分之和；一个人的力量是有限的，集体的力量是无穷的。因而，在挑选合作伙伴上花费更多的时间，有着更高的社交成本，这是社会环境使然。在成为优秀人才的路上，人们需要学习如何去了解他人、如何服从团队的安排、如何更好地与他人协作。相互协作使人们能更高效地做更多的事情，往往比一个人能完成的快得多，也多得多。

没有他们我什么都做不了
（信任并尊重伙伴们）

“我看到中国这里的生活一直在改善，那是因为在中国，人们都在一条船上，他们都想让这个国家的一切变得更好。”Biggi 见证了中国近 20 年来的飞速发展，并深深体会到中国人团结一心的强大力量。在 Biggi 自己的企业中也实施了类似的管理方针，试图让他的员工与他有共同的目标，团结一心。“在我的公司，我信任我的员工，我不在乎你什么时候来办公室，也不在乎你什么时候回家。如果你生病了，你可以请假，我只是信任你。”

Biggi 认为，与员工建立相互信任是成功管理的关键因素，足够的信任与尊重能让员工时刻保持做事的激情，为公司的发展竭尽全力，员工将成为和他在同一条大船上的伙伴，向着共同的目标前进。“我们公司有一个信任的环境，我会用心来告诉你，在我们公司你能够做得更好，你当然也会得到更多。而当你在我的公司开始工作，我会想着如何帮你创造一条晋升的路，你只需要负责去做得更好，做得更好，以及做得更好。”

Biggi 给予他的员工足够的信任与足够的尊重，带动他们一起热爱他们的工作和公司。在这家公司中，员工不用被琐事影响。“如果你有急事了，我不需要知道真正发生了什么，那是你的私生活，我信任你。比如你的父母来上海了，我理解你需要时间和你的家人在一起，我会让你去休息一天。我知道我必须给你一些自由，我不会让你成为另一个永远在电话那头的家人”。

卡尔·罗杰斯心理理论中提到，被积极关注的给予充分信任与尊重的人们将更能深刻地领会到自身的价值，他们更能漫无拘束地发挥出自己的无限潜能，有着更高的工作效率。这在 Biggi 的企业中体现得淋漓尽致。员工们只需要考虑如何在有限的时间工作得更努力一些，让整个公司团队变得更好一些，他们可以尽情地发挥他们的创意，去思考问题的解决方案，信任与尊重解放了他们的潜能，释放了他们的能量，也提高了他们的工作效率。

"我信任并重视我的每一个员工，没有我的员工我什么都做不了，这要感谢他们付出的辛勤劳动。"Biggi 在采访中一再强调。

疫情中的威定海鲜
（做个值得被信任的人）

当谈到疫情对公司贸易造成的影响时，Biggi 眉头紧锁："新冠肺炎疫情期间，海洋运输变得十分艰难。因为中国国内正专注于阻止病毒的传播，所以进口商品现在变得十分困难，产品很难进入国内，我很担忧运输人员能否会好好地对待这些产品。"

和众多企业一样，威定海鲜在疫情中也遇到了很大的麻烦，例如进关的严格审查，以及国际运输的重重障碍。这些曾经并不起眼的问题现如今都变成了负担，重重地压在了 Biggi 身上。但幸运的是，疫情的到来给 Biggi 关上了一扇门，却在别处为他打开了一扇窗。"事实上，我认为我们从未有过比这更好的机会去向个人家庭销售海鲜并与想吃健康食品的人做生意了。"当对健康的威胁步步紧逼时，人们终于意识到提升日常健康意识的重要性，越来越多的人开始关注食品健康。毕竟，健康饮食可以带来更好的免疫力，更好地对抗强大的病毒。"我们是一家信誉很好、诚实守信的公司，产品质量也一直很优秀。我们有自己的故事去告诉人们鱼从哪里来，是怎么处理的，这些都是公开透明的，所以人们愿意相信我们。现在，他们更加注重健康，也知道我们的海鲜对健康有益，所以产生了更多的需求，而我的公司正在努力抓住这个机会。"一直以来积攒的信誉优势，在疫情期间以一种意想不到的方式为威定海鲜带来了额外的红利，Biggi 抓准了时机，成功帮助公司在疫情中止损并获利。

不止如此，Biggi 在疫情期间还额外帮助了一些他的老朋友们。"2020 年，我给我的一些客户们一年的时间来筹钱归还欠款，因为我想帮助他们度过最艰难的时期，他们会记得在这最艰难的时候，我们在他们身边。在你用心与别人合作的过程中，你也许会损失一些钱，但赢得了人心。"正如采访中 Biggi 所说的，那些被帮助的人会回想起在最艰难的时候有人帮助过他们，他们明白 Biggi 是位值得信任与尊重的合作伙伴。也许在当下看来，Biggi 损失了一些利益，但放眼未来，相信 Biggi 会收获更多的合作者，得到更多的回报，交到更多可以信赖的朋友，尤其在中国，这是非常值得的。

获得 FHC 烹饪艺术大赛委员会主席朱一帆授予的中国最佳海鲜食品奖

见证中国的发展与转变（信任我们的国家）

过去 20 年，中国的发展与转变是巨大的，工人平均工资涨了 10 倍有余。现在，中国人可以去想、去做自己想做的事。尽管有时还会因为找不到工作岗位而辗转反侧。但人们不再会因为战争而流离失所，也极少因为要补贴家用而辍学打工。不容置疑，一切都在慢慢地变得更好。令人兴奋的是，许多在华的外国企业家都一路见证并高度赞赏中国这些年来的飞速发展和巨大变化，Biggi 也是如此。“是的，我见证了在过去 17 年里这个国家巨大的发展，一切都变得那么的干净，一切都很安全，交通也很便利。中国人来自同一个团队，为同一个国家以及人民的利益而工作。”Biggi 十分赞赏中国十余年来的管理进步，他非常关注中国市场，并且表示，在未来中国百分之百会是威定海鲜公司的主要市场。“我为现在我们两国之间的实际关系感到自豪和感激。当我在中国的任何地方告诉人们我是一个冰岛人时，大家都会知道冰岛，知道冰岛是一个好国家。在这个大国几乎每个人都知道我们这样一个小国。”

采访最后，Biggi 谈到冰岛是第一个与中国达成自由贸易协定的欧洲国家。他真切希望冰岛与中国有更多的交流沟通，可以更多地互相理解，互相学习，成为更好的朋友。“我们将继续在中国发展我们的公司，讲述更好的故事，提供更好的服务。”

中冰建交至今已有 50 年之久。1971 年中冰建交时，中国正值百废待兴之际，冰岛也正处于发展初期。50 年时过境迁，中冰两国的发展至今已与往昔大不相同。中国经济飞速发展，成为世界第二大经济体，冰岛也逐渐发展经济多元化，旅游业飞速发展，成为人类幸福指数排名第四的国家。在当下世界经济全球化的发展趋势下，相信中国与冰岛两国一定能拥有美好的发展未来，成为越发亲密的、全方位的合作伙伴。

Biggi 作为已经来到中国 17 年之久的外国企业家，深谙中国市场中的处世之道，是有着强大经营管理实力、名副其实的优秀企业家，是年轻一代经营管理人的学习偶像。衷心祝愿 Biggi 及他的威定海鲜公司战胜新冠肺炎疫情的负面影响，达成他的美好夙愿，在中国讲述属于他的更为精彩的故事。

（黄梓杰　麻中怡　牛晓梦）

Understanding, Trusting and Respecting

— Interview with Biggi Stefansson, CEO of IS Seafood

"Long distance separates no bosom friends." I believe Mr. Biggi must be such a bosom friend of China worldwide. Mr. Biggi, named Biggi Stefansson in full, is a talent entrepreneur from Iceland in Nordic Europe. He is the founder and CEO of IS Seafood Trading (Shanghai) Co., Ltd., and the Chairman of Icelandic Business Forum in China.

As a successful seafood trade entrepreneur, Mr. Biggi has been dedicated himself to the Chinese market for more than 10 years. Over the years, in addition to being in charge of relevant trading affairs of IS Seafood, he has actively promoted the China-Iceland friendly people-to-people exchanges, playing a unique role and making positive contributions to the development of China-Iceland people-to-people diplomacy. Based on China-Iceland culture integration, Biggi designed a unique Chinese name for himself — Peng Jiarui.

Starting with My Job at the Age of Eight (Knowing What We Need to Do)

Mr. Biggi was born in a small fishing town of 1,200 people in the northernmost of Iceland. His father was a captain and Biggi himself became fully qualified captain on the age of 20. At that time, his great grandfather was the captain of a Chinese fishing boat. Biggi and his father inherited this family business and kept working on it.

Under the influence of family, different from most of us, Biggi started work very early: "When I was eight years old, I realized that my parents were under heavy economic pressure, so I began to make money by distributing leaflets to people, and I didn't want to be a burden on them. So they didn't have to worry about me or bother discussing things about me."

At the age of 14, the little Biggi got in the fishing boat following his father, which kicked off his fishing career in the first stage. "You cannot imagine that's what a 14-year-old kid is doing. At that time, I worked 18h and rest 6h a day. That is to say, I could sleep for a maximum of 5h a day." The work on the fishing boat was highly intense, and the uninterrupted work was almost full of the daily life of the little Biggi who was just 14 years old at that time, so he hardly had any spare time and energy to even think about how to play. However, it brought him some unique "wealth": "You will know how money comes from, and how much money you can get if you work hard with so much energy. So I think it (work) is a good 'school' and is extremely important."

Perhaps this is what many juniors lack now. Most young people under the age of 20 in China have almost never worked aside from going to school. In winter and summer vacations, they rush to different cram schools. The young in China should know where the money comes from and what they need to do.

Biggi said, "Maybe you will ask me if I regret. I thought about it. Perhaps I have a chance to be an innocent child for a little longer. But I still have a wonderful childhood."

Deciding to Do What I Really Understood Later (Knowing My Real Position)

When we were young, maybe every one of us said: "I want to do something great, proving to all the adults that I can!" "I want to make a unique innovation that only I can think of, giving everyone a shock!"

When starting a business for the first time, Biggi also said in high spirits: "I remember I told you that I want to do something completely different from the roots of my family doing seafood business when I first came to China. But then I learned that I had competitive advantage in selling seafood coming from many generations of fisherman and fishing vessel owners comparing to others." In work, Biggi gradually understood that it was woefully inadequate to survive in the Chinese market only by high spirits, and being competitive was large required for entry to the Chinese market. Later, he began to seek his real position. "If you want to start a business, there may be something you need to consider: Is there room for you to develop in the industry? Is it your service or your product that makes you more competitive?" "Will you like the industry engaged? Is this the thing you're keen on? If you have no enthusiasm, why are you going to do it?"

Mr. Biggi and his seafood

The Tao Te Ching says: "Those who know others are only smart, while those who know themselves are truly wise. Those who overcome others are only competent, while those who exceed themselves are really powerful." At present, starting a business is still quite popular among the younger generation. "Making my own business as I am still young" is an unchanging belief for generations of young entrepreneurs. However, before deciding to start a business in a certain industry and getting ready to know it, people must seriously think about these questions: Where does my core competitiveness come from? Is this the thing I am keen on? Do I really like the industry? Do I know my real position here? Questions mentioned by Biggi in the interview are as follows: Why should I do it? Am I competitive? Do I really like it? These are his sincere suggestions to young entrepreneurs. For every junior who is about to enter into the society, maybe it is worth serious consideration. When Biggi was young, he thought about his real position, and decided to do what he was really good at and what he really wanted to do.

"The best decision I made was to do something I really understand, so I finally chose to return to the seafood market. But I don't regret. China is the most competitive market in the world and I want to survive here."

Interpersonal Relationship from the View of Biggi (Knowing the People Around You)

When we discuss China's commercial market, it is unavoidable to mention "relationship". For a long time, the complex interpersonal relationship has become a key word in China's economy and trade. Mr. Biggi mentioned this in the interview without exception. "You know, in China, there is one thing important called relationship, and you need to establish interpersonal relationships with people. There was an American salesman in my company, who needed to attend 20 meetings every day. He is outstanding in America but poor in China."

Chinese people always want to discuss business cooperation after having a certain understanding of both parties in trade, which is somewhat different from foreign businessmen. Some foreign businessmen may think that establishing relationships is time-consuming, laborious, boring and inefficient. "I told the American salesman: Take it easy, try to communicate with them, know them, have tea with them, chat with them and build relationships with them, which takes quite some time." "We always have a mutual understanding before doing business. People don't like to come by and say hello, and then discuss business directly. In that case, we don't understand each other." To get a mutual understanding, in China, sometimes we need to spend several hours on tea and chat, and then spend a short time in deciding whether to make cooperation. Actually, it seems quite unreasonable, but it is very worthy. In China, cooperation is often more than itself.

Chinese society is a collective society, and a society of mutual help. “If there is anything I can do to help each other, please feel free to contact me” and “The more friends you have, the more options you have in your life” are often said by many Chinese people. Chinese people believe that unity is strength; the whole is greater than the sum of the parts; the strength of one person is limited, while the strength of the collective is inexhaustible. Therefore, more time is spent in choosing partners, and solid social relationship cost is higher, which is due to the social environment. On the way to becoming an elite, people need to learn how to understand others, comply with the arrangement of the team and cooperate with others better. Through cooperation, people can do more things more efficiently, compared by what one person can do.

I Can Do Nothing Without Them (Trusting and Respecting Your Partners)

“I see that life here in China has been improving all the time, because in China, people are all in the same boat and want to make everything in the country better.” Biggi witnessed the rapid development of China in the past 20 years, and deeply understood the great strength of Chinese people to unite as one. Biggi also implemented a similar management policy in his own enterprise, trying to make his employees share the same goals with him and unite as one. “In my company, I trust in my employees. I don’t care when you come to the office or when you go home. If you are ill, you can ask for leave. I just believe in you.”

Biggi believes that the key to management success is to build mutual trust with employees. With sufficient trust and respect, employees can be passionate about doing things at all times and exert all their energies for the development of the company. Employees will become his partners in the same boat and work together toward common goals. “Our company has an environment of trust, I will attentively tell you that you can do better in our company, and you will certainly get more. When you start to work in my company, I will think about how to help you create a career development path. What you just need to do is doing better, better and better.”

Biggi gives his employees enough trust and respect, which drives them to love their work and their company. In the company, employees don't have to be influenced by any distractions. "If something is urgent happens to you, I will not need to know what really has happened, because it's your private life, and I trust you. For example, if your parents come to Shanghai, I will give you a day off because I understand that you need time with your family. I know I have to give you some freedom, and I won't let you become another family member forever on the other end of phone."

According to the theory of psychology of Carl Ranson Rogers, people who are actively concerned and given full trust and respect will be abler to deeply understand their own value and freely display their unlimited potential with higher work efficiency. This is truly reflected in Biggi's enterprise. Employees just need to consider how to work harder in limited time to make the whole company team better. They can give full play to their creativity and think about solutions to problems. Trust and respect liberate their potential, release their energy and improve their work efficiency.

"I trust and value every employee of mine. I can do nothing without my employees. Thanks to their hard work." was repeatedly stressed by Biggi in the interview.

IS Seafood Under the Effect of COVID-19 (Being a Trustworthy Person)

When talking about the impact of COVID-19 on the company's trade, Biggi frowned: "During the outbreak of COVID-19, it has been difficult to perform sea transportation. Because China is concentrating on preventing the spread of the virus, it is very difficult to import goods now, and it is difficult for products to enter the country. I am worried whether the staff of transportation treats these products properly."

Like many enterprises, IS Seafood has also been in great troubles during the outbreak, such as strict inspection of customs entry and considerable obstacles in international transportation. Now, these problems that were inconspicuous have become a heavy burden on Mr. Biggi. Fortunately, a window has been opened for Biggi elsewhere, although a door has been closed after the outbreak. "In fact, I don't think we have ever had a better opportunity to sell seafood to individual families and do business with people who want to eat healthy food." When the threat to health is pressed on at every stage, people finally realize the importance of improving their daily health, more and more people begin to focus on food health. "We are a reputable and honest company, with excellent product quality. We have our own stories to tell people where the fish comes from and how it is handled. These are all open and transparent, so people are willing to believe us. Now, they attach more importance to health, and they also know that our seafood is good for health, so there are more demands. At this time, my company is trying to seize this opportunity." During the outbreak, the reputation advantage accumulated all the time has brought extra bonuses to IS Seafood in an unexpected way, and Biggi has seized the opportunity, thus successfully helping the company stop losses and make profits.

Additionally, Mr. Biggi also did some of his old friends a favor during the outbreak. "In 2020, I gave some of my customers a year to raise money for debt repayment, because I wanted to help them get through the most difficult time, and they would remember that we were there in the most difficult time. During attentive cooperation with others, you may lose some money, but you win the support from others." As Biggi said in the interview, those who were helped would recall that someone assisted them in the most difficult time, and they would understand that Biggi is a trustworthy and respected partner. It maybe seems that Biggi has lost some benefits at present, but I believe Biggi will gain more partners, get more returns and make more reliable friends in the future. Especially in China, it is very worthwhile.

Witnessing the Development and Transformation of China (Trusting Our Country)

In the past 20 years, China's development and transformation have been earthshaking, and workers' average wages have increased by more than 10 times. Today, Chinese people can think and do what they want to do. Although sometimes people toss and turn because of being shut out of work, they no longer become destitute and homeless by the war, and they rarely drop out of school to work for supporting their families. Of course, everything is getting better gradually. To one's excitement, many foreign entrepreneurs in China have witnessed and highly appreciated China's rapid development and great changes over the years, so has Mr. Biggi. "Yes, I have witnessed the great development of the country in the past 17 years. Everything becomes so clean and safe and the traffic is very convenient. Chinese people come from the same team and work for the interests of the same country and people." Biggi is very appreciative of China's management progress over the past 10 years. He pays close attention to the Chinese market and thinks that China will be absolutely the main market of IS Seafood in the future. "I feel proud and grateful to the actual relationship between our two countries. When I tell people that I am an Icelander everywhere in China, everyone knows about Iceland and thinks that Iceland is a good country. In such a big country, almost everyone knows such a small country."

In the end, Biggi mentioned that Iceland was the first European country to reach a free trade agreement with China. He really hoped that Iceland and China could make more exchanges and communication, understand and learn from each other, and become better friends. "We will continuously develop our company in China, to tell better stories, render better services."

It has been 50 years since the establishment of diplomatic relations between China and Iceland. During the establishment of diplomatic relations in 1971, China was turbulent and in ruins, while Iceland was also in the early stage of development. Times have passed and circumstances have changed after 50 years, and China and

Iceland have not been what they used to be upon years of development. China's economy has grown rapidly, becoming the second largest in the world. Iceland also gradually realizes diversification of economy, with rapid development of the tourist industry, becoming the fourth country in human happiness index. Under the current development trend of international economic globalization, I believe that China and Iceland will have a bright development prospect and become more and more intimate and all-round partners.

As a foreign entrepreneur who has been in China for 17 years, Mr. Biggi is very familiar with the philosophy of life in the Chinese market. He is an outstanding entrepreneur worthy of the name, with strong management strength, and an idol for the younger generation of managers. I sincerely wish Mr. Biggi and his IS Seafood to overcome the negative impact of COVID-19, achieve his beautiful long-cherished wish, and tell more wonderful story of him in China.

(Huang Zijie Ma Zhongyi Niu Xiaomeng)

12

心无旁骛，不断探索

——访冰岛商业咨询公司 MAR Advisors 总裁 Magnus Bjarnason

Magnus Bjarnason

“勇敢尝试，胜于原地踏步”这是Magnus Bjarnason人生的真实写照，也是他在采访中不断向我们传递的一种品质和精神。这位来自冰岛的企业家，他的一生都在勇于尝试，不断地探索，书写自己的历史。“世之奇伟、瑰怪，非常之观常在于险远，而人之所罕至焉。”没有会当凌绝顶，怎会体验到一览众山小的壮观？人活着就应该不断探索，未知的世界过于奥妙，探索的脚步应该不断前行。

无论是在学习中还是工作中，这种不断探索的精神都在Magnus Bjarnason身上体现得淋漓尽致。Magnus在美国读完了大学，并取得优异的成绩，但他不满足于当时的状况，他知道自己需要的是什么，自己需要准备什么。于是，他勤奋刻苦、奋发图强，在1991—1992年于美国雷鸟商学院获得了工商管理硕士和国际商务硕士，这为以后Magnus在商界的成功奠定了坚实的基础。Magnus早期在政府部门担任官员，后转行于商界，并在商界不停转换职务角色，探索属于他自己的职业之路。

要成为一名企业家，不仅要有良好的职业素养，同时还要有优异的业务能力。在这一点上，Magnus一直做得很好。他为人和善，热情务实，待人诚恳，工作不墨守成规，具有极强的创新意识。在采访中，Magnus不仅分享了他在事业上的发展，还提到了他的国际大家庭。他兴趣爱好广泛，对生活充满热爱。作为一名热爱中国的冰岛友人，Magnus积极推动中冰两国之间的友好交流，为两国间长远安定的发展贡献力量。

不断创新，勇敢尝试

大学生活可以说是Magnus Bjarnason人生中的一个重大转折点，在那里，Magnus Bjarnason 找到了探索新事物的价值。“大学时代，我最引以为傲的是我不断尝试和探索了很多事情，结识了新的朋友，我认为这是对我有好处的。”Magnus 在采访中说道。同时，Magnus 也对今天的学生们提出了宝贵的建议。Magnus 认为，年轻人应该要敢于面对新鲜事物，一直保持着一种渴望探索的心理，要不断地探索新鲜事物并保持开放，他还鼓励学生们坚定信念。他在采访中说道：“不管你们处于一种什么水平，只要你们坚定信念，努力工作，为了成功，你必须专注，知道自己的角色是什么，计划做并且集中注意力，你们终究会成为你们想要成为的样子。”

Magnus Bjarnason 丰富多彩的学习经历和国际化经历使得他在 1997 年加入冰岛外交部。1997—2003 年，他先后担任了冰岛驻美大使馆北美贸易专员、冰岛驻纽约总领事。2003—2005 年，任冰岛驻华公使衔参赞。当然，在卸任外交部门的相关职务之后，Magnus 没有忽略去学习新事物的重要性，他从政界转向商界，缔造了一个又一个的商业传奇。这也是 Magnus 在人生中寻找到的又一条正确的道路。

Magnus（左三）出席 2007 年中冰地热资源开发报告会（咸阳）

不断地发展自身，不断地转换角色。Magnus Bjarnason 说，“在生活和事业中尝试不同的事情是非常重要的”，他真的做到了。受益于大学期间所学的专业知识，Magnus 很快在 2005—2008 年担任了 Glitnir 银行美洲与亚洲董事总经理，此后还担任过总部位于纽约的冰川全球合作伙伴（Glacier Global Partners）金融公司的首席执行官。不管担任什么职务，Magnus 始终认为他的职责就是去发展新业务。2010—2013 年，他任职于冰岛最大的可再生能源公司——冰岛国家电力公司（Landsvirkjun），担任市场营销和业务发展的执行副总裁，2011 年任法里斯（Farice）的非执行委员会成员，2012—2014 年担任冰岛集团（Icelandic Group）董事会成员和冰岛集团首席执行官兼总裁，2015 年担任克维卡银行（Kvika Bank）常任董事，2019 年任冰岛海鲜国际（Iceland Seafood

International）董事会主席。即使在成为企业家后，他所涉及的范围广纳了银行、能源、海鲜等领域，但是他始终认为这并不影响他的工作。相反，他将自己看作是一位商业发展者，他知道他需要做些什么来帮助客户。

在谈到对于中国企业家的印象时，Magnus 认为，两国企业家之间并没有太大的区别，反而是有很多相似之处，因为无论冰岛企业家还是中国企业家，都必须专注自身事业，不断探索企业发展的道路。对于中国企业家来说，这一点尤其重要，这样才能在中国这个偌大且竞争激烈的市场占得一席。

翻看 Magnus Bjarnason 的工作经历，你会惊叹于他的职业生涯，但正是这种不断地求索，造就了 Magnus Bjarnason 传奇的职业履历。我们每一个人从小都拥有着对未知事物了解的渴望，但是在长大后，经过现实的规则束缚，很多人失去了尝试新事物的勇气，更多的人选择了墨守成规，被束缚在成长的道路上。而 Magnus Bjarnason 则截然相反，他真正诠释了正确的探索会让人们的生活充满动力，帮助人们走向正确的人生方向。

怀揣激情，热爱生活

Magnus Bjarnason 有一个幸福的国际家庭，他有四个孩子和五个孙子。不同于其他普通家庭的家长，从小接受过美国高等教育的 Magnus 深深地知道孩子在外面独自闯荡的重要性，他从不束缚他们，他把积极探索新事物的理念传输到他的家庭中去。在良好的教育和家庭环境下，Magnus 的孩子分别在不同的国家生活和发展，组成了一个国际大家庭。他的女儿住在伦敦；二儿子在美国担任沃尔玛的高管；三儿子一直在越南做生意；最小的儿子正在慕尼黑攻读硕士学位，而 Magnus 也经常因为工作的原因在全球不同的地方开展合作，所以 Magnus 非常珍惜并享受与家人们待在一起的时光。地球因为亲情仿佛变得没有这么辽阔，即使生活在地球的不同地方，但是他们依然在互相思念着远方的亲人，尤其是在疫情过

在华期间 Magnus（右二）与家人出游

后，所有的感情更是显得弥足珍贵。Magnus Bjarnason 认为，人生在世，需要体会爱与被爱的力量，需要亲情、友情和爱情的滋润，这样的人生才算是完整、圆满。他将自己的生活活成了一杯热酒，永远热烈地走在追梦路上，也及时地享受身边的美好与温情。

看望当地民居

Magnus Bjarnason 作为一位十分热爱中国的冰岛友人，在采访中多次强调自己对中国文化和环境的热爱，也见证了中国十几年的飞速发展。Magnus 在采访中说道："1997 年我第一次来到中国北京，让我印象最深刻的是北京的街头到处都是自行车和行人，那时的北京是一座完全不同的城市。在过去的 20 年里，中国发生了翻天覆地的变化，我看到了中国各个城市的飞速发展。不仅是一线城市，二、三线城市也发生了翻天覆地的变化。对我来说，来到中国是一次改变我生活的经历，也正因如此，我深深地爱上了这里，爱上了这个平静而祥和的国度。"

生活充满乐趣，Magnus 面对生活充满了对未来道路的向往，他笑着直言自己有很多的爱好，他喜欢滑雪、打高尔夫球、游泳、打网球等等。正是这种多姿多彩的生活让 Magnus 热爱自己，热爱世界。不管遇到什么样的障碍与困难，他都能以积极的态度和出色的判断力、领导力渡过难关。或许就像 Magnus 自己说的那样，如果你喜欢你正在做的事情，你会变得更好，努力找一些令人愉快的事情，这是最重要的。因为如果你喜欢你所做的事情，你就会擅长它，并做得更好。

心无旁骛，滴水穿石

纵览 Magnus 的职业生涯，我们可以看到他在所工作的部门都有着优异的表现，从冰岛外交部参赞、驻华公使衔参赞到冰岛国家电力公司执行副总裁、冰岛集团首席执行官，再到冰岛海鲜国际董事会主席，以及作为

MAR 顾问公司的创始合伙人，是什么造就了如今的 Magnus Bjarnason。

从我们的访谈中不难看出，专注的做事风格是 Magnus Bjarnason 成功转型的关键。“你必须集中精力，当你创业时，你必须有一个明确的重点。在任何情况下，为了成功，你必须要有专注力，你必须明确自己的优势和劣势、你在其中扮演的角色是什么。最重要的事情就是集中注意力做出计划。”

与中石化新星签署地热合作协议（前排右二）

“专注”是 Magnus 在采访中提及次数最多的词语之一。“不要试图做太多的事情，一次只做一件事，然后把它做好”。Magnus 一直强调做事情要专心，想要在某些方面取得成果就一定不能三心二意，而是应该脚踏实地、心无旁骛地专注于要做的事情上。

Magnus Bjarnason 在经营如今的 MAR Advisors 之前，曾从事过许多不同类型的工作。1997 年，在当时的冰岛外交部长的邀请下，Magnus 进入外交部并执行的第一个任务就是海外服务，即支持冰岛企业在国际市场上的产品和服务推广。自此，Magnus 远赴美国并爱上了外交服务工作。他专注于此并坚持奋斗，从日常工作中发现外交工作的乐趣，吐故纳新，不断提升自身的外交能力、语言沟通交往能力，更重要的是发现时机的能力。在北美工作的第 6 个年头，也就是 2003 年，Magnus 来到了正在经历改革开放的中国。他意识到中国是当时快速发展的经济体，正在经历一个非常独特的转变。“能够让我们中的一些人生活在中国”，正是鉴于中国自身的高速发展，才吸引到了像 Magnus 这样有能力的人将目光投向中国。

由于 Magnus 的专业主要涉及工商、商务、贸易等领域，因此 Magnus 在告别了冰岛外交部后加入了一个国际化的银行——冰岛 Glitnir 银行。“2005 年我决定离开外交部，加入 Glitnir 银行，负责为中国、北美的客户提供海鲜和可再生能源方面的服务”。正是有了这些工作经验，Magnus 不仅提升了专业水平，还增加了对于海鲜和可再生能源的认识，这为其后来的工作奠定了基础。在与中国和北美的客户进行沟通交流的过程中，Magnus 发现了其中的商机。海外市场对天然海鲜的需求量高且注重质量，而冰岛海鲜正拥有得天独厚的条件来满足海外市场。因此，为客户开发新业务和发展业务就成了 Magnus 的主要工作。“我把自己看作是一个商业发展项目，我有着丰富的成功经验。对我来说，从什么样的公司跳槽都没有问题。无论是在商业银行还是在政府的能源公司，工作性质都是一样的。我的角色是开发新业务和发展业务，你只需要解决某些问题。我认为，我在这方面的长期的经验和做法对我的客户有帮助。”在采访中 Magnus 建议，想要创业的年轻人一定要专注，因为没有什么事情是轻轻松松就能做成功的，如果还没成功就想转移注意力到其他事情上，那么什么事都做不成。

中冰友好，共创未来

众所周知，冰岛是一个几乎无污染、最接近纯天然的国度，清洁能源、海鲜产品、纯净矿泉水等都是冰岛所富有的资源，同时也是冰岛主要出口产品。冰岛吸引着中国游客前往遥远的冰岛旅游、欣赏自然风光。在中冰建交 50 年里，双方进行的贸易往来愈发朝着更多元、更深入的方向发展。尤其是在中国国务院政府工作报告指出碳达峰、碳中和工作目标后，中国企业对于清洁能源的需求直线上升；冰岛企业对于中国高科技产品的需求也日益增长。因此，促进中冰双边贸易往来就成为近年来中冰两国政府外交工作的重点。Magnus 在谈及与中国企业进行业务往来的经历时，认为中国市场竞争十分激烈，因此成功的中国企业家都是聪明又有趣的人。

在担任冰岛驻华公使衔参赞的两年里，Magnus 去过许多省市。与 1997 年初识的中国不同，进入 21 世纪的中国如同乘上了高速列车般飞速发展，不仅越来越多的中国人能通过英语等国际性语言与外国人交流沟通，而且中国的产品也逐渐从成本优势转换为质量优势，这吸引着海外企业对中国产品的需求越来越高。读万卷书的同时也要行万里路。Magnus 通过实际调查了解到中冰两国企业的业务需求，搭建了一个中间服务平台，作为双方沟通和协商的桥梁，该平台帮助中国和冰岛许多企业实现了贸易往来，这极大地促进了中冰交往，实现了共赢。

在进行业务往来时，不可避免地会遇到中冰两国在语言、文化、习惯等方面的差异，而消除其中的误解并帮助双方提高沟通效率正是 Magnus 的工作重点。例如，他在访谈中提到冰岛企业家往往很难意识到中国有多大，而中国企业家往往很难意识到冰岛有多小，也就是说，双方对于对方的大小都没有直观的感受和理解。因此，在涉及业务时，对业务量大小认知偏颇的情况时有发生。但总体来说，冰岛和中国企业家有很多相似之处，甚至相差无几。正是企业家之间的默契使得即使相距甚远也能成为友好的合作伙伴。目前 MAR 公司的几大核心业务中就包含与中方的合作，如 Magnus 谈到的在中国政府的支持下，与中石化合资在中国建设地热区域供热系统的中石化绿源地热能开发有限公司，如今已是中国最大的地热集中供热公司；再如 MAR 为中国领先的 IT 和研发公司华为在冰岛的数字化和技术战略提供战略咨询。Magnus 始终认为，中国企业是冰岛企业的友好伙伴，并将中国视为他的希望，期待"能够帮助冰岛投资者更多地投资于中国的海鲜分销"，同时促进中国企业找到更多中国以外的商业机会，也许并不仅仅是在冰岛。

谈到对于未来中国和冰岛两国合作展望，Magnus 认为，一方面，在未来 5 到 10 年内，将看到冰岛公司将冰岛等地的海鲜产品销往中国市场；另一方面，将看到更多的中国人到冰岛投资，比如在新技术领域。对于未来的美好期待，不仅需要两国企业家努力达成合作，更需要两国政府从外交政策层面达成共识。良好的国际关系需要各国共同努力。因为当今世界局势动荡，因此想要保持友好交往必须付出努力。Magnus 认为，在促进冰中贸易合作与交流方面，政府或行业协会需要持续加大投入，建立基于信任的良好关系是两国贸易往来的基础。

在采访的最后，Magnus 表示，期待与中国企业更多合作与交流，在更多业务上取得丰硕的合作成果。同时，他还热情欢迎中国人民前往美丽的冰岛旅游。Magnus 对中冰建交 50 周年高度关注，衷心希望未来能继续为推动中冰关系做出实际贡献。他坚信，他的人生乐章将更加激昂，而中国与冰岛的双边关系也会拥有更加灿烂的明天！

（闫星耀　郭亚亚）

Focus on Exploring

— Interview with Magnus Bjarnason, President of MAR Advisors

"Brave attempt is better than standing still" is a true portrayal of Magnus Bjarnason's life, and it is also a kind of quality and spirit he constantly conveyed to us in the interview. The entrepreneur from Iceland has been brave in trying, exploring and writing his own history all his life. The world's wonderfully majestic and extraordinary landscapes are often found in places that are dangerous, remote and rarely visited. If you don't reach the top, how can you hold all mountains in a single glance? People should keep exploring when they are alive. The unknown world is too mysterious, and the pace of exploration should keep moving forward.

Magnus Bjarnason

Magnus Bjarnason embodies this spirit of continuous exploration in both his studies and work. Mr. Magnus got a bachelor's degree in the United States and achieved excellent results. But he didn't stop there at that time. He was clear what he dreamed of and what preparations he needed to make. Therefore, he was determined to make more arduous efforts. From 1991 to 1992, he successively obtained an

MBA and an MIB from Thunderbird School of Global Management, laying a solid foundation for his future success in business sector. Mr. Magnus worked as an official in government departments before switching to business. Through the transformation of different business roles at different stages, Mr. Magnus has accumulated rich business experience and explored his business path.

To be an entrepreneur, he or she should not only have good professional quality, but also have extraordinary business ability. Mr. Magnus has always done a good job in this point. He is kind-hearted, enthusiastic, pragmatic, and very sincere to others. When working, he is not a conformist and has a strong sense of innovations. In the interview, Mr. Magnus not only shared his career development, but also mentioned his international family. He has a wide range of interests and hobbies and full of love for his life. As an Icelandic friend who loves China, Mr. Magnus actively promotes the friendly exchanges between China and Iceland. At the same time contributes to the long-term and stable development of the two countries.

Continuous Innovation and Bold Attempt

College was a major turning point in Magnus Bjarnason's life, where he found the value of exploring new things. "What I am most proud of in college is that I keep trying and exploring many things constantly and making new friends. I think it is good for me." Mr. Magnus said in the interview. At the same time, Mr. Magnus also provided valuable advice to the students today. Mr. Magnus believed that young people should dare to face new things, always keep a kind of desire to explore, constantly explore new things and keep open, and he also encouraged students to strengthen their faith. He said in the interview, "I think when you're young, it's time to be used to explore new things, you should always remind yourself, whether you are at the university, the undergraduate or the graduate level, whatever level it is. But you can become whatever you want, just matter of hard work."

Mr. Magnus's learning experience and internationalization experience led him to join the Icelandic Ministry for Foreign Affairs in 1997. From 1997 to 2003, he served as the North American Trade Commissioner and the Consul General in New York. From 2003 to 2005, he served as the Minister-counsellor of Iceland in China. Of course, after stepping down from relevant position in the diplomatic service, Mr. Magnus did not neglect the importance of learning new things. He turned from the diplomatic service to business, creating one business legend after another. This is another correct path that Mr. Magnus has found in his life.

Constantly develop hisself and change roles. Magnus Bjarnason said that "it is very important to try different things in life and career", and he really did it. Benefiting from his professional knowledge in college, Mr. Magnus soon served as the managing director in Americas and Asia of Glitnir Bank from 2005 to 2008, and later on served as the CEO of the Glacier Global Partner, which is a finance company based in New York. No matter what position he holds, Mr. Magnus always thinks that his duty is to develop new business. From 2010 to 2013, he worked for Landsvirkjun, Iceland's largest renewable energy company, as the executive vice president for marketing and business development of the Landsvirkjun, then as a non-executive board member of the Farice in 2011. Later on, he served as the CEO and president of Icelandic Group in 2012–2014 while being a member of its board of directors and a permanent director of the Kvika Bank in 2015. In 2019, he became the Chairman of the board of directors of the Iceland Seafood International. Even covering a wide range of fields such as banking, energy and seafood after becoming an entrepreneur, he always thinks that this does not affect his work. On the contrary, he regards himself as a business developer, and he knows what he needs to do to help customers.

When talking about the impression of Chinese entrepreneurs, Mr. Magnus believed there was no big difference between entrepreneurs of the two countries, but rather that there were many similarities, and that both Icelandic and Chinese entrepreneurs must focus on their own business and constantly explore the path of business development. For Chinese entrepreneurs, this is especially important in order to gain a foothold in the large and competitive market in China.

Looking through Magnus Bjarnason's work experience, you will be amazed at his career. However, it is this constant search that has created Mr. Magnus's legendary career resume. Every one of us has a desire to know the unknown since childhood, but after growing up, many people lose the courage to try new things as a result of the bondage of reality, and more people choose to stick to convention and are bound on the road of growth. Mr. Magnus is totally different. He really explained that the correct exploration would make people's lives full of motivation and help people move towards the right direction of life.

Love Life with Passion

Mr. Magnus has a happy international family with four children and five grandchildren. Unlike other parents of ordinary families, Magnus Bjarnason, who has received American higher education since childhood, deeply knows the importance of wandering about outside alone for children. He never binds them, and he transmits the idea of actively exploring new things to his family. With good education and family environment, the children of Mr. Magnus live and develop in different countries, forming an international family. His daughter lives in London, the second son develops his career in the USA where he serves as a WalMart executive. The third son has been developing new businesses in Vietnam, the youngest son is studying for a master's degree in Munich, and Mr. Magnus often cooperates in different places around the world for work reasons, so Mr. Magnus really enjoys spending time with his family. Because of affection, the earth seems to be less vast. Even though living in different parts of the earth, they still miss each other's distant relatives. Especially after the epidemic, all the feelings are even more precious. Mr. Magnus believes that we need to appreciate the power of loving and being loved, and to be nourished by family, friendship and love in our life time. This kind of life is complete and satisfactory. He lives his life as a cup of hot wine, always walking enthusiastically on the road of chasing dreams, and enjoying the beauty and warmth around him in time.

Magnus Bjarnason, as an Icelandic friend who loves China very much, repeatedly emphasized his love for Chinese culture and environment in the interview, and also witnessed the rapid development of China over the past dozen years. Mr. Magnus said in the interview: "I first came to Beijing, China in 1997. What impressed me most was that the streets of Beijing were full of bicycles and pedestrians, and it was a completely different city then. In the past 20 years, China has undergone radical changes, and I have seen the rapid development of various cities in China. Not only first-tier cities, but also second-and third-tier cities have undergone earth-shaking changes. For me, coming to China is an experience that changes my life, and because of that, I deeply fell in love with this place and this peaceful country."

Life is full of fun. Magnus Bjarnason is full of yearning for the way ahead in facing life. He smiled and said that he has many hobbies, and he likes skiing, playing golf, swimming, playing tennis and so on. It is such colorful life that makes Mr. Magnus love himself and the world. No matter what kind of obstacles and difficulties he encounters, he can tide over the difficulties with positive attitude, excellent judgment and leadership. Perhaps, as Mr. Magnus himself said, if you like what you are doing, you will become better and try to find something pleasant, which is the most important thing. It is because that if you like what you are doing, you will be good at it and do it better.

Constant Effort Brings, Success Without Distractions

Looking at Mr. Magnus's career, we can see that he has excellent performances in the departments he worked in. From the Counsellor and the Minister Counsellor of the Icelandic Ministry for Foreign Affairs to the executive vice-president of National Power Company of Iceland, CEO of Iceland Group, Chairman of the board of directors of the Iceland Seafood International, as well as a founding partner of MAR Advisors, what made Magnus Bjarnason today?

Our interview shows that a focused work style is the key to Magnus Bjarnason's successful transformation. "You have to be focused. When you're building a business, you must have a clear focus. In all instances, in order to be successful, you must be focused, and you must be clear about your strengths and weaknesses and what role you play in it. The most important thing is to focus and plan."

"Focus" is one of the words most frequently mentioned by Mr. Magnus in the interview. "Don't try to do too many things, do one thing at a time, and do it well." Mr. Magnus has always stressed that we should do things with concentration. If we want to achieve results in some aspects, we must not be half-hearted. Instead, we should be down-to-earth and focused on what we want to do.

Magnus (front row, first from the right) focused on the meeting

Magnus Bjarnason worked in several different types of jobs before running present MAR Advisors. In 1997, at the invitation of Icelandic Foreign Minister, his first mission to enter Icelandic Foreign Ministry was overseas services, namely, supporting the promotion of products and services of Icelandic enterprises in the international market. Since then, Mr. Magnus has traveled to the United States and fell in love with diplomatic service. He focused on this and found the fun of diplomatic service from his daily work. He got rid of the stale and took in the fresh. And constantly he improved his diplomatic ability, verbal communication skills, and more importantly, the ability to find opportunities. In the sixth year of working in North America, in 2003, Mr. Magnus came to China, which was undergoing reform and opening up. He realized that China was a fast growing economy going through a very unique transformation. "I was able to make some of us living in China." It is because of its own rapid development that has attracted capable people like Mr. Magnus to China.

Since Mr. Magnus' major mainly covers the fields of industry, commerce, trade and so on, he joined an international bank, Icelandic Glitnir Bank, after leaving from the Icelandic Ministry for Foreign Affairs. "I decided to leave the Foreign Service in 2005 and join the international bank, whether become responsible for our service to customers in China, North America, in seafood and renewable energy." With this experience, Mr. Magnus not only improved his professional level, but also increased his understanding of seafood and renewable energy, which laid the foundation for his subsequent job. In the process of communicating with customers in China and North America, Mr. Magnus discovered the business opportunities. Overseas markets have a high demand for natural seafood and pay attention to its quality, while Iceland seafood has unique conditions to meet overseas markets. Therefore, developing new business and expanding business for customers have become Mr. Magnus's main job. "I regard myself as a business development project with a wealth of successful experiences. It has been no problem for me to move from different companies. Whether working in commercial banks or in energy companies, the nature of the work is same. My role was to develop new business and to expand business. You need to have certain things that you work on. And I think that my quite long experience and doing that is helping my clients today." In the interview, Mr. Magnus suggested that young people who want to start a business must be focused, because nothing can be done easily. If they want to divert attention to other things before they succeed, nothing can be done.

Promote China-Iceland Friendship and Create the Future Together

On a state visit to China Magnus (second from the left) and Olafur Ragnar Grimsson (second from the right), former president of Iceland

As we all know, Iceland is a country with almost no pollution and the closest to pure nature. Clean energy, seafood products, pure mineral water, etc. are Iceland's rich resources and its main export products. Chinese tourists are attracted by Iceland, and fly to distant Iceland to enjoy the natural scenery. In the 50 years since the establishment of diplomatic relations between China and Iceland, the trade between both sides has been developing in a more diversified and deeper direction. Especially after the goal of peak carbon dioxide emissions and carbon neutralization pointed out in the government work report of the State Council of China, Chinese enterprises' demand for clean energy has risen perpendicularly. Icelandic enterprises' demand for Chinese high-tech products has also been increasing day by day. Therefore, promoting bilateral trade between China and Iceland has become the focus of diplomatic work of the Chinese and Icelandic governments in recent years. When talking about his business with Chinese enterprises, Mr. Magnus thinks that

Chinese entrepreneurs are smart and interesting people. "They have to be extremely smart in order to succeed, because China is a very competitive market".

Mr. Magnus has been to many provinces and cities during his two years as the Icelandic Minister Counsellor to China. Unlike the first know China in 1997, China in the 21st century is booming like riding a high-speed train. Not only more and more Chinese people are able to communicate with foreigners through international languages such as English, but also Chinese products are gradually shifting from cost advantage to quality advantage, which attracts overseas enterprises to have higher and higher demand for Chinese products. While reading more books, you should also make more field visits to truly feel the temperature of the world. Mr. Magnus set up an intermediate service platform after learning the business needs of enterprises in China and Iceland. As a bridge for communication and negotiation, the platform helped many enterprises to achieve trade contacts and greatly promoted the contacts between China and Iceland. It achieved a win-win situation.

Inevitably, when doing business exchanges, there will be differences in language, culture and habits between China and Iceland. Eliminating misunderstandings and helping both sides improve communication efficiency are Mr. Magnus's key emphasis in work. For example, he mentioned in the interview that it is often difficult for Icelandic entrepreneurs to realize how big China is, as well as difficult for Chinese entrepreneurs to realize how small Iceland is. That is to say, both sides have no intuitive feeling and understanding of each other's size. Therefore, when it comes to business, the amount of business is biased sometimes. But overall, Icelandic and Chinese entrepreneurs have many similarities, or even few differences. It is the tacit understanding among entrepreneurs that makes them friendly partners even if they are far apart. At present, several core businesses of MAR include cooperation with China. For example, Mr. Magnus mentioned that Sinopec Luyuan Co., Ltd. is currently the largest geothermal central heating company in China. It is a joint venture founded by MAR and Sinopec with the support of the Chinese government. Another example is that MAR provides strategic advice for digitalization and technology strategy in Iceland of Huawei, the leading IT and R&D company in China. Mr. Magnus always thinks that Chinese enterprises are friendly partners of Icelandic enterprises, and regards China as his hope. He expects to "help Icelandic investors invest more in seafood distribution in China" and to promote Chinese enterprises to find more business opportunities outside China, perhaps not just in Iceland.

Talking about the prospect of China-Iceland cooperation in the future, Mr. Magnus believes that, on the one hand, Icelandic companies will sell seafood products from Iceland and other places to the Chinese market in the next 5 to 10 years; on the other hand, more Chinese people will invest in Iceland, such as in new technologies. Good expectations for the future require not only the entrepreneurs of the two countries to work hard to reach cooperation, but also the two governments to reach an agreement from the aspect of foreign policy. Good international relations need the joint efforts of all countries. Since the world is in ongoing turmoil at present, efforts must be made to maintain friendly communication. Mr. Magnus believes that the government or industry associations need to continue to invest in based relationships between people to promote trade cooperation and communication between Iceland and China. Trade between the two countries is based on trust and good relationships among people.

At the end of the interview, Mr. Magnus expressed his expectation for more cooperation and communication with Chinese enterprises, and achieved fruitful cooperation results in more businesses. At the same time, he also warmly welcomed Chinese people to travel to beautiful Iceland. Mr. Magnus pays close attention to the 50th anniversary for the establishment of diplomatic relations between China and Iceland, and sincerely hopes that he can continue to make practical contributions to the promotion of China-Iceland relations in the future. He firmly believes that his life movement will be more passionate, and the bilateral relationship between China and Iceland will have a more brilliant tomorrow!

(Yan Xingyao　Guo Yaya)

13

众志成城，砥砺前行

——访青岛怡之航物流有限公司总裁吕磊杰

吕磊杰

古语有言："乘众人之智，则无不任也；用众人之力，则无不胜也。"当我们谈及如何经营管理企业时，青岛怡之航物流有限公司总裁吕磊杰坚定地告诉我们："团队。我认为企业管理依靠的是一个团队而非某一个人。"

伟大的事情可以通过集体努力来完成。一个人的能力是有限的，但一群人的潜能却是无限的，当他们团结起来时，他们将创造一种令人敬畏的力量并克服所有困难。在这个纷繁复杂的社会，人们总是身处团队却又忘记团队。吕磊杰从事物流行业多年，在行业中几经磨炼，他用丰富的经验和卓越的成绩告诉我们团队的重要性。采访时，吕磊杰在讲述自己时是低调的，但在谈及团队和企业时，他的言语却是丰富而奢华的。这大概就是为什么吕磊杰能始终如一地保持着对物流行业的热爱吧，不仅仅是他对物流行业的兴趣使然，也是他内心深刻无瑕的团队精神使然。

成立之初，砥砺奋进

"合抱之木，生于毫末；九层之台，起于累土；千里之行，始于足下。"2005 年，冰岛第一家物流公司，也是最大的物流公司 Eimskip 在青岛设立了怡之航分部——青岛怡之航物流有限公司，主要负责亚洲冷链物流市场的开拓。一个成功的企业需要坚实的基础，只有在坚实的基础之上，才能造就宏伟的建筑。而青岛这个美丽富饶的城市就是怡之航亚洲总部的基

吕磊杰主持怡之航中国 2021 年度集团工作会议

础，它为怡之航在亚洲的发展创造了得天独厚的优势。从区位特点上看，青岛地处山东半岛东南部，东、南濒临黄海，拥有得天独厚的地理位置优势。吕磊杰向我们强调，青岛拥有中国最大的冷藏箱出口基地，同时又是中国非常重要的集装箱生产基地和水产加工基地，每年都会有各大船舶公司在青岛启动新项目。与此同时，在区域经济上，山东省既是中国的经济大省，又是农业大省和对外出口贸易大省，水果、蔬菜、水产品常年出口到世界各地，市场潜力巨大，而青岛作为山东省的经济中心，设立物流中心是水到渠成的。从发展战略角度上看，吕磊杰说道："2005 年之前，冰岛 Eimskip 公司的业务仅限于在欧洲。2005 年在中国成立了分公司后，总公司可以把北大西洋的业务、北欧的业务、西北欧的业务快速地延展到亚洲地区，这是一个很有价值的、具有战略意义的选择。"同时，他还补充道："怡之航的发展对于提升青岛在韩国、日本的物流竞争力有极大帮助。"

然而，在 2005 年，中国在冷链物流方面还存在许多问题与困难。比如，冷链技术不够先进，物流发展还比较滞后。"机会是留给有准备的人的"，同样地，机会也是留给有准备的团队的。在采访中，吕磊杰高度评价了他的团队，简短的几句话却让我们感受到了吕磊杰在团队工作中的严谨与认真，同时他向我们讲述了他们团队的工作氛围。吕磊杰表示，在日常工作中，他们的工作氛围十分和谐，但对员工的要求是严格的，员工必须经过最专业的培训。吕磊杰说："我们比较注重企业的文化管理，传播总部的企业文化，并坚持将管理理念传递给每一位员工，让每一位员工清楚企业的发展方向。"在吕磊杰的带领下，团队善于学习、执着不移，每个成员都毫无顾虑地奉献自己全部的力量，这种力量汇聚为一股更加强大的合力，使他们团结一心、奋勇向前。当一个出色的团队团结、优秀、不断进取，具备了学无止境的态度，那这个团队可以称得上是无敌。

在谈到青岛怡之航物流有限公司的成立与发展时，吕磊杰着重向我们介绍了刘涛——青岛怡之航物流有限公司的第一任总裁。通过吕磊杰的介绍，我们了解到刘涛多年旅居国外，2004 年刘涛怀着满腔的热忱抱负和一颗赤子之心，毅然决然地回到中国，将怡之航物流品牌和业务引入中国。在青岛怡之航物流有限公司成立初期，从公司选址、市场扩展、业务发展和人才招聘等大小事宜，刘涛均是亲力亲为。刘涛一直将怡之航视为自己的孩子一般，看着它出生，看着它成长，看着它独当一面。怡之航也从最初的 6 人的团队发展到 100 多人，这不仅是刘涛呕心沥血付出的结果，也是怡之航所有人乘风破浪、不断奋斗而取得的结果。吕磊杰在采访中表示，他非常敬佩刘涛的谋略和眼光，刘涛严谨的工作态度和高尚的人格品质，是怡之航企业文化的最好的印证。吕磊杰是继刘涛之后、怡之航中国的第二任总裁。自上任以来，他以身作则、恪尽职守，为怡之航的进一步发展鞠躬尽瘁，为团队的壮大尽心竭诚。

吕磊杰说："实际上，我们面临的工作压力还是比较大的，因为我们的销售团队、运营团队、财务团队、市场团队以及其他团队都有着非常高的指标，而且我们在日常管理方面都盯得很紧。""有志者事竟成，破釜沉舟，百二秦关终属楚"就是对吕磊杰团队最好的描述。在中冰建交 50 周年之际，青岛怡之航物流有限公司被认定为山东省跨国公司地区总部，而通过 2021 年山东省跨国公司地区总部认定的外资企业只有 5 家。"宝剑锋从磨砺出，梅花香自苦寒来。"吕磊杰和他的团队始终不忘初心，砥砺前行。

紧跟时代，深入布局

"现在顾客在购买生鲜类食品时，都会倾向于使用保温袋或者冰袋；商家在送货时也非常注重食品食材的保鲜。从中我们可以体会到，消费者对食材的保鲜冷藏意识在不断提高，对保鲜冷藏技术的需求也在不断发展。这背后不仅是消费质量的提升，也是冷链物流发展的机遇。"吕磊杰在采访中这样说道。

的确，随着中国经济的快速发展和居民生活水平的提高，消费者的关注重点也在渐渐变化，从以前的注重数量，到如今的注重质量。追求更高的服务效率、更高的产品质量、更创新的服务模式是当前的消费特点。随着消费者对生活品质追求的提升，所消费的粮食、蔬菜、瓜果、禽蛋肉制品等产品的运输方式也正在发生质的改变，对产品保鲜、保质的要求使得冷链物流需求更加旺盛。吕磊杰从事物流行业多年，凭借着丰富的知识经验和敏锐的洞察力，他深刻地明白，唯有与时俱进，保持清醒的头脑，才能稳中求进。面对消费者观念的转变，吕磊杰说道："消费者对食材新鲜度的要求越来越高，从吃饱到吃好，食品消费正逐步走向品质化、健康化阶段，这些都将直接加速冷链物流的发展。"

与此同时，"互联网 +"概念的出现和不断实践，构建线上线下有效结合，已经成为多数冷链物流公司的生存之道。

怡之航的机械设备在港口工作

面对中国冷链物流行业崭新的行内业态和激烈的行业竞争，吕磊杰率领青岛怡之航公司广泛开展 B2B 业务，深入布局国际电商冷链物流市场。"目前，怡之航将业务重心放到了国际段运输，在国际物流、国际货运代理运输领域，我们更多应用 B2B 电商平台，服务范围涵盖水产加工企业、海外捕捞公司等。对于 B2C 电商业务，目前还没有直接联系，但是存在间接联系，因为进出口货物的销售最终会通过 B2C 电商平台来实现的。"

中国和冰岛两国在冷链物流方面达成的合作，不仅仅是人才、技术、资金上的合作，更是商业资源、物流网络的合作。吕磊杰认为："物流行业实际入门的门槛比较低，但是如果想把它做好做精又不是那么容易"。青岛怡之航公司之所以能够做大做强并不是因为其拥有最先进的冷链物流技术，而是因为合作之初冰岛 Eimskip 所带来的庞大的网络关系和成熟的物流平台。在此基础上，青岛怡之航公司构建了自己独特的辐射亚太地区的冷链物流贸易网络。

时代在发展，社会在发展，人们的思想也在发展。作为青岛怡之航物流有限公司的总裁，吕磊杰深知怡之航只有与时俱进才能勇立潮头。在这种思想的指引下，怡之航将不断开拓新的业务、拓展新的市场。

迎击疫情，展望未来

2020 年，新冠肺炎病毒在全球蔓延，随着全球疫情的大流行，国际物流服务供应链越来越重要，全球海运业在应对新冠肺炎疫情方面发挥着至关重要的作用。据估计，全球 80% 以上的贸易量和 70% 以上的贸易价值是由全世界 5 万多艘商船运出的。在后疫情时代，全球冷链物流运输业受到了一定程度的影响。作为中国冷链物流百强企业的青岛怡之航物流有限公司也面临着考验。特别是青岛怡之航物流有限公司作为山东省国际物流进出口重点物流企业，承担着恢复贸易的重要责任。要恢复贸易，就要让员工在安全的环境下办公，为了避免疫情给公司业务的发展带来不利影响，怡之航制定了严格的防疫措施，在遵守国家防疫政策的基础上，怡之航还订购了大量的防护用品，规定出差归来的员工必须居家办公。在一段时间内，怡之航还向员工颁布了旅行禁令，禁止员工出差，将一切异地业务转移到线上进行。面对从海外运来的货物，怡之航也采取了一整套的防护措施，不仅由专门的专业人员处理，而且也会要求员工与货物仓库保持距离，更多地使用机械设备进行操作。

吕磊杰（右四）和同事们庆祝怡之航成立 108 周年

除此之外，吕磊杰在担任青岛怡之航总裁之际便立即开始完善公司的运营体系，面对突如其来的疫情，他说："疫情给我们的工作模式带来巨大的改变，大家只能选择在家办公，青岛怡之航物流有限公司基于比较完善的操作系统，将疫情造成的损失降到最低，在公司业务方面受到的影响也调整到了最小。"

与此同时，在后疫情时代，青岛怡之航公司并不局限于目前的公司业务范围及规模，尽管青岛怡之航已经分别在大连、深圳、厦门、上海等地设立分支机构，但吕磊杰对于公司未来发展有着由东向西的构思。由于目前中国东西部冷链物流发展极不平衡，中国冷库总量 63% 位于东部，而中西部地区冷库数量不足，无法满足日常需求。对于这个战略机遇，在谈及未来打算时，吕磊杰说："之前的发展重心以及分支机构设立在东部沿海，是因为沿海地区的经济比较发达，配套设施比较完善，有充足的冷库，做物流业务相对来讲又是港口城市，离码头很近，这就是东部得天独厚的优势。

而青岛怡之航一直在寻求机会，因为国家提出了向西部发展的战略，并且现在铁路运输十分便利，我们关注四川、重庆以及中欧班列较为发达的西安，同时也思考过利用长江的优势与港口城市相连接。但这些业务需要较深厚的积淀才能完成。”

老子说：“祸兮福之所倚，福兮祸之所伏。”事物的发展总是有两面性。新冠肺炎疫情确实对怡之航的物流业务有影响，但这种影响不是永远的，这种影响也不全是坏事。疫情对于怡之航来说，更像是一次考验，一次由量变到质变的考验。当风雨退去，狂风渐停，迎接它的将是彩虹。

企业发展，人才为急

任正非曾说：“当你用一个人的时候，先别管这个人强还是不强，你要告诉我，你想让他做什么，也就是说他的能力是否与你想让他做的事情匹配。”

在当今社会，在激烈的行业竞争中，人才对于企业的重要性不言而喻，吕磊杰在采访中也多次高度评价他的团队。“企”之一字，有“人”为企，无“人”为止。人才是企业的根基，是企业活力的源泉，一个企业得先有人，才能发展，才能创造，才能称得上是企业，无人只能“止业”。而“人”之一字，过则为“入”，欠则为“八”，交叉则为“×”，只有一撇一捺合理放置，才为“人”，才是有效的人才。

当我们问到在面试时最看重什么时，吕磊杰毫不犹豫地回答：“我们选择合适的人。”在吕磊杰眼中，应试者都很优秀，但优秀并不代表合适。俗话说：“三百六十行，行行出状元。”每个行业有每个行业的特点，每个人也有每个人的特点，有的人在IT领域可以称霸一方，但在新闻编辑方面却一窍不通。就像吕磊杰所说的那样，把合适的人放在合适的岗位。

吕磊杰认为，除了合适以外，综合素质也是一个必不可少的因素。素质既包括身体素质，也包括心理素质，要想真正胜任一个岗位，不仅需要健康的身体，也需要强大的内心。吕磊杰在采访中坦言称：“我们公司相对来说较为年轻化，所以在原则性的问题上是决不妥协的，我们对

中秋节 怡之航公司内挂满灯笼

员工的要求是严格的，实际上每个团队都有很高的指标任务。但我们也非常注重对员工的关怀，公司设有一个员工俱乐部，这完全是由年轻人来负责的。”俗话说：“月圆则缺，器满则倾。”一个既有原则又有自由的工作氛围，一个张弛有度的管理层，是培养人才的最好温床。没有人才的成长，也就没有企业的成长。怡之航将人才管理做到了极致。吕磊杰说道：“我们每个月都会安排固定的时间去举办一些活动，包括一些节假日，都是由员工俱乐部来负责，基本上都是年轻人来主办。”在进行本次采访之前的准备工作中，我们了解到了怡之航的抖音账号和微信公众号，通过怡之航的这些网络账号可以看到公司员工的工作日常和举办的庆祝活动，从中不难看出怡之航和谐融洽的工作氛围和严谨认真的工作态度。

吕磊杰超强的战略思维和领导力像是怡之航的远光灯，而吕磊杰团队的高职业化素养以及在业务工作中的细致入微，像怡之航的近光灯。二者相辅相成，共同推进了怡之航的高速发展。

采访之前，吕磊杰曾多次说过：“我个人没什么值得说的，希望大家可以多关注我们公司，关注我们的这个行业。”当时只觉得是谦虚，但到了正式采访时，我们才真正体会和明白。当我们询问吕磊杰个人爱好等问题时，他的语言总是简短而匮乏；但当吕磊杰讲到团队、公司和行业时，却总是侃侃而谈、谈吐如流。从他热情的分享中可以深刻地体会到他对团队、公司和物流行业的挚爱。也正是因为这一点，吕磊杰始终坚持学习、不断进取，并要求他的团队持续学习和进步。采访的自始至终，“学习”和“团队”是吕磊杰谈及次数最多的词语，他总是有很多的感悟和心得。不断学习可以促进团队的进步，促进团队高效、高质地获得更为卓越的成果，而团队又使得学习的成果变得更加丰硕和完善。采访最后，吕磊杰再次强调：“当团队是一个善于学习的团队时，就变得与众不同了。当我们的团队通过不断学习，锁定了发展方向，每个人都清楚我们的方向所在，并能够执着地沿着正确的方向前进，就形成了强大的合力。”

（李云蝶　张惟晰）

Forging Ahead with the Unity of Will

— Interview with Lyu Leijie, Managing Director of Eimskip Logistics (Qingdao) Co., Ltd.

As the old saying goes, "Everything can be done with the wisdom of all men; all successes can be achieved with the strength of all people." When we talked about how to manage a company, Lyu Leijie, Managing Director of Eimskip Logistics (Qingdao) Co., Ltd. firmly told us, "The team. I think business management depends on a team rather than an individual."

Great things can be accomplished through collective efforts. A person's ability is limited, but the potential of a group of people is unlimited. When they unite, they will create an awesome power and overcome all difficulties. In this complex society, people are always in a team but forget the team. Lyu Leijie has been engaged and honed in the logistics industry for many years. With his rich experience and outstanding achievements, he demonstrates us the importance of a team. During the interview, Lyu Leijie was low-key when he talked about himself, but his words were rich and luxurious when he talked about the team and the company. This is probably why Lyu Leijie has always maintained his passion for the logistics industry, not only because of his interest in the industry, but also because of his profound and strong teamwork spirit.

Advance Bravely at the Early Stage

"Tall oaks grow from little acorns. Building a high-rise begins with mounds of soil. A journey of a thousand li begins with the first step." In 2005, Eimskip, the first logistics company and also the largest logistics company in Iceland, set up a branch in Qingdao, named Eimskip Logistics (Qingdao) Co., Ltd., which is mainly responsible for the development of cold chain logistics market in Asia. A successful enterprise needs a solid foundation. Only on a solid foundation can it is possible to make a grand building. Qingdao, a beautiful and affluent city, is exactly the foundation of Eimskip's headquarters in Asia, which has created unique advantages for Eimskip's development in Asia. In terms of geographical location, Qingdao is located in the southeast of Shandong Peninsula, bordering the Yellow Sea in the east and south, with unique geographical advantages. Lyu Leijie told us that Qingdao has the largest export base for reefer containers in China, and is also an important reefer container production base and aquatic product processing base in China. Every year, major shipping companies will start new projects in Qingdao. In terms of regional economy, Shandong Province is not only a major economic province of China, but also a major agricultural province and a major export trade province. Its fruit, vegetables and aquatic products are exported around the world all the year round, with a huge market potential. Therefore, Qingdao as the economic center of Shandong Province has mature conditions for establishing a logistics center. In terms of development strategy, Lyu Leijie said, "Before 2005, the business of Eimskip was limited to Europe. After the branch office was established in China in 2005, the head office can rapidly expand its business from North Atlantic, North Europe and North West Europe to Asia. This is a valuable and strategic choice." At the same time, he added, "The development of Eimskip has greatly enhanced Qingdao's competitiveness in logistics in the republic of Korea and Japan."

However, in 2005, there were still many problems and difficulties in cold chain logistics in China. For example, the cold chain technology was not advanced enough, and the development of logistics still lagged behind. "Opportunities are always reserved for people who are prepared." Similarly, opportunities are always reserved for teams who are prepared. During the interview, Lyu Leijie spoke highly of his team, and we could feel his rigorous and earnest attitude in teamwork from his short and concise speech. He also talked about the working atmosphere of his team. Lyu Leijie said that they have a harmonious working atmosphere in the daily work even though the requirements for employees are strict, and employees must undergo the most professional training. Lyu Leijie said, "We pay more attention to the management of corporate culture, spread the corporate culture of the headquarters, and insist on conveying the management concept to all employees, so that every employee can clearly understand the development direction of the company." Under the leadership of Lyu Leijie, the team is good at learning and persistent, and each member can dedicate all of their strength, which then converges into a more powerful joint force, enabling them to unite as one and step ahead. When an excellent team is united, keeps improvement and holds an attitude of endless learning, the team will become invincible.

When talking about the establishment and development of Eimskip Logistics (Qingdao) Co., Ltd., Lyu Leijie introduced Liu Tao separately, the first Managing Director of the company. According to Lyu Leijie's introduction, Mr. Liu Tao had lived abroad for many years, and then he returned to China in 2004 with full enthusiasm and ambition, and introduced the brand and business of Eimskip to China. In the early days of the company, Mr. Liu Tao took care of every corporate affair personally, from site location, market expansion, business development to talent recruitment. Mr. Liu Tao has always regarded Eimskip as his own child, fully participating in its birth, growing up, and standing alone. Now Eimskip has developed from a team of six persons to more than 100 members. This is not only the result of Mr. Liu Tao's hard work, but also the result of the painstaking and continuous efforts of all Eimskip staff. In the interview, Lyu Leijie said that he really admired Mr. Liu Tao's intelligence and vision, as well as his rigorous work attitude and noble personality, which are the best evidence of Eimskip's corporate culture. Lyu Leijie is the second Managing Director of Eimskip China after Liu Tao. Since he took office, he has been leading by example and fulfilled his duties scrupulously, and has fully devoted himself to the further development of Eimskip and the growth of the team.

On the occasion of the 50th anniversary of the establishment of diplomatic relations between China and Iceland, Lyu Leijie (first from the right) attended the celebration reception of the Icelandic embassy

"In fact, we are under great pressure because we have high performance indicator requirements for our sales team, operation team, finance team, marketing team and other teams," Lyu Leijie said. "And we keep a close eye on the day-to-day management." "Where there is a will, there is a way. Cutting off all means of retreat, Qin's territory finally belonged to Chu." This is the best description of Lyu Leijie's team. On the 50th anniversary of the establishment of diplomatic relations between China and Iceland, Eimskip Logistics (Qingdao) Co., Ltd. was assessed as the regional headquarters of multinational companies in Shandong Province, while there were only five foreign-funded enterprises identified as the regional headquarters of multinational companies in Shandong Province in 2021. "Sharpening makes a mighty sword, and cold makes a blooming wintersweet." Lyu Leijie and his team always keep their original intention in mind and go forward.

Keep Abreast of the Times and Make Intensive Layout

"Now customers tend to use thermal insulation bags or ice packs when buying fresh foods, and merchants also pay much attention to the preservation of food ingredients when delivering goods. We can realize from this trend that consumers' awareness of the freshness and cold storage of food ingredients is constantly enhancing, and their demand for freshness and cold storage technology is also constantly developing. This is not only the improvement of consumption quality, but also an opportunity for the development of cold chain logistics." Lyu Leijie said in the interview.

Indeed, with the rapid development of China's economy and the improvement of living standards, the focus of consumers is gradually changing from quantity to quality. The current consumption characteristics include pursuit of higher service efficiency, higher product quality and more innovative service models. As consumers pursue better quality of life, the transportation modes are undergoing fundamental changes for grain, vegetables, fruit, egg products and other products. The requirement for freshness and quality of products leads to a stronger demand for cold chain logistics. Lyu Leijie has been working in the logistics industry for many years. By virtue of his rich knowledge and experience and keen insight, he clearly understands that only by keeping abreast of the times and keeping your mind clear can the company make steady progress. In response to the change in consumers' concept, Lyu Leijie said, "Consumers have increasingly higher requirements for the freshness of food ingredients, from fulling up to eating well, and food consumption is gradually moving toward the stage of quality and health. These changes will directly accelerate the development of cold chain logistics."

At the same time, the emergence and continuous practice of the concept of "Internet +" and the effective combination of online and offline have become the key to the survival of most chain logistics companies.

Lyu Leijie (front row, fifth from the left) and his colleagues celebrated the 100th anniversary of the establishment of Faroe Ship, a subsidiary of Eimskip Group

Facing the new business types and fierce competition in China's cold chain logistics industry, Lyu Leijie leads Eimskip Logistics (Qingdao) Co., Ltd. to extensively carry out B2B business and make an intensive plan in the international e-commerce cold chain logistics market. "At present, Eimskip focuses its business on international transportation. In the field of international logistics and international freight forwarding transportation, we have more applications of B2B e-commerce platforms, with services covering aquatic products processing enterprises and overseas fishery companies. For B2C e-commerce business, there is no direct connection at present, but there is indirect connection, because the sales of imported and exported goods will be finally arranged through B2C e-commerce platforms to a large extent."

The cooperation in cold chain logistics between China and Iceland not only covers talents, technology and funds, but also covers commercial resources and logistics network. Lyu Leijie said, "The logistics industry has a low entry threshold, but it is not easy to do it well." The reason why Eimskip Logistics (Qingdao) Co., Ltd. can grow bigger and stronger is not attributed to its most advanced cold chain logistics technology, but because of the huge network and mature logistics platform brought by Eimskip at the beginning of the cooperation. On this basis, Eimskip

Logistics (Qingdao) Co., Ltd. has built its own unique cold chain logistics network covering the Asia-Pacific region.

The times are developing, the society is developing, and people's thoughts are also developing. As the Managing Director of Eimskip Logistics (Qingdao) Co., Ltd., Lyu Leijie knows that Eimskip can become an industry leader only if it keeps pace with the times. Under the guidance of this philosophy, Eimskip will continuously explore new business and expand new market.

Tackle the Epidemic and Look Ahead

In 2020, the COVID-19 epidemic broke out around the world. With the spread of the global pandemic, the international logistics service supply chain was becoming increasingly important, and the global shipping industry was playing a vital role in responding to the outbreak. It is estimated that more than 80% of global trade volume and more than 70% of trade value is shipped by more than 50,000 vessels worldwide. In the post-epidemic era, global cold chain logistics has been affected to a certain extent. As one of the top 100 cold chain logistics enterprises in China, Eimskip Logistics (Qingdao) Co., Ltd. is also facing a test. In particular, Eimskip Logistics (Qingdao) Co., Ltd., as a key import and export logistics enterprise of Shandong Province, undertakes the important responsibility of resuming trade. To resume trade, employees need to work in a safe environment. In order to avoid the negative impact of the epidemic on the company's business development, Eimskip formulated strict anti-epidemic measures. On the basis of abiding by national anti-epidemic policies, the company also purchased a large number of protective articles and stipulated that employees returning from business trips must work at home for a certain days. For a period of time, Eimskip also issued a travel ban which prohibited employees from business travel and required them to handle all foreign business online. For goods shipped from abroad, Eimskip took a full set of protective measures, such as assigning specialized personnel to handle the goods, requiring employees to keep a distance from warehouses, and making more use of machinery and equipment for operation.

In addition, Lyu Leijie began to improve the company's operation system immediately after he became the Managing Director of the company. In the face of the sudden epidemic outbreak, he said, "The epidemic has brought tremendous changes to our operation mode. We can choose to work at home. By applying a relatively perfect operating system, Eimskip Logistics (Qingdao) Co., Ltd. minimized the losses caused by the epidemic and the impact on the company's business."

Moreover, in the post-epidemic era, Eimskip Logistics (Qingdao) Co., Ltd. is not limited to its current business scope and scale. Although the company has set up branches in Dalian, Shenzhen, Xiamen and Shanghai respectively, Lyu Leijie has an idea for further developing the company from east to west. Due to the unbalanced development of cold chain logistics in eastern and western China, 63% of cold storage is located in eastern China, while there is not enough cold storage in central and western China to meet the daily demand. Facing this strategic opportunity, Lyu Leijie said when talking about the future plan, "The previous development focus and branch offices are located in eastern coastal areas, because these areas are relatively developed economically and have perfect supporting facilities and sufficient cold storage for developing logistics business. Besides, many cities are port cities and close to terminals. This is the unique advantage of the East. Eimskip Logistics (Qingdao) Co., Ltd. has long been seeking opportunities. As the State has put forward the strategy of developing to the west and now railway transportation is very convenient, we pay much attention to Sichuan, Chongqing and Xi'an, where China-Europe freight trains are relatively developed. At the same time, we are also considering the connecting with port cities through the Yangtze River. However, we should accumulate more to carry out these businesses."

Lao-tzu said, "Misfortune might be a blessing in disguises." There are always two sides to the development of things. It is true that the COVID-19 outbreak has affected Eimskip's logistics business, but the impact is not permanent, and it is not all bad. The epidemic is more like a test for Eimskip, a test from quantitative change to qualitative change. When the storm recedes , we will finally see the rainbow.

Talents Are Essential to Company Development

Ren Zhengfei once said, "When you use a person, never mind whether this person is highly competent or not first, you have to tell me exactly what you want the person to do, that is, whether his/her ability matches what you want him/her to do."

In society today, in the face of fierce industry competition, the importance of talents to enterprises is self-evident. Lyu Leijie spoke highly of his team many times in the interview. An enterprise can develop only with the support of talents. Talent is the foundation of an enterprise and the source of enterprise vitality. An enterprise must have talents to boost development and creation; otherwise, it will end up with suspension of development. However, excellent talents are not necessarily right talents. Only when talents are arranged in proper positions can they become effective talents.

When we asked what he valued most during interview, Lyu Leijie responded without hesitation, "We choose the right person." In the opinion of Lyu Leijie, the candidates are excellent, but being excellent does not mean being suitable. As the saying goes, "No matter what career you choose, you can be the best." Each industry has its own characteristics, so does each person. Some people can be a master in the IT industry, but they know nothing about news editing. As Lyu Leijie said, put the right people in the right positions.

Besides being suitable, Lyu Leijie believed that comprehensive quality is also an essential factor including both physical quality and psychological quality. To be truly competent for a position, it not only needs a healthy body, but also a strong heart. During the interview, Lyu Leijie said, "Our company is relatively young, so we will never compromise on matters of principle, and we have strict requirements for employees. In fact, we set high performance indicators for each team. But we also focus much on caring for our staff. The company has set up a staff club, which is entirely managed by young people." As the saying goes, "When the moon is full, it will fall; when a container is full, it will spill out." A working atmosphere with both principle and freedom and a well-balanced management are the best environment for cultivating talents. Without the growth of talents, there will be no growth of enterprise. Eimskip has achieved the ultimate in talent management. "Every month, we will arrange fixed time to hold some activities, including some holidays and festivals, which are all operated by the staff club, majorities are young people," Lyu Leijie said. In the preparation for this interview, we learned about Eimskip's Tik Tok account and WeChat public account, through which we can see the daily work and celebration activities of the employees of Eimskip. It is not difficult to see the harmonious working atmosphere and rigorous and earnest working attitude of Eimskip from these accounts.

Lyu Leijie's extraordinary strategic thinking and leadership are like the high beam of Eimskip, while his team's high professionalism and attention to details in work are like the low beam of Eimskip. The two complement each other and jointly promote the high-speed development of Eimskip.

Prior to the interview, Lyu Leijie said many times, "I have nothing more to say about myself, I hope you can pay more attention to our company and the industry." At that time we felt that he was modest, but during the formal interview, we really understood what he meant. When we asked Lyu Leijie about his hobbies and other questions, his words were always short and concise, but when talking about the team, the company and the industry, he always talked a lot frankly with assurance. From his enthusiastic sharing, we can deeply feel his love for the team, the company and the logistics industry. It is precisely because of such love that Lyu Leijie always persists in learning, constantly moves ahead, and requires his team to continuously learn and make progress. From the beginning to the end of the interview, "learning" and "team" were the words Lyu Leijie mentioned the most frequently, and he always had a lot of personal insights. Continuous learning can promote the progress of the team and help the team to achieve more outstanding performance efficiently with high quality, while the team also makes the learning results more colorful and perfect. At the end of the interview, Lyu Leijie stressed again, "When the team is good at learning, it becomes different. Through constant learning, we can lock the direction of development and move forward tenaciously in the right direction, and everyone knows where our direction is, thus forming a strong joint force."

(Li Yundie　Zhang Weixi)

14

脚踏实地铸英才，坚守责任成大业

——访北京华尚园贸易有限公司总经理刘崇山

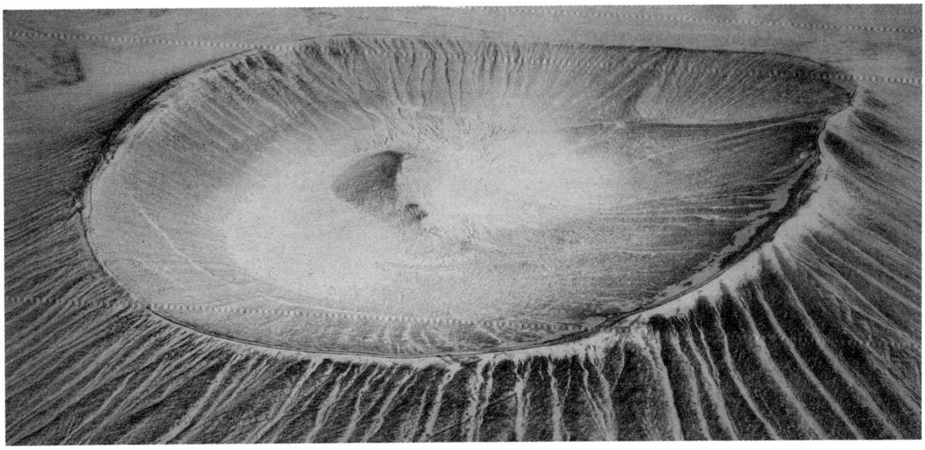

刘崇山手持冰岛天然泉水

爱因斯坦曾经说过："对一个人来说，他所期望的不是别的，而仅仅是他能全力以赴和献身于一个美好的事业。"在一个人的一生中，他所从事的工作占据了他的大部分时间，若是能够找到自己感兴趣、愿意为之付出一切努力的事业，那是一件极其幸福的事情。刘崇山在事业初始时，机缘巧合下了解到Iceland Spring这一品牌，开启了与冰岛天然泉水的故事篇章。企业发展的这些年，经历过困难，有过瓶颈期，也有成功的喜悦。正如梁启超所说："人生须知负责任的苦处，才能知道有尽责的乐趣。"经历多年磨砺之后，刘崇山更加看重"责任"二字，对企业负责，对消费者负责，唯有脚踏实地做实事，才能称得上是一个负责任、有担当的人。

巧遇良机，明者因时而变

"人生成功的秘诀是，当好机会来临时，立刻抓住它。"刘崇山与冰岛天然泉水的故事便印证了这句话。在机遇来到面前时，能够适时抓住机遇并加以利用，是走向成功的秘诀。2014年刘崇山从部队退伍后，来到北京打拼，通过朋友介绍得知Iceland Spring这一品牌，借此了解到冰岛天然泉水。当时水行业市场前景广阔，刘崇山意识到这个行业隐藏的机遇，并对它产生了兴趣。与此同时，北京华尚园贸易有限公司的团队也在吸纳新的人才，刘崇山就此成为团队中的一员。2010年，冰岛天然泉水在上海世博会上展出，首次出现在大众视野中。当时，公司团队便看中了冰岛天然泉水的品质，希望与冰岛泉可以达成合作。为了进一步了解产品，董事长带领团队到冰岛实地考察，了解了冰岛天然泉水的源头、生产流程、工艺标准等等，最终决定将 Iceland Spring 引入中国，自此冰岛天然泉水进入中国大众的生活。北京华尚园贸易有限公司成为其中国国内的总代理，至此也是国内唯一的独家代理商。

冰岛天然泉水之所以能够得到人们的认可，是因为它的源头、生产和运输流程都有自己独特的工艺与优势。冰岛对环境保护非常看重，因此冰岛是一个基本没有污染的国度。冰岛独特的环境和泉水品质是得天独厚的优势。冰岛天然泉水取自冰岛首都雷克雅未克附近的郊区，泉水纯净、天然，不添加任何人工物质，相对于其他矿泉水而言，口感更柔和，饮水体验更好。更为重要的是，冰岛天然泉水的天然 pH 值为 8.88，属于弱碱性矿泉水，可以帮助身体调节酸碱平衡，作为日常饮水更为健康。冰岛水厂也非常重视泉水运输过程中的接触问题，泉水被压出泉口后直接进入灌装设备，为避免泉水与重金属接触发生反应，部分采用了特殊的陶瓷管道运输，保证每一瓶天然泉水从源头一直到瓶盖被打开，都不被任何人接触。这种纯天然的品质保证也是公司团队所看重的，做产品就要做高品质的产品，做服务更要带给消费者最好的体验，做到无愧于己、无憾于人。

Iceland Spring 冰岛天然泉水

业精于勤，永不止步

团队带领冰岛天然泉水于 2016 年进入中国大众的视野，最初极少有人了解这款产品，遑论大批量地采购。因此，他们在推广冰岛天然泉水的过程中花费了大量时间与成本。企业在让大众了解冰岛天然泉水的过程中做出过多种尝试。他们曾经通过与其他企业合作加强对冰岛天然泉水的宣传，与负责海运工作的怡之航国际物流公司分享冰岛天然泉水，等等。其中有的举措收到了良好的效果，但也不乏不尽如人意的结果，这是做企业的必经之路，这些经历使刘崇山积累了丰富的经验，也成为他未来企业发展宝贵的财富。

为了扩大天然纯净的冰岛天然泉水的知名度，增进客户对冰岛天然泉水的了解，企业时刻关注着行业内的产品宣传机会。2016 年，北京华尚园贸易有限公司参加了第二十届中国国际健康产业博览会，公司团队携 Iceland Spring 冰岛天然泉水参加博览会，产品一经展出就受到了热烈关注，冰岛驻华大使馆公使参赞拉格纳尔·鲍德松先生（Ragnar Baldursson）作为特邀嘉宾详细介绍了冰岛天然泉水独具的健康特性。同年，团队带着冰岛天然泉水参加了第五届广州国际品水大赛，独具特色的冰岛天然泉水依靠自身的纯净天然博得一致好评，在参展的众多产品中拔得头筹，获得金奖。让刘崇山高兴的是，多次参展使冰岛天然泉水已经逐渐为国人所熟知，产品品质得到专业水平的认可，最初的希冀得以实现。

作为冰岛天然泉水在中国国内的总代理商，刘崇山希望提高冰岛天然泉水在中国消费者中的了解度和认可度，通过代理商、经销商团队以及线上线下相结合来发掘更多的家庭型客户。2018 年，在开拓市场过程中，公司曾定有一个目标，实现中国有一万个家庭每月持续性采购冰岛天然泉水，达到每月有较大的固定采购体量。由于冰岛天然泉水在泉水采集、灌装过程中使用独特技术，并且生产天然泉水产品中所需的瓶身、木制托盘、瓶盖等产品需要从国外进口，冰岛国内并不对这些产品组织生产。产品包装所需瓶身、瓶盖均由外国设计师进行独特的实验设计制造，在检测上采用欧美标准来检验，因此在产品的生产包装过程中产生了较高的成本。另外，在将冰岛天然泉水通过海运运输到中国国内时，运输路途遥远，这也在一定程度上提高了冰岛天然泉水的成本。刘崇山与冰岛水厂进行日常需求沟通时大多是以邮件的形式进行。冰岛水厂按照自己的运行规律来生产。冰岛天然泉水一年内有固定的生产月份。如果有产品需求，刘崇山必须提前 3 个月发邮件沟通说明需求，冰岛水厂进行生产排期的安排。这需要中方提前沟通、提出产品规格和数量的需求，然后再安排生产的运营模式也导致了产品生产周期较长，相对而言，增加了时间成本。此外，独特纯净的品质和独具匠心的包装共同形成了冰岛天然泉水的特色，高标准的产品更易得到消费者的青睐，但同时，由于这种高端追求也使得冰岛天然泉水在市场上的定价是普通矿泉水的数倍，对于团队而言，将产品推广给大众的难度也更高。

在谈到产品贸易中遇到的困难时，刘崇山表示，遇到难题不能退缩，要迎难而上去解决问题。他提到国家在产品进口贸易中给予了支持。在2014年7月1日开始生效的《中华人民共和国政府和冰岛政府自由贸易协定》中，对进口冰岛的绝大多数商品实行零关税政策，这极大地促进了冰岛天然泉产品在中国的推广与销售。他说："国家已经给了企业很好的贸易政策。我们不能一直向国家伸手要政策，还是要努力提高企业的效益，用优质的服务和严谨的态度回报消费者，把企业团队做大做强。"作为冰岛天然泉水的销售总代理公司总经理，刘崇山更多地注重销售方面，面向消费者提供更好的服务，在产品运输过程中注重运输时效和安全问题，将自己角色内的工作努力做到最好。另外，在宣传产品的过程中尝试创新产品推广方式。冰岛天然泉水在经历几年时间的推广后，在国内市场中已经具有了一定的熟悉度和认可度，这与刘崇山团队前期做出的种种努力和尝试是分不开的。

2020年全球新冠肺炎疫情暴发之后，正常经济活动受到了影响，尤其是国际贸易方面，中冰路途遥远，导致冰岛天然泉水贸易遇到的阻力更大。全世界是一个命运共同体，新冠肺炎疫情的存在，需要各国携手共同抗击疫情，只有全球的大环境是安全的时候，消费者才会对产品真正放心。公司面临的就是这样的大环境，产品的安全问题是重中之重。当产品运抵海关后，会进行严格的消毒流程，保证产品的外包装没有受到污染，产品从海关运输至企业仓库后也需要进行消毒检测，并安排专门人员定时定点进行消毒，这些事情都是最基础也是最重要的。刘崇山说："产品有安全保证，这样客户才能放心，一定要让客户对我们充分信任，相信我们能把所有的事情做好。"正是由于刘崇山负责任的态度和做法，产品得到了消费者的认可和信任，疫情发生的这两年内，冰岛天然泉水的销量反而有了一定的增加。在刘崇山看来，这是多方面因素综合产生的结果。首先，冰岛天然泉水的高品质是大家有目共睹的，这是最坚实的基础。其次，自2016年开始，对冰岛天然泉水的多方面推广也发挥了重要的作用，团队把好品质产品分享出去，经过时间的积累和成本的投入，消费者更加了解了这款产品。这次新冠肺炎疫情也提醒人们要更注重身体健康，对于吃的食物、选的衣服、用的日用品等等都更注重品质，人们的消费观在潜移默化中更偏向于选择放心、健康的高品质产品。

目前，冰岛天然泉水在中国国内的市场较好，产品从冰岛水厂运输发出，通过海运到达中国一般需要 2 个月的周期，而每次订购的产品在国内很快就会脱销。这种向好的市场环境也给了刘崇山很大的信心，反馈出人们对冰岛天然泉水的喜爱。之前团队做出的规划是有一万个家庭能够固定持续地采购冰岛天然泉水，但现在，在市场环境逐步改善的情况下，他们有信心将未来的规划做成倍的提升，给自己定一个新目标，努力让国内更多的消费者能够享受到这种好品质的水。采访中刘崇山还谈到，推广一种产品并不仅仅是推广产品本身，更重要的是让消费者体会到产品背后的内涵，可以让大家更多地了解冰岛。很多人去冰岛旅游后都爱上了冰岛天然泉水，希望回国后也能喝到，常常会有人询问大使馆可不可以供应冰岛天然泉水。这些细节都表明冰岛天然泉水在中国具有广阔的前景，消费者会从一款产品出发，进而对其背后的出处产生兴趣，进一步了解并喜欢上冰岛这个美丽的国家。

沟通达共识，协调求进步

刘崇山（左一）与公司董事长（左二）、冰岛驻华大使易卜雷（左三）及其夫人、冰岛驻华使馆商务代表杨力合照

自公司与冰岛企业进行合作以来，大使馆举办过多次中冰企业家交流活动，也有一些企业家之间的私人聚会，企业家朋友间保持着较为频繁的交流和沟通。中冰建交 45 周年和建交 50 周年时，大使馆都举办过大型的中冰建交周年庆活动，每一次活动刘崇山都会去参加，并借此机会与其他企业家分享和交流。刘崇山开展冰岛业务以来，先后得到了三任冰岛驻华大使的关怀与支持，并有幸在 2019 年作为冰岛企业代表参加了与来访的冰岛前外交部长

格维兹勒于尔·索尔·索尔达松的见面会。无论是外长，或者是各位大使，他们一直都鼎力支持中冰企业家的活动，积极推进各方的沟通与反馈，使中冰双边贸易更为顺畅，合作氛围也更加轻松。

刘崇山和他的团队十分注重国内消费群体的感受，为了让客户得到最好的产品和服务，他积极地与冰岛企业进行沟通，确定贸易往来的最优策略。在与冰岛企业家沟通时，一些冰岛企业家可以用中文来交流，令刘崇山很是惊喜，在沟通时避免了许多不便。这也充分体现了中国和冰岛间的友好交往以及日益紧密的双边关系。

在与冰岛企业家沟通过程中，刘崇山感触最深的是每个企业家最看重的就是负责，做产品的企业最看重的是产品的品质，做服务的企业最看重的是服务的质量。对刘崇山而言，服务是第一位的，让高品质的产品能够被大众认识、接受、认可，让选择这款产品的消费者得到最优质的服务是他全力以赴所追求的。

君子务本，立本而道生

身为一名“90 后”，刘崇山有一颗炽热的报国之心。年轻时参军入伍，将自己的青春和一腔热血挥洒在祖国的土地上。军旅生涯结束后，他开始了自己的经商之路。后来，经朋友介绍了解了冰岛天然泉水 Iceland Spring，一步步开启了与冰岛的合作。刘崇山对祖国的发展感触颇多。他认为，各行各业的发展在本质上都是一样的。只有自己的团队有足够的实力，国家有强大的后盾支撑，企业才会有长远的发展，而个人通过努力也会有好的成绩。他还提到，企业要将消费者的感受放在第一位，用优质的服务回报消费者、回报社会，祖国给予我们贸易方面的优惠政策支持，我们也要用自己的力量为国家的经济发展做出贡献。

在社会发展日新月异的今天，各行各业都在吸纳人才。刘崇山认为，在工作中没有捷径可走，唯一的准则便是脚踏实地、扎扎实实地磨炼本领，人才自有用武之地。上学时要认真学习，用知识武装自己，参加工作后要踏踏实实干好每一项工作，一步一个脚印地向前走，结果定不会辜负有心人。除此之外，他还强调，身体是革命的本钱，保持良好的休息状态，强健体魄，以积极向上的精神风貌投入学习工作中，往往效果也是事半功倍的。

刘崇山在自己的行业中所取得的成就无疑是出类拔萃的，但他始终保持着一种谦逊的态度，从不认为自己取得了傲人的成绩。在提到这段时间的热词“躺平”和“内卷”时，他也有自己独特的见解。他认为，一个人在学习和工作的过程中可能会出现一个疲劳期或瓶颈期，由于各种压力而无法前进，从而出现“躺平”这种现象。但他也强调，自己不会选择“躺平”。如果他在遭遇困境时就此停下脚步，很可能会被行业所淘汰，在任何时候他都要保持勇于上进的心态。对于“内卷”，真正有能力的人都不会提倡“内卷”，我们需要的是良性的进步。或许别人认为自己的状态已经达到了平稳期，继续成长进步的其他人就变成了“内卷”，但事实上，我们应该时刻都保持学习和进步的状态。新年伊始，我们不只是年龄长了一点，方方面面都要有进步和成长。时代一直在进步，我们也要与时俱进。正如老师在学校所教诲的，不会的事情就要问，现在也是一样的。我们需要保持求知欲和上进心。

正是秉持这样认真务实、勇于上进的态度，刘崇山始终坚守作为冰岛天然泉水中国总代理的责任担当，向消费者提供优质的服务，与大众分享高品质的产品，在行业和在社会中做出表率，勇于担当，脚踏实地做好每一件事。天行健，君子以自强不息。年轻的力量、年轻的思维像冰岛潺潺清泉一样注入身心，不论面对怎样的困境，我们都不应轻言放弃。刘崇山在执着奋斗中实现着他的人生价值，在奉献担当中收获了真诚、坦荡和满足。

（朱昱茹　闫星耀　张楚玲）

Talents Born from Solid Work and a Great Career from Sense of Responsibility

— Interview with Liu Chongshan, General Manager of Beijing Hua Shangyuan Trading Co., Ltd.

Einstein once said: "For a man, what he expects is nothing else, but that he can devote himself to a good cause." In a person's life, the work he is engaged in occupies most of his time. If he can find a career that he is interested in and is willing to make all efforts for it, it's an extremely happy thing. At the beginning of his career, Liu Chongshan learned about Iceland Spring by chance, which opened a chapter of his story with Iceland Spring. In these years of the enterprise development, the enterprise has experienced a lot. There are difficulties, bottleneck period and the joy of success in pursuing development. As Liang Qichao said, "Only when you know the hardship of responsibility in life can you know the pleasure of being responsible." After years of honing, Liu Chongshan pays more attention to responsibility. He shall be always responsible for his enterprise and consumers. Only by doing solid work in a down-to-earth manner can he be called a responsible and accountable man.

With a Chance Encounter, a Wise Man Changes as Time Changes

"The secret of success in life is to seize a good opportunity as soon as it comes." The story of Liu Chongshan and Iceland Spring confirm the remark. When the opportunity comes, the secret to success is to seize it and make full use of it. After Liu Chongshan retired from the active military service in 2014, he came to Beijing to struggle for his cause. He learned of the brand Iceland Spring through the introduction of his friends, thus he also knew of natural Icelandic springs. At that time, the market prospect of the water industry was promising. Liu Chongshan realized the hidden opportunities of the industry and became interested in it. At the same time, the team of Beijing Hua Shangyuan Trading Co., Ltd. was also recruiting new talents, so Liu Chongshan was on the team. In 2010, Iceland Spring were exhibited at the Expo 2010 Shanghai China and first became known to a wider public. At that time, the quality of natural Icelandic springs struck the team's fancy, so the team hoped to establish cooperation with Iceland Spring. In order to further know about the product, the chairman led the team to Iceland to make a field visit and find out the source, production process and process standards of natural Icelandic springs. Afterwards, the team decided to introduce Iceland Spring into China at last. Since then, Iceland Spring has entered the life of the Chinese public. Beijing Hua Shangyuan Trading Co., Ltd. has become the general agent of the product in China and the only exclusive agent of the product in China.

The reason why natural Icelandic springs are recognized by Chinese people is that their source as well as the process of production and transportation boasts their own unique technology and advantages. Iceland attaches great importance to environmental protection. Therefore, Iceland is a basically pollution-free country. Iceland's unique environment and spring quality enjoy exceptional advantages. Natural Icelandic springs come from the suburbs near Reykjavik, the capital of Iceland. The springs are pure, natural and rich in natural minerals any artificial substances. Compared with other mineral water, and natural Icelandic springs taste softer and customers have a better drinking experience. More importantly, the natural pH value of 8.88 which belongs to weakly alkaline mineral water, and natural Icelandic springs can help the human body regulate the acid-base balance, so natural Icelandic springs are healthier daily drinking water. Icelandic water plant also attaches great importance to the contact problem in the transportation process of natural Icelandic springs. Pressed out of the spring vent, natural Icelandic springs directly enters the filling equipment. In order to avoid the reaction between spring and heavy metals, some special ceramic pipeline transportation is adopted to ensure that each bottle of natural springs is not contacted by anyone from the spring source to the opening of the bottle cap. The pure and natural quality assurance is also valued by our company team. When marketing products, we must deal in high-quality products, when offering services, we must bring consumers the best experience, thus we can build our self-worth and live up to the others' expectation.

Efficiency Comes from Diligence and Continuous Struggle

Led by the team, Iceland Spring was known to the Chinese public in 2016. At first, few people knew about the product, let alone large-scale procurement. Therefore, the team spent a lot of time and cost in promoting natural Icelandic springs. The enterprise has made various attempts in the process of making the public know about Icelandic Spring. They once strengthened the publicity of Iceland Spring through cooperation with other enterprises, shared natural Icelandic springs with Eimskip International Logistics Co., Ltd., which is responsible for ocean shipping, and so on. Some of these measures have achieved good results, but there are still few unsatisfactory results. It is the only way which must be passed in the running process of an enterprise. These experiences not only made Liu Chongshan gain rich experience but also became his valuable asset for the development of enterprises in the future.

In order to increase the publicity of natural and pure Icelandic springs and enhance customers' awareness of natural Icelandic springs, the Enterprise always pay attention to the opportunities for the product promotion in the industry. In 2016, Beijing Hua Shangyuan Trading Co., Ltd. participated in the 20th China

International Health Industry Expo. The team took Iceland Spring natural Icelandic springs to the Expo. Once the product was displayed, they received warm attention. As a special guest, Mr. Ragnar Baldursson, Minister-Counselor of Embassy of Iceland in China, explained in detail the unique health characteristics of natural Icelandic springs. In the same year, the team took natural Icelandic springs to participate in the Fifth Guangzhou International Water Tasting Competition. The unique natural Icelandic springs received unanimous praise for its pure nature, took the lead among many products in the exhibition and won the Gold Award. Liu Chongshan is delighted that natural Icelandic springs has been gradually known to Chinese people, the product quality has been recognized by the professional institutions, and the initial expectation has been fulfilled.

As the general agent of natural Icelandic springs in China, Liu Chongshan hopes to expand the awareness and recognition of natural Icelandic springs among Chinese consumers. So he explored more family customers through the combination of agents, dealer team and online and offline activities. In 2018, in the process of market exploitation, the Company set a goal of the continuous purchase of natural Icelandic springs every month by 10,000 families in China to achieve a large fixed purchase volume every month. Unique technology is adopted in the collection and filling process of natural Icelandic springs, and the bottle body, wooden tray, bottle cap and other products that are required in the production of natural spring products are imported from abroad, which are not produced in Iceland. The body and cap of bottles that are required for product packaging are manufactured by the unique experimental design conducted by foreign designers, and inspected with European and American standards. Therefore, higher costs are incurred in the production and packaging process of products. In addition, when natural Icelandic springs is transported to China by sea, the transportation route is long, which also increases the cost of natural Icelandic springs to a certain extent. Most of the communication for daily demand between Liu Chongshan and the Icelandic water plant is conducted in the form of e-mail. The Icelandic water plant produces the products according to its own operation law. There are fixed months for the production of natural Icelandic springs within a year. If there is a product demand, Liu Chongshan must send an email three months in advance to inform the product demand, and the Icelandic water plant can arrange the production schedule. This operation mode requires Chinese agent to communicate in advance, put forward the demand for product specifications and quantities, and then the manufacturer arranges product production, which leads to a long production period and relatively increases time cost. Besides, the unique and pure quality and exquisite packaging together form the characteristics of natural Icelandic springs. High-standard products are more easily favored by consumers. However, due to this high-end pursuit, the price of natural Icelandic springs in the market is several times higher than that of ordinary mineral water, which makes it more difficult for the team to promote the products to the public.

When talking about the difficulties encountered in product trade, Liu Chongshan said that they should not shrink back in the face of difficulties but rise up to solve them. He mentioned that the state had given support in the import trade of products. In the *Free Trade Agreement Between the Government of the People's Republic of China and the Government of Iceland* that has come into force from July 1, 2014, the zero tariff policy of the vast majority of goods imported Iceland has been implemented as well, which has greatly boosted the promotion and sales of Iceland Spring products in China. He said, "The state has given enterprises good trade policies. We can't always ask for policies from the state, but we should strive to improve the enterprise benefit, reward our consumers with excellent service and rigorous attitude, and make our enterprise team bigger and stronger." As the general manager of the general sales agent of natural Icelandic springs, Liu Chongshan pays more attention to sales, better services to consumers, transportation timeliness and safety in the process of product transportation, and exerts himself to do his best at work in his role. Besides, he also tries to innovate the way of product promotion in the process of promoting products. After several years of promotion, Iceland Spring has gained a certain degree of familiarity and recognition in the domestic market, which is inseparable from the efforts and attempts made by Liu Chongshan's team in the early stage.

After COVID-19 epidemic broke out across the world in 2020, the normal economic activities, especially international trade, was affected. The long distance between the China and Iceland caused greater resistance to natural Icelandic springs trade. The whole world is a community of shared destiny. The existence of COVID-19 needs all countries to work together to fight against the epidemic. Only when the global environment is safe, consumers will truly feel relieved. The Company is now facing such an environment, and the safety of products is the top priority. After the products are transported to the customs, a strict disinfection process will be carried out to ensure that the outer packaging of the products is not polluted. After the products are transported to the enterprise warehouse from the customs, disinfection testing will also be conducted, and special personnel will be arranged to disinfect at fixed times. All these procedures are the most basic and important. Liu Chongshan said, "Only when the products enjoy safety assurance can customers rest assured. We must make sure customers have fully trust in us and believe that we can do everything well." It is definitely because of Liu Chongshan's responsible attitude and practice that the products could be recognized and trusted by consumers, and the sales of natural Icelandic springs have increased to a certain extent in the past two years. In Liu Chongshan's view, it is the comprehensive result of various factors. Firstly, the high quality of natural Icelandic springs is obvious to all, which is the most solid foundation. Secondly, since 2016, the promotion of natural Icelandic springs has also played an important role. The team has shared the products with good quality. After the accumulation of time and cost investment, consumers have a better understanding of the product. The COVID-19 epidemic also reminds people to pay more attention to not only health but also the quality of food, clothing and daily necessities. People's consumption concept is more inclined to select a safe and healthy product under the subtle influence.

At present, natural Iceland Spring has a good market in China. It generally takes two months to reach China by sea after the products are transported from Icelandic water plants. The products will be sold out very soon each time in China. The positive market environment not only reflected Chinese people' favor of natural Icelandic springs but also gave Liu Chongshan great confidence. The previous plan made by the team is that 10,000 families can purchase natural Icelandic springs regularly and continuously. But now, under the gradual improvement of market environment, they are confident to double the previous plan for their future plans. By setting a new goal for themselves, they would strive to make more domestic consumers can enjoy the high-quality water. In the interview, Liu Chongshan also said that the promotion of a product is not only just a promotion, making consumers feel the deep connotation behind the product is also significant, which could make Chinese people know more about Iceland. After traveling to Iceland, many people fall in love with natural Icelandic springs and desire to drink them after returning home. People often ask whether the Embassy can supply natural Icelandic springs. These details show that natural Icelandic springs have broad prospects in China. Starting from a product, consumers will become interested in the source behind it and further know about and like Iceland, a beautiful country.

Communication for Consensus and Coordination for Progress

Since the establishment of the cooperation between the Company and Icelandic enterprises, the embassy has held many exchange activities between Chinese and Icelandic entrepreneurs, and some entrepreneurs have arranged private gatherings, thus entrepreneurial friends maintain frequent communication. On the 45th and 50th anniversary of the establishment of diplomatic relations between China and Iceland, the embassy held large-scale activities to celebrate the anniversary of the establishment of diplomatic relations between China and Iceland. Liu Chongshan participated in every activity and took the opportunity to share and communicate with other entrepreneurs. Liu Chongshan has obtained care and support from three terms of ambassador of Iceland to China since he started his business in Iceland. He was lucky to participate in the meeting with visiting Gudlaugur Thor Thordarson, former Icelandic Foreign Minister as a representative of Icelandic enterprises in 2019. Whether foreign ministers or ambassadors, they have always fully supported the activities of Chinese and Icelandic entrepreneurs. They promoted the communication and feedback of all parties actively to make the bilateral trade between China and Iceland smoother and the cooperation atmosphere more relaxed.

A group photo of Liu Chongshan (first from the right) together with Mr. Gudlaugur Thor Thordarson (first from the left), former Icelandic Foreign Minister

Liu Chongshan and his team attach importance to the feelings of domestic consumer groups. In order to let customers receive the best products and services, he communicated with Icelandic enterprises actively to determine the best strategy for trade. When he communicated with Icelandic entrepreneurs, some Icelandic entrepreneurs could speak in Chinese, which surprised Liu Chongshan and avoided a lot of inconvenience in communication. The communication fully reflects the friendly exchanges and increasingly close bilateral relations between China and Iceland.

In the process of communicating with Icelandic entrepreneurs, what Liu Chongshan felt most deeply is that every entrepreneur regards responsibility most important. The most important thing for enterprises dealing in products is the quality of products, and the most important thing for enterprises offering services is the quality of services. In Liu Chongshan's opinion, service comes first. It is his full pursuit to make high-quality products known, accepted and recognized by the public and let consumers who select the product get the best service.

A Gentleman Putting Basic Principles First Will Illuminate the Way Forward

As a generation after 1990s, Liu Chongshan has a passionate heart of serving the country worthily. When he was young, he joined the army to devote his youth and energy to the motherland. Then he began his own business after retiring from the active military service. Later, he learned about Iceland Spring, a natural Icelandic springs, via the introduction by his friends, and opened cooperation with Icelandic enterprises step by step. Liu Chongshan has a lot of thoughts and feelings about the development of the motherland. He believes that the development of all trades and professions is essentially the same. Only when the teams of their own have sufficient strength and are supported by powerful country can the enterprises develop for a long term, and the individuals also have good achievement after personal efforts. He also mentioned that enterprises should not only put consumers' feelings first, rewarding their consumers and the society with high-quality services, but also use their own strength to contribute to the economic development of motherland who gives preferential policies on supporting enterprises in trade.

Today, with the rapid development of society, all trades and professions are recruiting talents. Liu Chongshan believes that there is no shortcut in work. The only criterion for the talents to display their abilities is first to practice skills one step at a time in a down-to-earth. When you go to school, you should study hard and arm yourself with knowledgc. After taking a job, you should do every thing in a thoroughgoing manner and move forward one step at a time. The result will not fail to the one who sets his mind on it. Besides, he also stressed that good health is a prerequisite for work. Good rest, strong physique and learning and working with a positive spirit often yield twice the result with half the effort.

There is no doubt that the achievements which Liu Chongshan made in his industry are outstanding, but hc is still always humble and never thinks he has made extraordinary achievements. He also has his own unique opinions when referring to the hot words "lying flat" and "rat race" during this period. He held that an individual might indeed enter a fatigue period or bottleneck period in the process of study and work and be unable to proceed due to various pressures, thus the phenomenon of "lying flat" appeared. But he also emphasized that he would not choose to "lying flat". If he stopped at the time of encountering difficulties, he was likely to be eliminated by the industry. He would maintain the mentality of making progress at any time. As for "rat race", competent and well-trained people will not advocate rat race. What we need is benign progress. Perhaps others think that their state has reached a stable period and continuous growth and progress have become "rat race", but in fact, we should always maintain the state of learning and making progress. At the beginning of the New Year, not only do we get a little older, but we will also make progress in all aspects. The times have been going ahead, and we should keep pace with the times. As teachers taught us at school, we have to ask for help when we don't know how to do. Now it's the same. We still need to maintain our thirst for knowledge and the urge for improvement.

Holding such a positive attitude, Liu Chongshan always sticks with his responsibility, as the general agent of natural Icelandic springs in China. He provides and shares the high-quality product with the public. He is willing to set an example in the industry and the society, and take responsibility to do everything down-to-earth. As Heaven's movement is ever vigorous, so must a gentleman ceaselessly strive along. Young strength and young thoughts are injected into our body and mind like the gurgling spring in Iceland. No matter what difficulties we face, we should not give up easily. Liu Chongshan is realizing his life value in his persistent struggle and has gained sincerity, magnanimity and satisfaction in his dedication.

(Zhu Yuru Yan Xingyao Zhang Chuling)

15

做这个时代坚定的理想主义者

——访冰岛极地绿色能源集团首席执行官 Sigurdur Atli Jonsson

"Hello"，来自 7777 公里之外的热情

Sigurdur Atli Jonsson

"Hello！"当我们还在调试网络设备时，猝不及防地收到了 Jonsson 这声漂洋过海的问候。

前一秒刚进入线上会议室的我们不只是惊叹于网速之快，丝毫不受中冰两国相隔 7777 公里的影响，更惊喜于这声问候里所洋溢着的热情与温暖，像是一只和平鸽不远万里衔来了冰岛的春天，让人如沐春风。然而，因为会议链接问题，在起初 5 分多钟的时间里，我们先是无法接收对方的视频画面，解决之后又接收不到对方的声音。网络信号的故障耗费了我们本就宝贵的采访时间，却也成了我们捕捉人物特质的一扇窗——在音画不齐的情况下，Jonsson 始终保持着十分耐心的态度，与作为采访发起人的我们一起努力、一起焦急、一起用手比画尝试，以便尽早实现这一场期待已久而远隔重洋的连接。

终于，我们成功开启了音画同步的线上采访，这时 Jonsson 热情洋溢的问候之音与他的微笑一起映入眼帘，他冰蓝色的眼睛带来的并不是北欧的清凉，而是扑面而来的亲和力和热情，以及一名企业家卓越的洞察力。

"污染无国界"，新能源企业里的理想主义者

冰川、极光、火山……提及冰岛时，这些是涌现在我们脑海里的第一印象。除此之外，冰岛还是国际能源署所统计的国家中可再生能源占比最高的国家，这片小小的土地拥有全球独一无二的地热开发技术。

冰岛是一座火山岛，拥有丰富的水能资源和地热资源，是一个几乎靠可再生能源就能运转的国家。你可能会感到不可思议，冰岛的电力系统已经完全是通过可再生能源发电。此外，为应对气候变化，冰岛致力于用可再生能源替代化石能源，其目标是到2050年完全摆脱对石油能源的依赖。

在谈到冰岛的能源转型成果时，我们可以明显地感受到Jonsson那份油然而生的自豪，其中，既源于他作为一名冰岛居民对祖国新能源伟大成就的骄傲，也源于他作为新能源行业龙头企业家的荣耀——Jonsson是冰岛极地绿色能源集团（Arctic Green Energy，以下简称AGE）的CEO。AGE是一家营利性绿色能源公司，公司成立之初的使命是以中外合资的方式在亚洲新能源新兴市场建立一家公司，从而输出冰岛在地热和其他可再生能源方面的开发运营成果。至今AGE在60个国家和地区为将近200万人提供区域性供热项目，拥有注册专利58项，减排与循环利用二氧化碳达到16亿吨，并且参与了联合国教科文组织的地热能源项目推广。

在采访中，Jonsson也提到了对中国新能源产业的看法。对于中国2060年前实现碳中和的目标，他精准地点破了中国碳减排问题的根本："在中国，最大的能源消耗就在制热、制冷两个方面，所以减少化石燃料在制热与制冷方面的使用，就是减少碳排放的核心，而这正是我们与中石化合作的内容。"同时，他也对中国完成这一目标充满信心，"如果你有雄心，就一步一步地去努力。无疑，中国正走在正确的道路上"。

这并非Jonsson口头一说的豪言壮志，而是对AGE与中国在绿色能源领域合作成果的肯定。AGE与中国合作的代表，就是著名的中石化绿源地热能开发有限公司（Sinopec Green Energy Geothermal Development Co.,Ltd.，以下简称SGE）。SGE成立于2006年，这是一家中外合资企业，其中AGE持有46.2%的股份，中石化持有53.8%的股份，以发展地热区域供热业务为核心并拓展至其他绿色能源利用技术。自陕西省咸阳市建立第一个项目以来，公司已将业务扩展到河北、山东和江苏等地。如今，SGE是全球最大的地热区域供热公司，在中国拥有35%的市场份额，以绿色、清洁和可持续的能源利用方式为超过200多万客户提供供暖服务。它的地热工程是世界上第一个获得联合国清洁发展机制注册的项目。到目前为止，其区域供热业务已减少近1140万吨的二氧化碳排放。

环保行业是一个闪烁着人道主义光芒的行业，从事这一行业的人也应是如此。在与Jonsson简短的交谈中，我们接收到了这一点："不只是为了我们的客户，而且是为了全人类，因为污染是没有国界的。”穿插在他对中国和冰岛两国新能源行业前景的论述中的这样一句话深深地触动了我们，“污染无国界”，这一阐述虽然简洁，却让人振聋发聩。商业活动的本质不仅包括商业本身，而且要考量人道主义的关心。只有这样，企业才能创造出可持续发展的商业战略，从而将资本和技术应用于最有价值的、最重要的事情上去。这也是 AGE 的价值观：不仅要成为一家营利性组织，还要成为让世界更加清洁、更加健康的一股力量。

成为一个关注人类命运共同体且具有社会责任心的企业，并不单单是一个口号，以 Jonsson 为代表的 AGE 企业成员一直在向着这一方向奋力前行。

他是一位热爱家人的企业家，一位热爱中国的冰岛友人

“事实上，我非常向往那次假期，因为我特别想让我的妻子和孩子到中国看一看。”Jonsson 向我们提起，他曾计划在 2020 年 4 月带家人来中国度假，但由于新冠肺炎疫情暴发，这个计划不得不搁置。我们注意到，Jonsson 在这次短暂的采访中多次提到了自己的家人。有这样一个采访问题：您认为在以往的经历中，有哪些事情可以被称为自己的人生节点呢？我们设置这一问题的初衷是想对他在官网上所列举的商业成就有进一步的了解，但他的回答既出人意料又打动人心：“应该是组成家庭和我的孩子诞生的那一天。”细想一下，这确实是我们人生中的重要时刻，不是吗？只是在这样一次商务采访中，一名企业家脱口而出这一答案时，我们不自觉地被打动了。对于很多人来说，谈及全球新冠肺炎疫情带来的影响时，他们总是忍不住抱怨，而 Jonsson 的第一反应居然是疫情使居家办公成了常态化，自己在这一办公模式下也可以很好地完成工作，尤其是还可以抽出更多的时间陪伴家人，享受陪伴孩子成长的时光。

Jonsson 多次提到的另一个词语是“中国”，对于中国他想谈的有很多。在他眼里，中国人民和冰岛人民有不少相似之处——“人们一样地乐于沟通，愿意与别人交往。我来到中国时，即使面对很多语言障碍，但也并未影响我与中国伙伴愉快的交流”。但不可否认，冰岛与中国也有很多差异之处，Jonsson 感觉最显著的差异就是地理空间。冰岛是一个大岛屿，行走在冰岛的街巷，你很容易遇到熟悉的人，而在地域辽阔的中国，这基本是不可能的。他来过中国很多次，到过北京、上海、雄安新区等地，感受到了

传统文明与现代成就在这些城市中的完美融合，因此，他想把这份奇妙的体验分享给自己的家人。

他还热情地介绍了自己的家乡。冰岛面积不大，但独特的地理位置给冰岛带来了许多得天独厚的优势，如丰富的海洋渔业资源。他热情地向我们推荐了冰岛的传统特色美食，烟熏鳟鱼、发酵鲨鱼肉，还有鲜嫩的烤羊排。除此之外，因为地处于美洲板块和欧亚板块的交汇处，冰岛还拥有丰富的地热资源，冰岛人民关于地热能的灵感也由 Jonsson 与 AGE 公司带到了中国，为地球另一端国度的人民带来了福祉。

回归到 Jonsson 的企业家角色，从他丰富的职业履历中，可以看到他的不断尝试、不断突破：

——任职 AGE 公司首席执行官及高级顾问；

——在职冰岛金融服务组织（Icelandic Securities）主席和冰岛私募股权投资公司（Umbreyting）董事会董事；

——曾担任三家金融服务公司的首席执行官，其中包括冰岛最大的投资银行 Kvika。

在金融行业的丰富经历对他在新能源行业的工作有着极大的帮助。在地热产业前期的研发阶段，钻井设备、土地使用等相关基础设施需要大量的资金支持，这对公司管理层在公司治理结构、寻找潜在投资方面的能力要求极高，而拥有丰富金融从业经验的 Jonsson 对此可谓是轻车熟路。但在他的眼里，金融行业与绿色能源行业给人带来截然不同的工作体验。“银行和金融服务公司通常是高度纪律化、组织化的，面对严格的监管框架没有任何自由施展的余地，这个行业汇聚着很多优秀的人，但却因严格的框架而缺少创新。新能源产业则不同，它更强调技术的研发与更新迭代，所以会给人更多的创新空间，尤其是后疫情时代，各国经济发展的不确定因素增多，国家将更加重视能源安全，以地热为代表的新能源因其可持续性将会迎来更好的机遇。”行内人士的视角令我们收获到了不一样的职业感受，同时也赞叹于他深刻的洞察力。

Jonsson 的跨行业发展无疑是成功的。在瞬息万变的商界，我们希望能从他的身上学到成功的秘诀。他告诉我们，最重要的是专注于自我，要勇敢尝试，不要给自己设限，也就是我们常说的勇于走出自己的舒适区。同时，他也将一些重要的人生体会分享给年轻人：“保持真我，不要吝啬用于个人生活的时间”。不难发现，这些都是他一直在躬行践履的事情，正是这些理念驱动着他勇敢地做出不一样的选择。

中冰携手，共谱下一个 50 年华章

谈到中国和冰岛在下一个 50 年的合作，Jonsson 务实而又不失风趣地提出了自己的希冀："我希望在不久的将来，中国和冰岛之间能够实现直航。"

中国与冰岛之间虽然相距遥远，但从中冰经济结构来看，中冰之间存在着巨大的合作潜力。2006 年以来，中国已连续多年成为冰岛在亚洲的最大贸易伙伴，中冰两国贸易往来不断增加。同时，在很多优势互补领域的合作已经开展并取得了丰硕的成果，与 AGE 公司在新能源领域的合作就是其中之一。因此，从长远来看，中冰两国之间存在着巨大的合作潜力与广泛的合作前景。

50 年来，正是在千千万万如 Jonsson 一般的两国人民的努力奋斗下，中冰两国互相帮助，在文化交流与碰撞中实现了两国经济的蓬勃发展。这也是冰岛研究中心这次采访活动的初衷，希望能将 Jonsson 们的成功经验分享给两国人民，为中冰两国未来的发展贡献一份力量。

（刘子涵　马伊丹　毛雨）

Being a Firm Idealist in the Era

— Interview with Sigurdur Atli Jonsson, CEO of Iceland Arctic Green Energy Corporation

"Hello", Enthusiastic Greeting from 7,777 km Away

"Hello!" Mr. Jonsson's greeting across the ocean suddenly heard when we were still commissioning the network equipment.

When we just entered the online conference room, we were not only amazed at the network speed even though there are 7,777 km away between China and Iceland but also surprised at the enthusiasm and warmth that are filled in Mr. Jonsson's greeting. It seems as if a peace dove carried the spring of Iceland in its bill, which makes us so delighted just like bathing in the spring wind. However, due to the problem of conference link, during more than five minutes, we couldn't accept each other's videos at first, and then we couldn't receive each other's audio. The disturbance of the Internet consumed our precious interview time, but it also became a window for us to capture the characteristics of characters — in the case of uneven video and audio, Mr. Jonsson not only maintained a very patient attitude but also made great efforts and gestures to realize the long-anticipated connection with us as soon as possible.

At last, we successfully started the online interview with audio-visual synchronization. At that time when Mr. Jonsson's warm greetings and his smile came into sight, his ice blue eyes didn't bring the coolness of northern Europe but the affinity and enthusiasm as well as the outstanding insight of an entrepreneur.

"Pollution Does Not Respect National Boundaries", an Idealist in the New Energy Enterprise

When it comes to talk about Iceland, the first impressions that come to our mind are glaciers, aurora and volcanoes. In addition, Iceland is also the country with the highest proportion of renewable energy around the world, based on the statistics from International Energy Agency (IEA). And in its small territory, has the unique geothermal development technology in the world.

As a volcanic island, Iceland is rich in hydropower and geothermal resources, so it is a country that can almost run by renewable energy. You may find it inconceivable that Iceland's power is completely generated from renewable energy. In addition, in response to climate change, Iceland is committed to replacing fossil energy with renewable energy, its goal is to completely get rid of its dependence on petroleum by 2050.

When talking about the achievements of Iceland's energy transformation, we could clearly feel his spontaneous pride, which stems not only from his self-confidence in the great achievements of the motherland's new energy as an Icelandic resident but also from his glory as a leading entrepreneur in the new energy industry. Mr. Jonsson is the CEO of Iceland Arctic Green Energy (hereinafter referred to as AGE). AGE is a profitable green energy company. Its mission at its founding is to establish a new energy company in Asia's emerging market in the form of Sino-foreign joint venture to export Iceland's achievement in the development and operation of geothermal and other renewable energy. The joint venture has 58 registered patents providing regional heating projects for over 2 million people in

60 counties and cities and the emission reduction of carbon dioxide reach 1.6 billion tons. In addition, it also participates in the Geothermal Training Program under the auspices of UNESCO.

Mr. Jonsson then talked about the carbon-neutral plan of the UN Climate Action Summit, especially China's goal of achieving carbon neutrality before 2060, and accurately laid bare the root of China's carbon reduction problem: "In China, the largest energy consumption is in heating and cooling, so the reduction in the use of fossil fuels for heating and cooling is the core of reducing carbon emissions, which is the exact content of our cooperation with Sinopec." Meanwhile, he is also confident that China will achieve its goal, "if you are ambitious, you should work hard step by step. Undoubtedly, China is on the right way."

This is not Mr. Jonsson's heroic utterance but an affirmation of the achievements of the cooperation between AGE and China in the field of green energy. The representative of the cooperation between AGE and China is the famous Sinopec Green Energy Geothermal Developmeng Co., Ltd. (hereinafter referred to as SGE). SGE founded in 2006, is a Sino-foreign joint venture, with 46.2% shares held by AGE and 53.8% shares by Sinopec. It focuses on the development of regional geothermal heating business and expands to the utilization technology of other green energies. Since the establishment of the first project in Xianyang City, Shanxi Province, the company has expanded its business to Hebei, Shandong and Jiangsu. Today, SGE is the world's largest regional geothermal heating company, with a 35% market share in China. It provides heating services to more than 2 million customers in a green, clean and sustainable way. Its geothermal project is the first project in the world that has been registered by the UN Clean Development Mechanism. Its regional heating business has reduced nearly 11.4 million tons of carbon dioxide emissions so far.

The environmental protection industry is an industry with shining humanitarianism, and so those engaged in this industry should be humanitarian. In a short conversation with Mr. Jonsson, we received this: "We work not just for our customers but for all mankind because pollution does not respect national boundaries." Such a sentence interspersed in his discussion on the prospect of new energy industry in China and Iceland deeply touched us, "pollution does not respect national boundaries", it can enlighten the benighted although this exposition is concise. The essence of commercial activities includes not only commerce itself but also humanitarian concerns. Only in this way can an enterprise create a commercial strategy for its sustainable development, and apply its capital and technology to the most valuable and important business. This is also the value of AGE: AGE is to become not only a profit-making organization but also the force to make the world cleaner and healthier.

Becoming an enterprise that pays attention to the community with shared future for mankind and a sense of social responsibility is not just AGE's value. AGE members represented by Mr. Jonsson have been working hard in this direction.

An Entrepreneur Who Loves His Family and an Icelandic Friend Who Loves China

"In fact, I really look forward to that holiday because I especially want my wife and children to travel to China." Mr. Jonsson told us that he had planned to bring his family to China for vacation in April 2020, but the plan had to be shelved as a result of the outbreak of COVID-19. We noticed that Mr. Jonsson mentioned his family many times in the short interview. There is such an interview question: what do you think can be called your life node in your past experience? Our original intention of setting the question was to further know about his commercial achievements listed on the official website, but his answer was both unexpected and touching: "It should be the days on which I formed a family and my child was born." After thinking about our past life, we think those days are really important moment in our life, aren't they? Only in such a business interview were we unconsciously moved when an entrepreneur blurted out the answer. For many people, when it comes to the impact of COVID-19, they were always can't help making complaints about it.

But Mr. Jonsson's first reaction is that COVID-19 epidemic has made home office a normalization. In this office mode, he can finish his work well and spend more time with his family and enjoy his time with his children.

Another word that Mr. Jonsson mentioned several times was "China", for he had a lot to say about it. According to him, there are a lot of similarities between the Chinese and the Icelandic people — "People there are also willing to communicate and interact with others. When I came to China, facing a lot of language barriers, but they didn't affect my pleasant exchanges with my Chinese partners." However, there are, of course, many differences between Iceland and China. A significant difference Mr. Jonsson felt the most is geographical space. Iceland is a large island, and it is easy to meet people you are familiar with while walking in the streets, which is almost impossible in the vast territory of China. He has been to China many times, such as Beijing, Shanghai and Xiong'an New Area. He has experienced the perfect combination of traditional civilization and modern achievements in these cities, and thus wanted to share this amazing experience with his family.

Mr. Jonsson warmly introduced his own hometown as well. Iceland is small in size, but its geographical location gives it many unique advantages, such as rich marine fishery resources. Mr. Jonsson recommended the traditional specialties of Iceland with enthusiasm, including smoked trout, fermented shark meat and tender lamb chops. In addition, Iceland is also rich in geothermal resources because it lies at the point where the American and Eurasian plates meet. Mr. Jonsson and AGE have brought the inspiration of the Icelandic people on geothermal energy to China to benefit people on the other side of the world.

Back to Mr. Jonsson's entrepreneur role, we can see his continuous attempts and breakthroughs from his rich career experience:

— CEO and Senior Consultant of AGE;

— Chairman of Icelandic Securities (an Icelandic financial services organization), and a member of the Board of Directors of Umbreyting (an Icelandic private equity company);

— Served as CEO of three financial services companies, including Kvika, Iceland's largest investment bank.

His rich experience in the finance was of great help to him in the new energy industry. In the early research and development stage of the geothermal industry, a large amount of capital support was needed for drilling equipment, land use and other related infrastructures, which requires company's management to be highly competent to corporate governance structure and seeking for potential investment, while Mr. Jonsson, who has extensive experience in finance, knew exactly how to do it. But he deemed it an entirely different working experience in finance and green energy industries. "Banks and financial services companies are often highly disciplined and organized. There's no room for manoeuvre in the face of a strict regulatory framework. This industry is home to a lot of excellent people but lacks innovation because of the strict framework. The new energy industry, on the other hand, places more emphasis on technological research and development and iteration, so it will give people more room for innovation. Especially in the post-COVID-19 era, countries will pay more attention to energy security as the uncertainties in their economic development increase. The new energy resources, such as geothermal, will have a better opportunity because of its sustainability." We've gained a different professional feeling from the perspective of an industry insider, and also admired his profound insight.

Mr. Jonsson's cross-industry development has certainly been a success. In this rapidly changing business circles, we hoped to learn from him the secrets of success. He told us that the most important thing was to focus on ourselves, to take risks and not put limits on ourselves, which was what we called stepping out of our comfort zone. He also shared some important life experience with young people: "Stay true to yourself and don't skimp on the time you have for your personal life". Obviously, these are the things he has always practiced. It is these ideas that have driven him to boldly make different choices.

China and Iceland Work Together for the Next 50 Years

Talking about China-Iceland cooperation in the next 50 years, Mr. Jonsson set out his expectation pragmatically and amusingly, "I hope there will be direct flights between China and Iceland in the near future."

Although the two countries are far away from each other, there is huge potential for cooperation between them from the perspective of their economic structure. Since 2006, China has been Iceland's largest trading partner in Asia for many years in a row, and the trade between them keeps increasing. At the same time, cooperation in many complementary fields has been carried out and achieved fruitful results, where the cooperation with AGE in the field of new energy is one of them. So in the long run, there is a huge potential and broad prospects for cooperation between China and Iceland, though the current cooperations is far from reaching a deeper and higher level.

Thanks to the hard work of millions of people like Mr. Jonsson over the past 50 years, China and Iceland have helped each other and brought about the vigorous development of bilateral economy through cultural exchanges and collisions. This is also the original intention of Icelandic Research Center to conduct this interview, hoping to share the successful experience of Mr. Jonsson with the people of China and Iceland and contribute to the future development of the two countries.

(Liu Zihan Ma Yidan Mao Yu)

致谢 | ACKNOWLEDGMENT

《中冰企业家风采录》一书的编辑工作于2021年6月正式开始，历经近一年的时间，于2022年5月完成。全书通过线上线下相结合的方式，采访并收集整理了中国和冰岛两国致力于中冰经贸往来的15位企业家的商务经历，共计约25万字。采访中，各位中冰企业家担当奉献的敬业精神、拼搏严谨的事业追求、格局宽厚的人格魅力，深深地感染着我们。在此，谨向受访企业家在百忙之中对本书的顺利完成给予的全力配合和大力支持致以最崇高的敬意！

在《中冰企业家风采录》的成书过程中，我们得到了中国驻冰岛历任大使王荣华、苏格、张卫东、金智健等的指点，以及中国驻冰岛前商务参赞陈贵生、薛茹三秘的鼎力相助；得到冰岛驻华使馆现任大使易卜雷（Thorir Ibsen)、前任大使古士贤（Gunnar Snorri Gunnarsson)及商务代表杨力的热心支持。同时，还得到山东省人民政府外事办公室主任蔡先金的建设性指导，济南大学校长张士强、副校长李光红的倾情鼓励，济南大学冰岛研究中心全体成员的通力协作，商学院学生孟伟、梁译文及英国雷丁大学亨利商学院博士生常凯文等23名志愿者的艰辛付出，以及许秋桃、高承、杨苏铁、薛冬、叶梓颐、张士涛、周星、朱美瑾等摄影师为本书提供的珍贵的、美轮美奂的摄影作品。山东译语国际教育咨询有限公司为本书提供了专业支持。在此一并对各位同仁及为本书出版谋划献计的中国经济出版社致以最诚挚的谢意！借此机会也衷心感谢社会各界多年来对济南大学冰岛研究中心的关心与厚爱！

《中冰企业家风采录》编委会

The editing work of the book *What They Say — Executives in China-Iceland Trade and Economic Cooperation* was officially started in June 2021. After nearly one year, it was completed in May 2022. Through online and offline interviews, we collected and sorted out the business experiences of 15 Chinese and Icelandic entrepreneurs dedicated to economic and trade exchanges between China and Iceland, totaling about 250 thousand words. During the interviews, we were deeply impressed with the spirit of brave shouldering and dedication, rigorous career pursuit, and generous personality charm of Chinese and Icelandic entrepreneurs. Now we would like to extend our highest respect to the interviewed entrepreneurs for their full cooperation and strong support for the successful completion of this book in their busy schedule!

In the course of compiling this book, we got precious advice from Chinese Ambassadors to Iceland Wang Ronghua, Su Ge, Zhang Weidong and Jin Zhijian. Former Counsellor Chen Guisheng and Third Secretary Xue Ru of Commercial Counselor's Office of Chinese Embassy in Iceland provided strong supports to help us overcome difficulties during interviews and compilation. Meanwhile, the incumbent Ambassador of Iceland to China Thorir Ibsen, former Ambassador Gunnar Snorri Gunnarsson, and Trade Representative Yang Li of the Embassy of Iceland in Beijing provided us enthusiastic supports. Cai Xianjin, Director of Foreign Affairs Office of Shandong Provincial People's Government provided constructive guidance. President Zhang Shiqiang and Vice President Li Guanghong of University of Jinan gave us hearty encouragements. All colleagues of Icelandic Research Center of University of Jinan under Ministry of Education of the People's Republic of China provided full cooperations. 23 volunteers, including Meng Wei, Liang Yiwen and other students from Business School of University of Jinan, as well as Ph.D. student Chang Kaiwen from Henley Business School of University of Reading worked hard to complete the book. The photographers, including Xu Qiutao, Gao Cheng, Yang Sutie, Xue Dong, Ye Ziyi, Zhang Shitao, Zhou Xing, Zhu Meijin provided their precious and beautiful photographic works for this book. Shandong Yiyu International Education Consulting Co., Ltd. provided professional supports for the book. Here, we would like to express sincere thanks to all of the above mentioned people and China Economic Publishing House for their contributions to the publication of this book! We also would like to take this opportunity to thank you from all walks of life for your long term concern and care for Icelandic Research Center of University of Jinan under Ministry of Education of the People's Republic of China!

Editorial Board of *What They Say — Executives in China-Iceland Trade and Economic Cooperation*